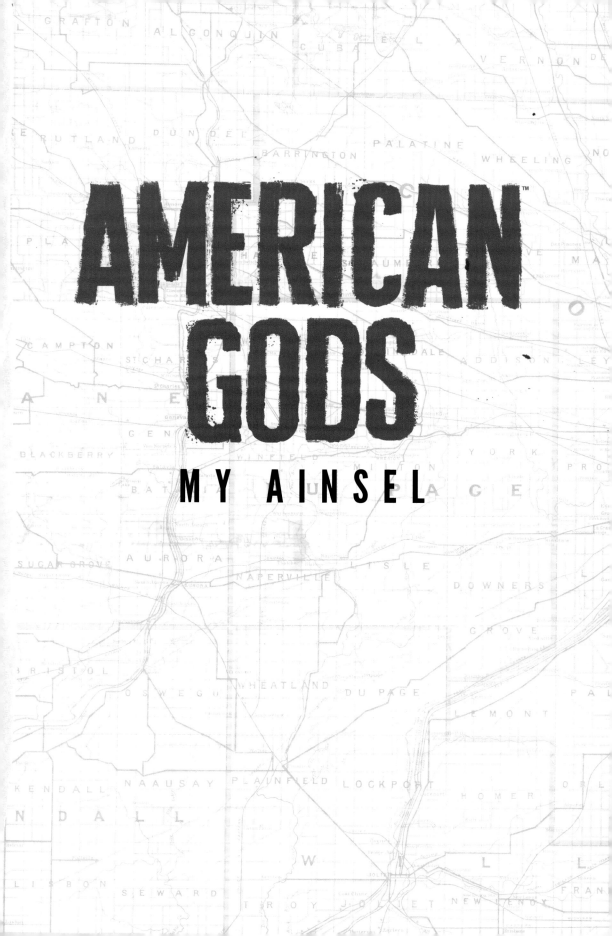

AMERICAN GODS™

MY AINSEL

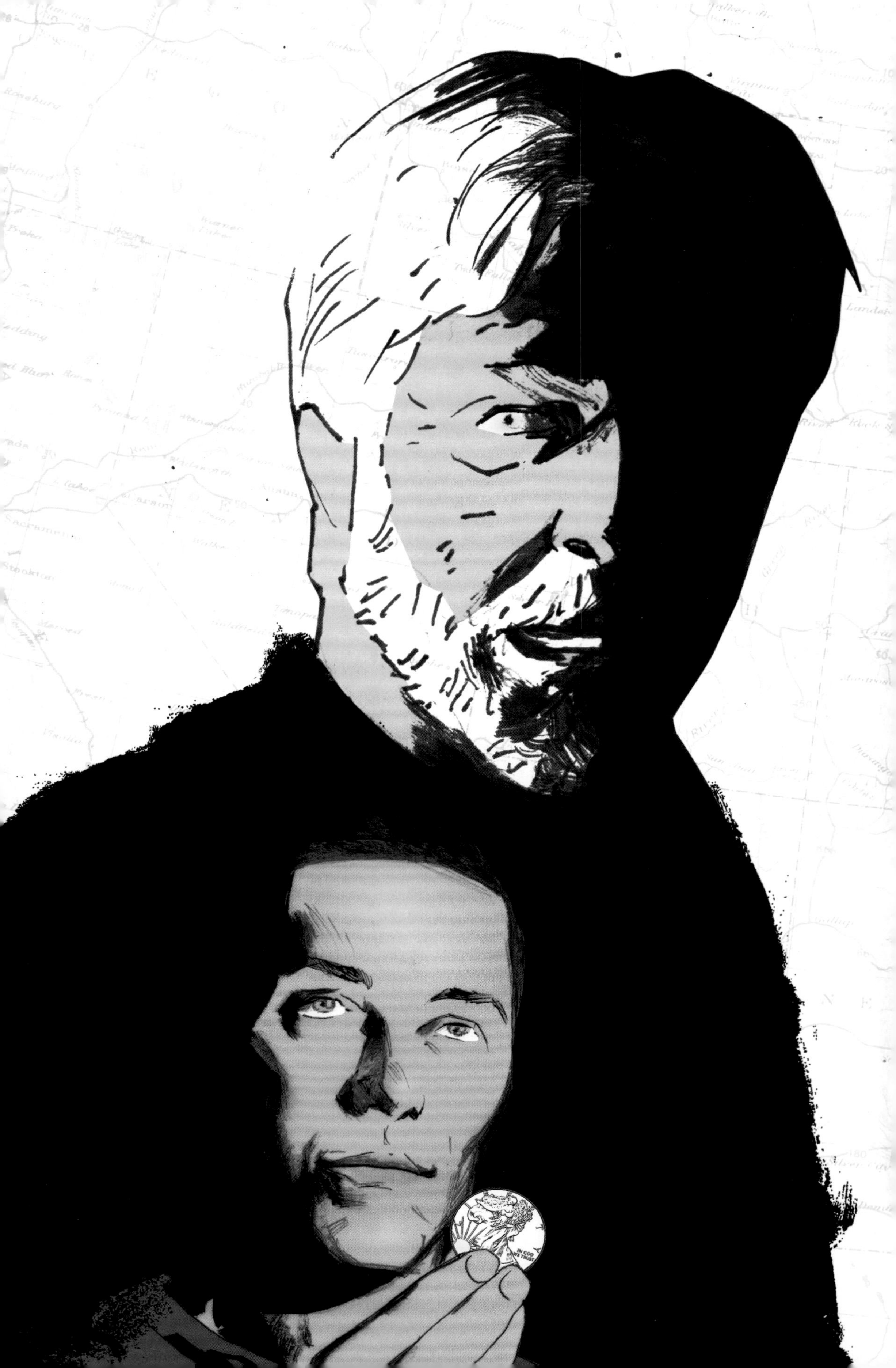

AMERICAN GODS™

MY AINSEL

Story and words by
NEIL GAIMAN

Script and layouts by
P. CRAIG RUSSELL

Art by
SCOTT HAMPTON

Colors by
JENNIFER T. LANGE

Letters by
RICK PARKER

Chapter title pages by **GLENN FABRY** with **ADAM BROWN**

Chapter design pages by **DAVID MACK**

Chapter Five art by **MARK BUCKINGHAM** and **CHRIS BLYTHE**

"Coming to America" from Chapter Nine by **GALEN SHOWMAN** and **LOVERN KINDZIERSKI**

Cover by **DAVID MACK**

DARK HORSE BOOKS

PUBLISHER MIKE RICHARDSON **EDITOR DANIEL CHABON** **ASSISTANT EDITOR BRETT ISRAEL**

DESIGNER ETHAN KIMBERLING **DIGITAL ART TECHNICIAN CHRISTIANNE GILLENARDO-GOUDREAU**

Facebook.com/DarkHorseComics Twitter.com/DarkHorseComics

Advertising Sales: (503) 905-2315
To find a comics shop in your area, visit comicshoplocator.com.

NEIL GAIMAN'S AMERICAN GODS™
© 2017, 2018, 2019 Neil Gaiman. Dark Horse Books® and the Dark Horse logo
are trademarks of Dark Horse Comics LLC, registered in various categories and
countries. All rights reserved. No portion of this publication may be reproduced
or transmitted, in any form or by any means, without the express written permission of Dark Horse Comics LLC. Names, characters, places, and incidents
featured in this publication either are the product of the author's imagination or
are used fictitiously. Any resemblance to actual persons (living or dead), events,
institutions, or locales, without satiric intent, is coincidental.

This volume collects issues #1 through #9 of the Dark Horse
comic-book series *American Gods: My Ainsel.*

Published by Dark Horse Books
A division of Dark Horse Comics LLC
10956 SE Main Street
Milwaukie, OR 97222

DarkHorse.com

First hardcover edition: April 2019
ISBN 978-1-50670-730-3

10 9 8 7 6 5 4 3 2 1
Printed in China

Library of Congress Cataloging-in-Publication Data

Names: Gaiman, Neil, author. | Russell, P. Craig, author, illustrator. |
  Hampton, Scott, artist. | Lange, Jennifer T., colourist. | Parker, Rick,
  1946- letterer.
Title: My Ainsel / story and words by Neil Gaiman ; script and layouts by P.
  Craig Russell ; art by Scott Hampton ; colors by Jennifer T. Lange ;
  letters by Rick Parker.
Description: First hardcover edition. | Milwaukie, OR : Dark Horse Books,
  April 2019. | Series: American Gods ; Volume 2 | "This volume collects
  issues #1 through #9 of the Dark Horse comic-book series American Gods: My
  Ainsel."
Identifiers: LCCN 2018049950 | ISBN 9781506707303 (hardback)
Subjects: LCSH: Comic books, strips, etc. | BISAC: COMICS & GRAPHIC NOVELS /
  Media Tie-In. | COMICS & GRAPHIC NOVELS / Science Fiction. | COMICS &
  GRAPHIC NOVELS / Horror.
Classification: LCC PN6728.A485 G28 2019 | DDC 741.5/973--dc23
LC record available at https://lccn.loc.gov/2018049950

CHAPTER ONE

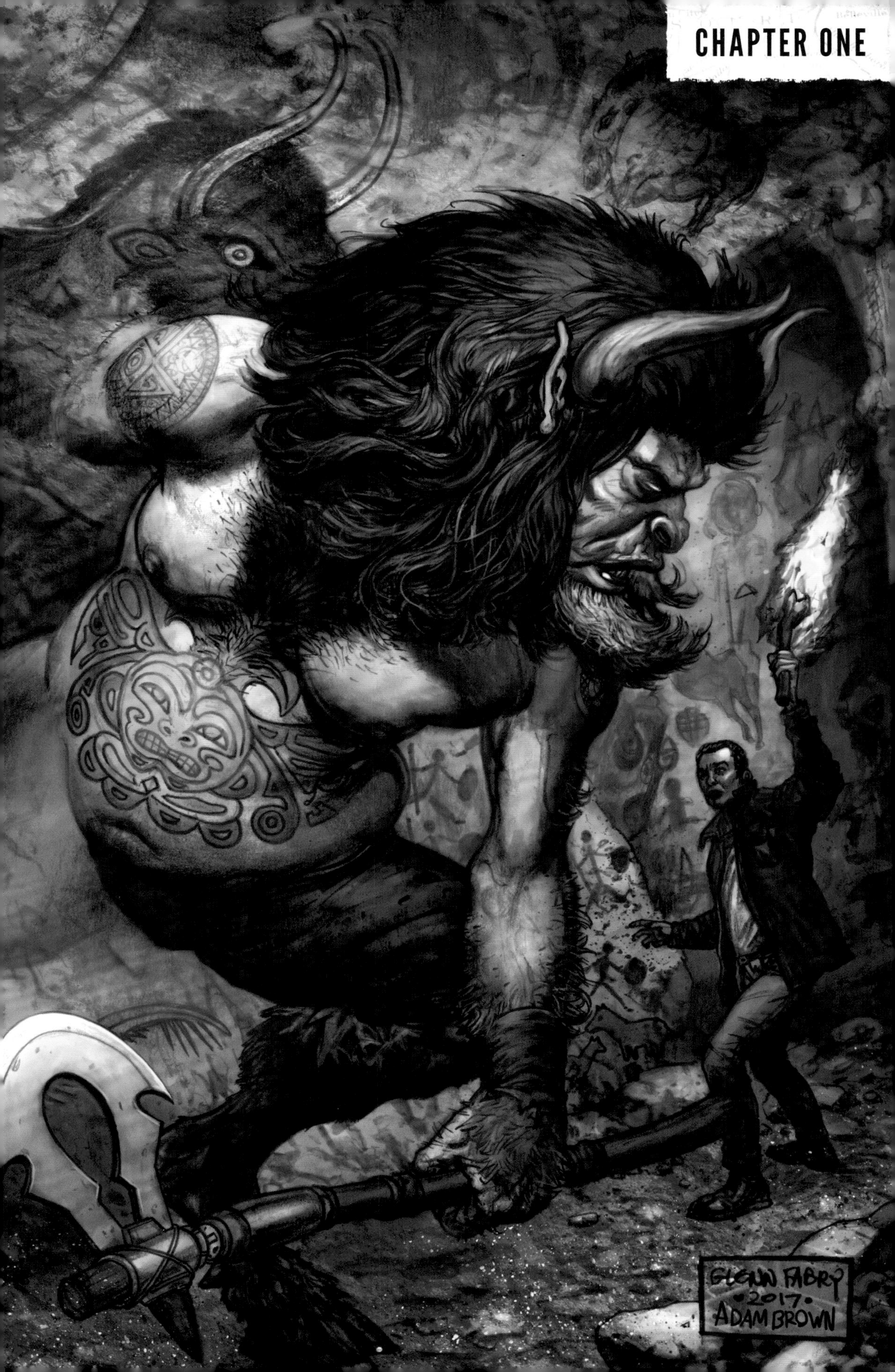
GLENN FABRY
•2017•
ADAM BROWN

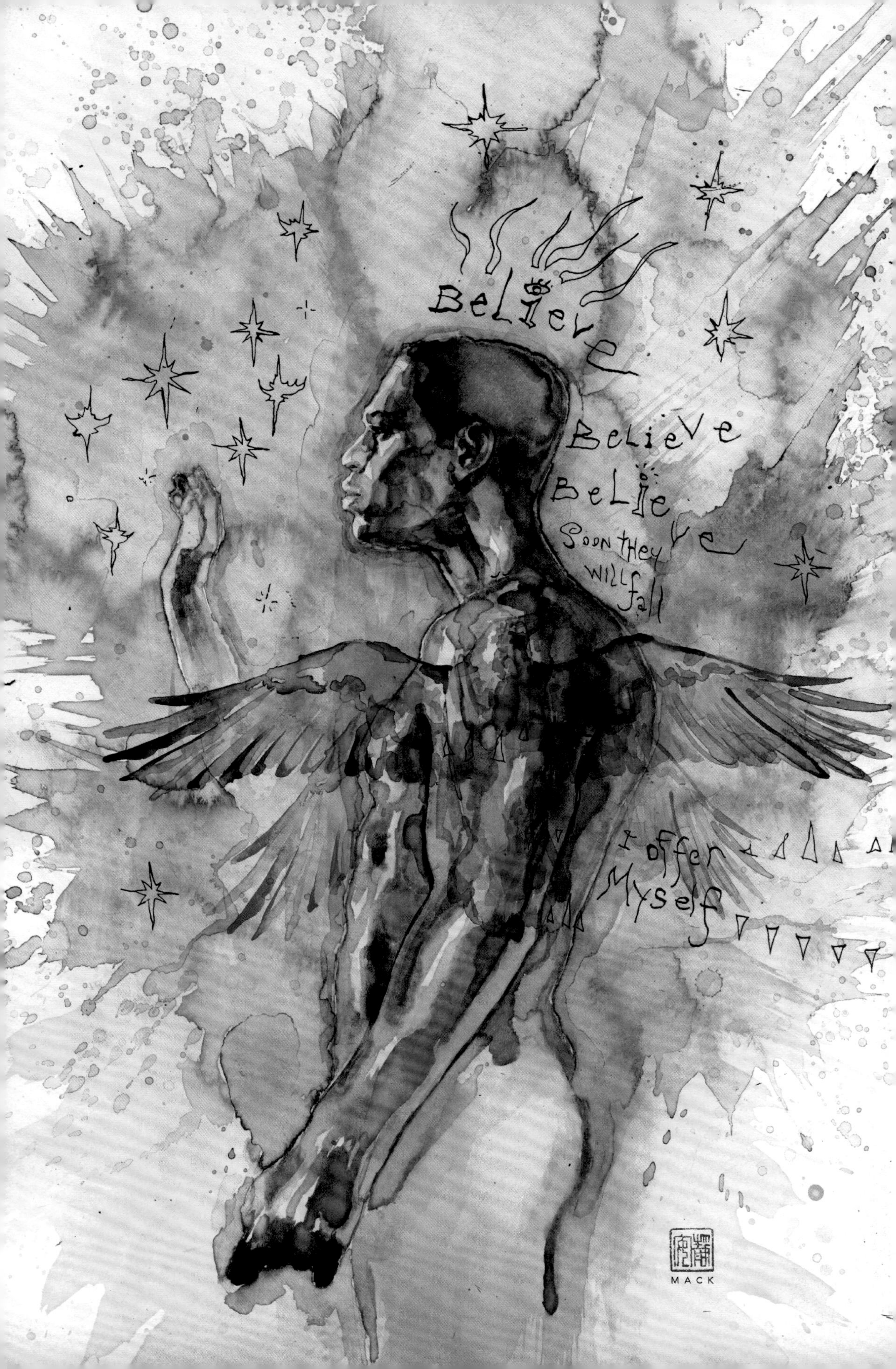
Believe
Believe
Believe
Soon they will fall
I offer Myself
MACK

WELCOME TO WISCONSIN

SO WHO WERE THE BUNCH THAT GRABBED ME IN THE PARKING LOT? MISTER WOOD AND MISTER STONE? WHO WERE THEY?

I THINK THAT THEY THINK THEY'RE THE WHITE HATS.

JUST SPOOKS, MEMBERS OF THE OPPOSITION.

OF COURSE THEY DO.

WEDNESDAY HAD ANNOUNCED THAT THEY WERE NOT TO TAKE FREEWAYS BECAUSE HE DIDN'T KNOW WHOSE SIDE THE FREEWAYS WERE ON, SO SHADOW WAS STICKING TO BACK ROADS. HE DIDN'T MIND. HE WASN'T EVEN SURE WEDNESDAY WAS CRAZY.

THE REALLY DANGEROUS PEOPLE BELIEVE THAT THEY ARE DOING WHATEVER THEY ARE DOING SOLELY AND ONLY BECAUSE IT IS WITHOUT QUESTION THE RIGHT THING TO DO.

AND YOU?

I'M DOING WHAT I'M DOING BECAUSE I WANT TO. SO THAT'S DIFFERENT.

HOW DID YOU ALL GET AWAY? OR DID YOU ALL GET AWAY?

WE DID, ALTHOUGH IT WAS A CLOSE THING. IF THEY'D NOT STOPPED TO GRAB YOU, THEY MIGHT HAVE TAKEN THE LOT OF US. IT CONVINCED SEVERAL OF THE PEOPLE SITTING ON THE FENCE THAT I MIGHT NOT BE COMPLETELY CRAZY.

SO, HOW DID YOU GET OUT?

I DON'T PAY YOU TO ASK QUESTIONS. I'VE TOLD YOU BEFORE.

SHADOW SHRUGGED.

LA CROSSE, WISCONSIN.

SUPER EIGHT

CHRISTMAS DAY WAS SPENT ON THE ROAD, DRIVING NORTH AND EAST. THE FARMLAND BECAME PINE FOREST. THE TOWNS SEEMED TO COME FARTHER AND FARTHER APART.

SHADOW PICKED CHEERLESSLY AT HIS DRY TURKEY CHRISTMAS LUNCH WHILE WEDNESDAY BECAME POSITIVELY EXPANSIVE— TALKING, JOKING, AND WHENEVER SHE CAME CLOSE ENOUGH, FLIRTING WITH THE WAITRESS.

EXCUSE ME, M'DEAR, BUT MIGHT I TROUBLE YOU FOR ANOTHER CUP OF YOUR *DELIGHTFUL* HOT CHOCOLATE?

FESTIVE, YET CLASSY.

AND I TRUST YOU WON'T THINK ME TOO FORWARD IF I SAY WHAT A MIGHTY FETCHING AND BECOMING DRESS THAT IS.

HEE ...

FETCHING. SOME THINGS MAY CHANGE. PEOPLE, HOWEVER... PEOPLE STAY THE SAME.

SOME GRIFTS LAST FOREVER, OTHERS ARE SWALLOWED BY TIME AND THE WORLD. MY FAVORITE GRIFT OF ALL IS NO LONGER PRACTICAL. STILL, SOME ARE TIMELESS— THE SPANISH PRISONER, THE PIGEON DROP, THE FIDDLE GAME...

THE FIDDLE GAME?

AH. THE FIDDLE GAME WAS A FINE AND WONDERFUL CON. IN ITS PUREST FORM IT IS A TWO-MAN GRIFT. IT TRADES ON CUPIDITY AND GREED, AS ALL GREAT GRIFTS DO.

YOU *CAN* ALWAYS CHEAT AN HONEST MAN, BUT IT TAKES MORE WORK.

SO ...

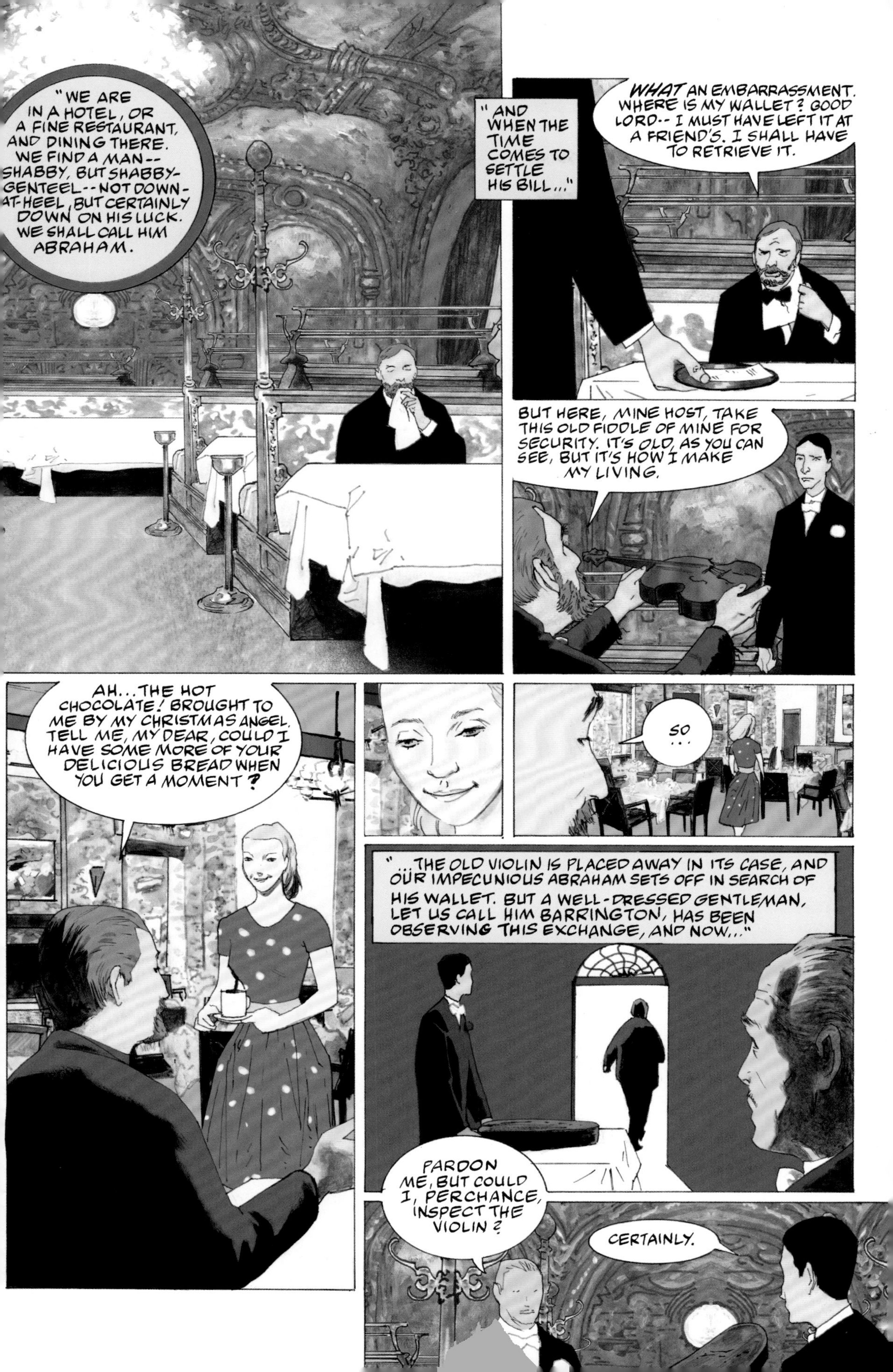
"WE ARE IN A HOTEL, OR A FINE RESTAURANT, AND DINING THERE. WE FIND A MAN-- SHABBY, BUT SHABBY-GENTEEL--NOT DOWN-AT-HEEL, BUT CERTAINLY DOWN ON HIS LUCK. WE SHALL CALL HIM ABRAHAM.
"AND WHEN THE TIME COMES TO SETTLE HIS BILL..."
WHAT AN EMBARRASSMENT. WHERE IS MY WALLET? GOOD LORD-- I MUST HAVE LEFT IT AT A FRIEND'S. I SHALL HAVE TO RETRIEVE IT.
BUT HERE, MINE HOST, TAKE THIS OLD FIDDLE OF MINE FOR SECURITY. IT'S OLD, AS YOU CAN SEE, BUT IT'S HOW I MAKE MY LIVING.
AH...THE HOT CHOCOLATE! BROUGHT TO ME BY MY CHRISTMAS ANGEL. TELL ME, MY DEAR, COULD I HAVE SOME MORE OF YOUR DELICIOUS BREAD WHEN YOU GET A MOMENT?
SO...
"...THE OLD VIOLIN IS PLACED AWAY IN ITS CASE, AND OUR IMPECUNIOUS ABRAHAM SETS OFF IN SEARCH OF HIS WALLET. BUT A WELL-DRESSED GENTLEMAN, LET US CALL HIM BARRINGTON, HAS BEEN OBSERVING THIS EXCHANGE, AND NOW..."
PARDON ME, BUT COULD I, PERCHANCE, INSPECT THE VIOLIN?
CERTAINLY.

"THE WELL-DRESSED MAN EXAMINES THE VIOLIN REVERENTIALLY, LIKE A MAN WHO HAS BEEN PERMITTED INTO A HOLY SANCTUM.

SO, THE VIOLIN IS RARE?

WHY, THIS IS-- IT *MUST* BE...

NO, IT CANNOT BE--

BUT *YES,* THERE IT IS ... THE MAKER'S MARK.

MY LORD, THIS IS *UNBELIEVABLE!*

INDEED IT IS, AND WORTH IN EXCESS OF A HUNDRED THOUSAND DOLLARS. I AM A DEALER IN SUCH THINGS, AND I WOULD PAY SEVENTY-FIVE THOUSAND DOLLARS FOR SUCH AN EXQUISITE PIECE. I HAVE A MAN ON THE WEST COAST WHO WOULD BUY IT TOMORROW...

OH, BUT MY *TRAIN.*

GOOD SIR, WHEN THE OWNER OF THIS INESTIMABLE INSTRUMENT SHOULD RETURN, PLEASE GIVE HIM MY CARD, FOR, ALAS, I MUST BE AWAY.

"AND WITH THAT, BARRINGTON LEAVES.

"MINE HOST EXAMINES THE VIOLIN, CURIOSITY MINGLING WITH CUPIDITY IN HIS VEINS, AND A PLAN BEGINS TO BUBBLE UP.

"BUT THE MINUTES GO BY, AND ABRAHAM DOES NOT RETURN.

"AND NOW IT IS LATE."

THEN, THROUGH THE DOOR, SHABBY, BUT PROUD, COMES OUR ABRAHAM, OUR FIDDLE-PLAYER, WAVING A WALLET THAT HAS SEEN BETTER DAYS.

"AND FROM IT HE TAKES THE MONEY TO PAY FOR HIS MEAL, OR HIS STAY, AND HE ASKS FOR THE RETURN OF HIS VIOLIN.

"MINE HOST RETURNS THE FIDDLE AND ABRAHAM TAKES IT LIKE A MOTHER CRADLING A CHILD."

TELL ME, HOW MUCH IS A VIOLIN LIKE THIS WORTH? FOR MY NIECE HAS A YEARNING ON HER TO PLAY THE FIDDLE, AND IT'S HER BIRTHDAY COMING UP IN A WEEK.

SELL THIS FIDDLE? NEVER! I'VE HAD HER FOR TWENTY YEARS, AND TO TELL THE TRUTH, SHE COST ME ALL OF FIVE HUNDRED DOLLARS WHEN I BOUGHT HER.

WHAT IF I WERE TO OFFER YOU A THOUSAND DOLLARS FOR IT?

WHERE WILL I EVER FIND ANOTHER THAT SOUNDS SO FINE? NOT A THOUSAND DOLLARS, NOT FOR FIVE THOUSAND.

"MINE HOST SEES HIS PROFITS SHRINKING, BUT YOU MUST SPEND MONEY TO MAKE MONEY."

EIGHT THOUSAND DOLLARS.

HOW CAN I SAY NO TO EIGHT THOUSAND DOLLARS?

"ESPECIALLY WHEN MINE HOST REMOVES NINE THOUSAND FROM A WALL SAFE."

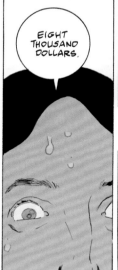

YOU'RE A GOOD MAN. YOU'RE A SAINT! BUT YOU MUST SWEAR TO TAKE GOOD CARE OF MY GIRL.

"AND RELUCTANTLY, HE HANDS OVER HIS VIOLIN."

BUT WHAT IF MINE HOST SIMPLY HANDS OVER BARRINGTON'S CARD AND TELLS ABRAHAM HE'S COME INTO SOME GOOD FORTUNE?

THEN WE'RE OUT THE COST OF TWO DINNERS.

LET ME SEE IF I'VE GOT IT STRAIGHT.

SO, ABRAHAM LEAVES, NINE THOUSAND DOLLARS RICHER.

HE AND BARRINGTON MEET UP, SPLIT THE MONEY, AND HEAD FOR THE NEXT TOWN.

I GUESS THE TRUNK OF THE CAR IS FILLED WITH HUNDRED-DOLLAR VIOLINS.

I PERSONALLY MADE IT A POINT OF HONOR NEVER TO PAY MORE THAN FIVE DOLLARS FOR ANY OF THEM.

NOW, MY DEAR, REGALE US WITH YOUR BUMPTIOUS DESSERTS ON THIS, OUR LORD'S NATAL DAY.

THERE'S APPLE PIE, APPLE PIE Á LA MODE -- THAT'S WITH A SCOOP OF VANILLA ICE CREAM -- CHRISTMAS CAKE, CHRISTMAS CAKE Á LA MODE, AND A RED AND GREEN PUDDING.

I'LL HAVE THE CHRISTMAS CAKE...

...Á LA MODE

HEE

NOTHING FOR ME.

NOW, AS GRIFTS GO, THE FIDDLE GAME GOES BACK THREE HUNDRED YEARS OR MORE. AND IF YOU PICK YOUR CHICKEN CORRECTLY, YOU COULD STILL PLAY IT TOMORROW ANYWHERE IN AMERICA.

I THOUGHT YOU SAID YOUR FAVORITE GRIFT WAS NO LONGER PRACTICAL.

I DID INDEED. HOWEVER, THAT IS NOT MY FAVORITE. NO, MY FAVORITE WAS CALLED THE BISHOP GAME.

IT HAD EVERYTHING: EXCITEMENT, SUBTERFUGE, SURPRISE. BUT ITS TIME HAS PASSED.

IT IS, LET US SAY, 1920 IN CHICAGO, PERHAPS, OR NEW YORK, OR PHILADELPHIA.

WE ARE IN A JEWELER'S EMPORIUM.

"A MAN DRESSED AS A CLERGYMAN-- AND NOT JUST ANY CLERGYMAN-- BUT A BISHOP IN HIS PURPLE-- ENTERS AND PICKS OUT A NECKLACE.

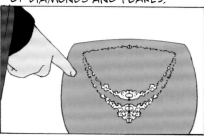

" IT IS A GORGEOUS CONFECTION OF DIAMONDS AND PEARLS,

" HE PAYS FOR IT WITH A DOZEN OF THE CRISPEST HUNDRED-DOLLAR BILLS.

"THERE IS A SMUDGE OF GREEN INK ON THE TOP-MOST BILL.

"THE STORE OWNER APOLOGETICALLY, BUT FIRMLY, SENDS THE STACK OF BILLS TO THE BANK TO BE CHECKED.

"SOON ENOUGH, THE STORE CLERK RETURNS WITH THE BILLS. THE BANK SAYS THAT NONE OF THEM ARE COUNTERFEIT."

I DO APOLOGIZE.

NOT AT ALL.

I WELL UNDERSTAND. THERE IS SUCH IMMORALITY AND LEWDNESS ABROAD IN THE WORLD, SUCH LAWLESS AND UNGODLY TYPES ABOUT, THAT WHAT MORE CAN ONE EXPECT?

" THE STORE OWNER DOES HIS BEST NOT TO PONDER WHY A BISHOP WOULD BE PURCHASING A DIAMOND NECKLACE WITH GOOD CASH MONEY.

" THE BISHOP BIDS HIM A HEARTY FAREWELL AND TURNS TO LEAVE...

...ONLY TO HAVE A HEAVY HAND DESCEND ON HIS SHOULDER."

WHY, SOAPY-- UP TO YOUR OLD TRICKS, ARE YOU?

BEGGING YOUR PARDON, BUT HAS THIS MAN BOUGHT ANYTHING FROM YOU?

CERTAINLY NOT. TELL HIM I HAVE NOT.

INDEED HE HAS. HE BOUGHT A PEARL AND DIAMOND NECKLACE FROM ME-- PAID FOR IT IN CASH AS WELL.

WOULD YOU HAVE THE BILLS AVAILABLE, SIR?

"SO THE JEWELER TAKES THE TWELVE HUNDRED-DOLLAR BILLS FROM THE CASH REGISTER AND HANDS THEM TO THE COP."

OH, SOAPY, SOAPY-- THESE ARE THE FINEST YOU'VE MADE YET.

YOU CAN'T PROVE NOTHING. THE BANK SAID THEY WERE ON THE LEVEL. IT'S THE REAL GREEN STUFF.

I'M SURE THEY DID, BUT I DOUBT THAT THE BANK KNEW THAT SOAPY SYLVESTER WAS IN TOWN, NOR OF THE QUALITY OF THE BILLS HE'D BEEN PASSING IN DENVER AND ST. LOUIS.

TWELVE HUNDRED DOLLARS' WORTH OF DIAMONDS AND PEARLS IN EXCHANGE FOR FIFTY CENTS' WORTH OF PAPER AND INK.

AND PASSING YOURSELF OFF AS A MAN OF THE CHURCH. YOU SHOULD BE *ASHAMED!*

" HE CLAPS THE HANDCUFFS ON THE BISHOP, WHO IS OBVIOUSLY NO BISHOP, AND HE MARCHES HIM AWAY.

" THE JEWELER GETS A RECEIPT, AND ASSURANCE THAT HE'LL GET THE $1,200 NECKLACE BACK AS SOON AS SOAPY COMES TO TRIAL. IT IS EVIDENCE, AFTER ALL.

" HE IS CONGRATULATED ON BEING A GOOD CITIZEN AND HE IS ALREADY THINKING OF THE TALE HE'LL HAVE TO TELL AT THE NEXT MEETING OF THE ODDFELLOWS.

" THE POLICEMAN MARCHES THE 'BISHOP' OUT OF THE STORE ON THEIR WAY TO A POLICE STATION THAT WILL NEVER SEE HIDE NOR HAIR OF EITHER OF THEM.''

WAS IT REALLY COUNTERFEIT?

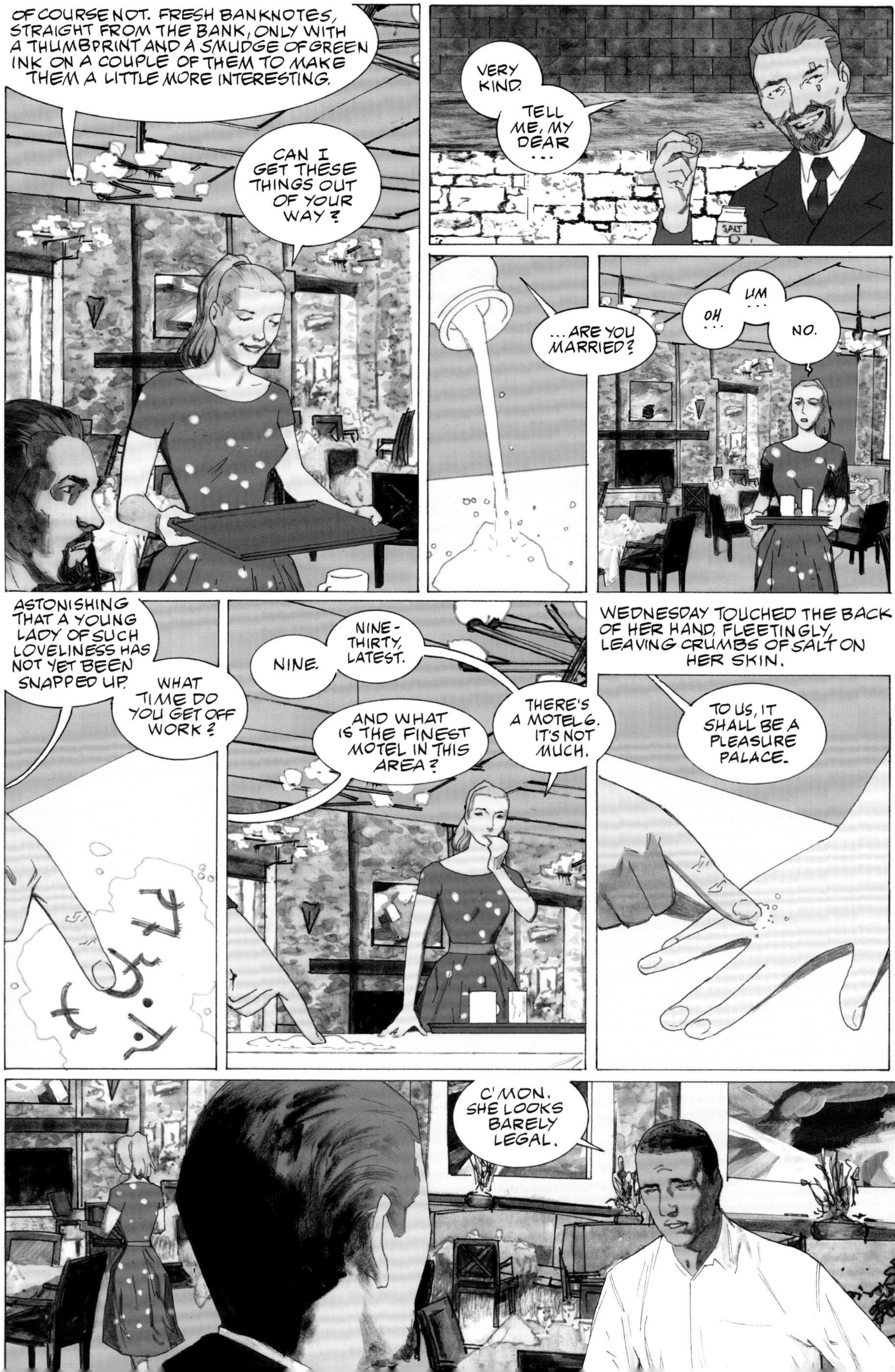
OF COURSE NOT. FRESH BANKNOTES, STRAIGHT FROM THE BANK, ONLY WITH A THUMBPRINT AND A SMUDGE OF GREEN INK ON A COUPLE OF THEM TO MAKE THEM A LITTLE MORE INTERESTING.
CAN I GET THESE THINGS OUT OF YOUR WAY?
VERY KIND.
TELL ME, MY DEAR . . .
SALT
...ARE YOU MARRIED?
OH . . .
UM . . .
NO.
ASTONISHING THAT A YOUNG LADY OF SUCH LOVELINESS HAS NOT YET BEEN SNAPPED UP.
WHAT TIME DO YOU GET OFF WORK?
NINE.
NINE-THIRTY, LATEST.
AND WHAT IS THE FINEST MOTEL IN THIS AREA?
THERE'S A MOTEL 6. IT'S NOT MUCH.
WEDNESDAY TOUCHED THE BACK OF HER HAND, FLEETINGLY, LEAVING CRUMBS OF SALT ON HER SKIN.
TO US, IT SHALL BE A PLEASURE PALACE.
C'MON. SHE LOOKS BARELY LEGAL.

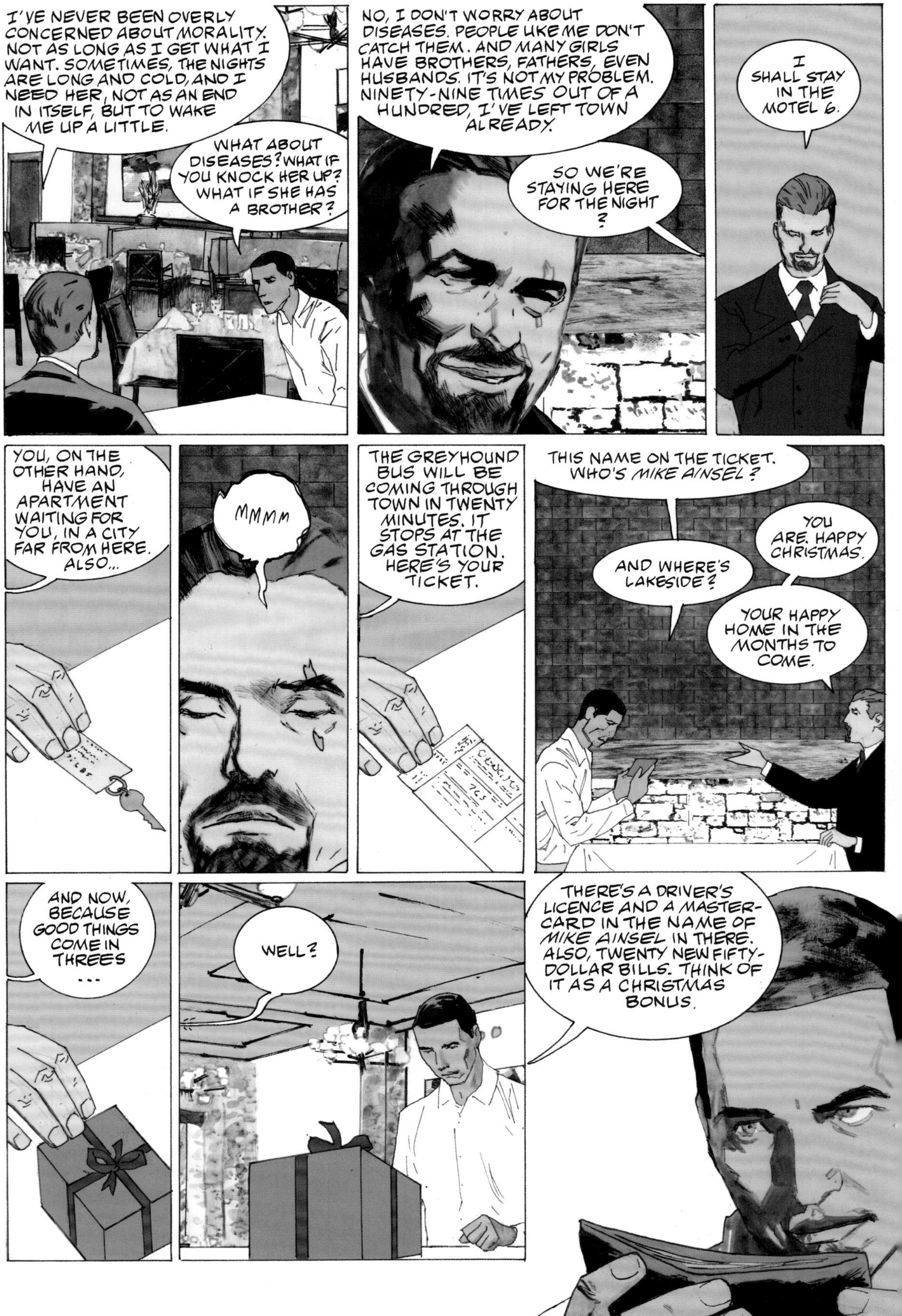
I'VE NEVER BEEN OVERLY CONCERNED ABOUT MORALITY. NOT AS LONG AS I GET WHAT I WANT. SOMETIMES, THE NIGHTS ARE LONG AND COLD, AND I NEED HER, NOT AS AN END IN ITSELF, BUT TO WAKE ME UP A LITTLE.
WHAT ABOUT DISEASES? WHAT IF YOU KNOCK HER UP? WHAT IF SHE HAS A BROTHER?
NO, I DON'T WORRY ABOUT DISEASES. PEOPLE LIKE ME DON'T CATCH THEM. AND MANY GIRLS HAVE BROTHERS, FATHERS, EVEN HUSBANDS. IT'S NOT MY PROBLEM. NINETY-NINE TIMES OUT OF A HUNDRED, I'VE LEFT TOWN ALREADY.
SO WE'RE STAYING HERE FOR THE NIGHT?
I SHALL STAY IN THE MOTEL 6.
YOU, ON THE OTHER HAND, HAVE AN APARTMENT WAITING FOR YOU, IN A CITY FAR FROM HERE. ALSO...
MMMM
THE GREYHOUND BUS WILL BE COMING THROUGH TOWN IN TWENTY MINUTES. IT STOPS AT THE GAS STATION. HERE'S YOUR TICKET.
THIS NAME ON THE TICKET. WHO'S *MIKE AINSEL*?
YOU ARE. HAPPY CHRISTMAS.
AND WHERE'S LAKESIDE?
YOUR HAPPY HOME IN THE MONTHS TO COME.
AND NOW, BECAUSE GOOD THINGS COME IN THREES ...
WELL?
THERE'S A DRIVER'S LICENCE AND A MASTER-CARD IN THE NAME OF *MIKE AINSEL* IN THERE. ALSO, TWENTY NEW FIFTY-DOLLAR BILLS. THINK OF IT AS A CHRISTMAS BONUS.

SHADOW FOUND IT HARD TO BELIEVE HOW MUCH COLDER IT HAD GOTTEN IN THE LAST FEW HOURS. AGGRESSIVELY COLD.

HEY, WEDNESDAY, BOTH OF THE SCAMS YOU WERE TELLING ME ABOUT-- THE VIOLIN SCAM AND THE BISHOP AND THE COP...

WHAT OF THEM?

THEY'RE BOTH TWO-MAN SCAMS. DID YOU USED TO HAVE A PARTNER?

YES. I HAD A PARTNER. A JUNIOR PARTNER. BUT, ALAS, THOSE DAYS ARE DONE.

THERE'S THE GAS STATION, AND THERE, UNLESS MY EYES DECEIVE ME, IS THE BUS.

YOUR ADDRESS IS ON THE KEY. IF ANYONE ASKS, I AM YOUR UNCLE, WITH THE UNLIKELY NAME OF EMERSON BORSON. I'LL COME FOR YOU WITHIN THE WEEK. WE SHALL BE TRAVELING TOGETHER. IN THE MEANTIME, KEEP YOUR HEAD DOWN, AND STAY OUT OF TROUBLE.

MY CAR?

I'LL TAKE GOOD CARE OF IT. HAVE A GOOD TIME IN LAKESIDE.

JESUS, YOUR HANDS ARE COLD.

SHADOW EXPERIENCED A DIZZYING MOMENT OF DOUBLE VISION:

HE SAW THE GRIZZLED MAN FACING HIM, BUT HE SAW SOMETHING ELSE: SO MANY WINTERS, HUNDREDS OF WINTERS, AND A GRAY WANDERER STARING IN THROUGH WINDOWS AT THE FIRELIGHT, AT A JOY AND A BURNING LIFE THAT WOULD NEVER BE HIS.

GO! ALL IS WELL, AND ALL IS WELL, AND ALL SHALL BE WELL.

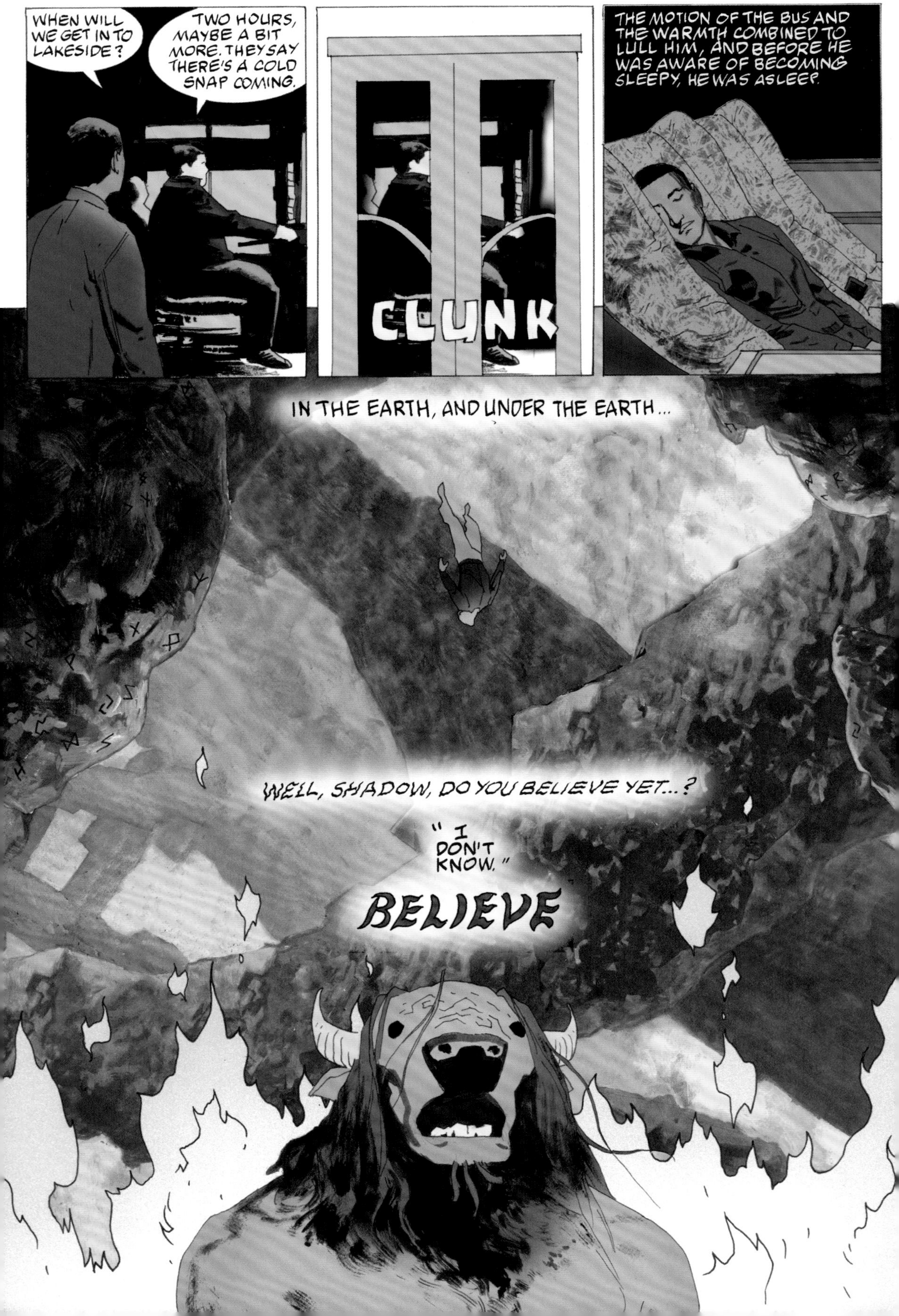
WHEN WILL WE GET IN TO LAKESIDE?
TWO HOURS, MAYBE A BIT MORE. THEY SAY THERE'S A COLD SNAP COMING.
CLUNK
THE MOTION OF THE BUS AND THE WARMTH COMBINED TO LULL HIM, AND BEFORE HE WAS AWARE OF BECOMING SLEEPY, HE WAS ASLEEP.
IN THE EARTH, AND UNDER THE EARTH...
WELL, SHADOW, DO YOU BELIEVE YET...?
"I DON'T KNOW."
BELIEVE

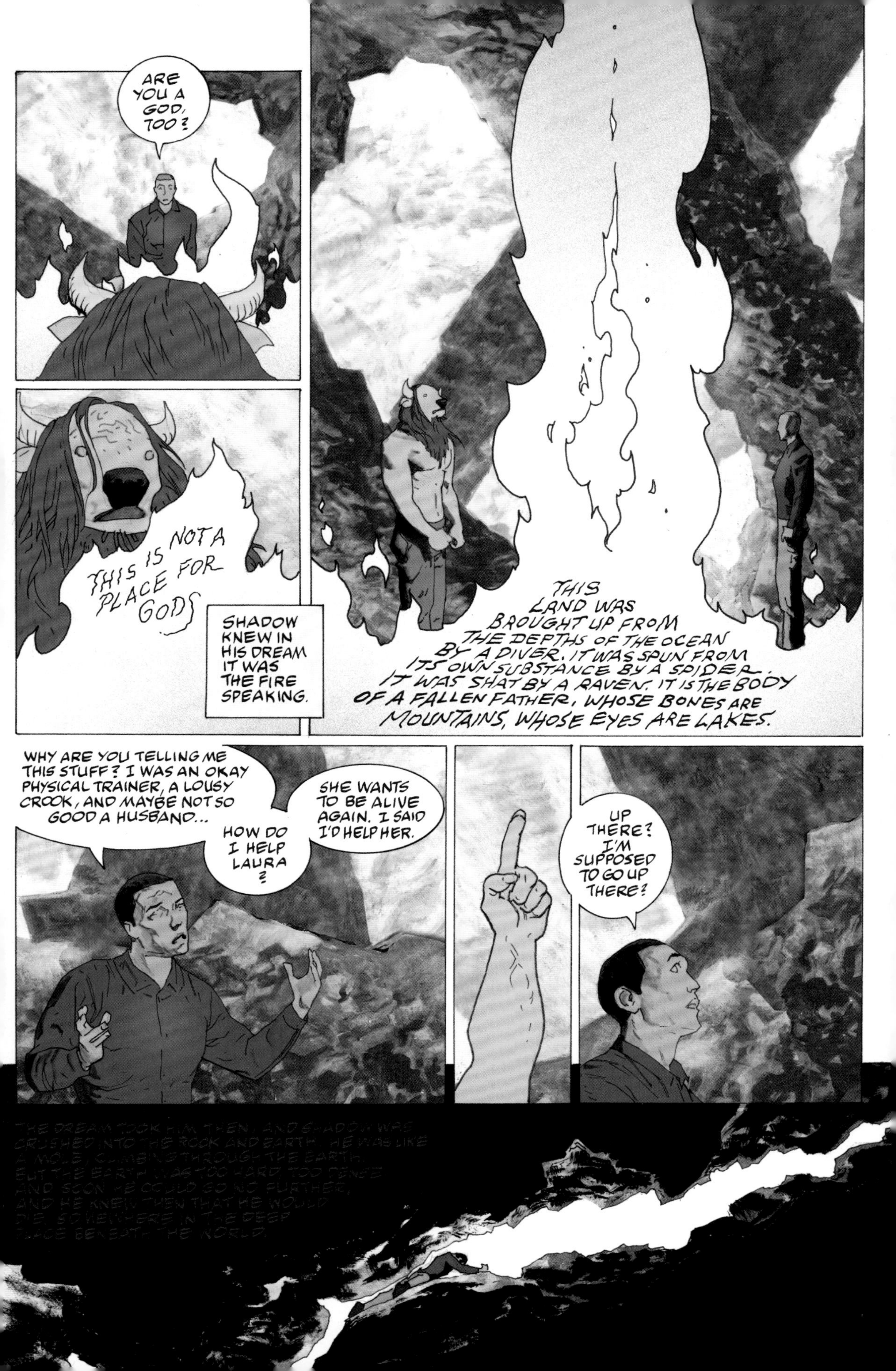
ARE YOU A GOD, TOO?
THIS IS NOT A PLACE FOR GODS
SHADOW KNEW IN HIS DREAM IT WAS THE FIRE SPEAKING.
THIS LAND WAS BROUGHT UP FROM THE DEPTHS OF THE OCEAN BY A DIVER. IT WAS SPUN FROM ITS OWN SUBSTANCE BY A SPIDER. IT WAS SHAT BY A RAVEN. IT IS THE BODY OF A FALLEN FATHER, WHOSE BONES ARE MOUNTAINS, WHOSE EYES ARE LAKES.
WHY ARE YOU TELLING ME THIS STUFF? I WAS AN OKAY PHYSICAL TRAINER, A LOUSY CROOK, AND MAYBE NOT SO GOOD A HUSBAND...
HOW DO I HELP LAURA?
SHE WANTS TO BE ALIVE AGAIN. I SAID I'D HELP HER.
UP THERE? I'M SUPPOSED TO GO UP THERE?
THE DREAM TOOK HIM THEN, AND SHADOW WAS CRUSHED INTO THE ROCK AND EARTH. HE WAS LIKE A MOLE, CLIMBING THROUGH THE EARTH, BUT THE EARTH WAS TOO HARD, TOO DENSE AND SOON HE COULD GO NO FURTHER, AND HE KNEW THEN THAT HE WOULD DIE, SOMEWHERE IN THE DEEP PLACE BENEATH THE WORLD.

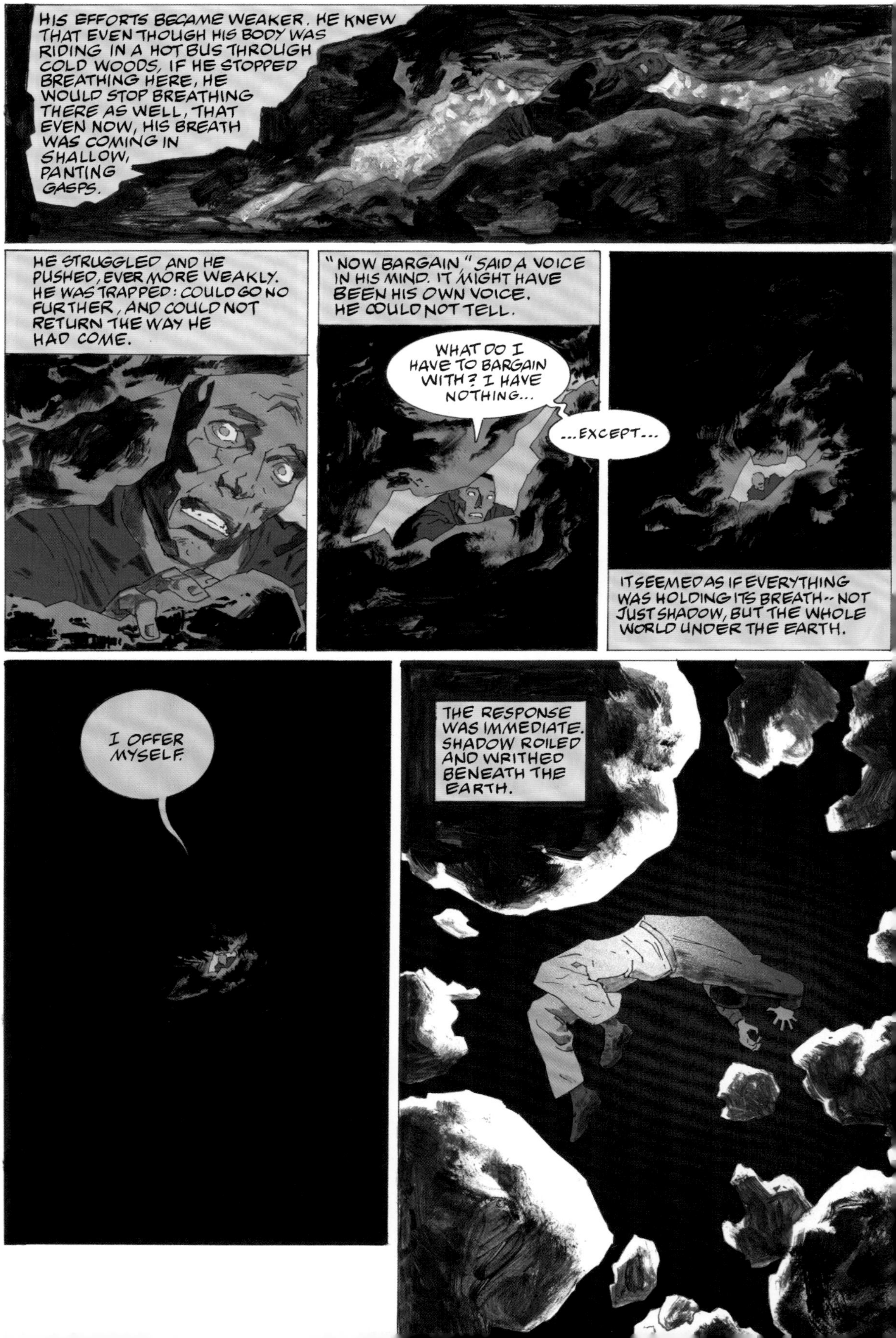
HIS EFFORTS BECAME WEAKER. HE KNEW THAT EVEN THOUGH HIS BODY WAS RIDING IN A HOT BUS THROUGH COLD WOODS, IF HE STOPPED BREATHING HERE, HE WOULD STOP BREATHING THERE AS WELL, THAT EVEN NOW, HIS BREATH WAS COMING IN SHALLOW, PANTING GASPS.
HE STRUGGLED AND HE PUSHED, EVER MORE WEAKLY. HE WAS TRAPPED: COULD GO NO FURTHER, AND COULD NOT RETURN THE WAY HE HAD COME.
"NOW BARGAIN," SAID A VOICE IN HIS MIND. IT MIGHT HAVE BEEN HIS OWN VOICE. HE COULD NOT TELL.
WHAT DO I HAVE TO BARGAIN WITH? I HAVE NOTHING...
...EXCEPT...
IT SEEMED AS IF EVERYTHING WAS HOLDING ITS BREATH-- NOT JUST SHADOW, BUT THE WHOLE WORLD UNDER THE EARTH.
I OFFER MYSELF.
THE RESPONSE WAS IMMEDIATE. SHADOW ROILED AND WRITHED BENEATH THE EARTH.

HE WAS BEING PUSHED TOWARD THE SURFACE. THE PRESSURE OF THE EARTH EXPELLING HIM, PUSHING HIM CLOSER TO THE LIGHT.

THE PRESSURE BECAME PAIN, IMPOSSIBLE TO BELIEVE, AND HE BEGAN TO SCREAM IN FEAR AND PAIN.

HE WONDERED, AS HE SCREAMED, WHETHER, BACK IN THE WAKING WORLD, HE WAS ALSO SCREAMING.

AND AS THE FINAL SPASM ENDED, SHADOW WAS ON THE GROUND, HIS FINGERS CLUTCHING THE RED EARTH, GRATEFUL ONLY THAT THE PAIN WAS OVER AND HE COULD BREATH ONCE MORE, DEEP LUNGFULS OF WARM SUMMER AIR.

IT WAS TWILIGHT AND THE STARS WERE COMING OUT, BRIGHTER AND MORE VIVID THAN ANY STARS HE HAD EVER IMAGINED.

SOON, THEY WILL FALL, AND THE STAR PEOPLE WILL MEET THE EARTH PEOPLE. THERE WILL BE HEROES AMONG THEM, AND MEN WHO WILL SLAY MONSTERS AND BRING KNOWLEDGE, BUT NONE OF THEM WILL BE GODS.

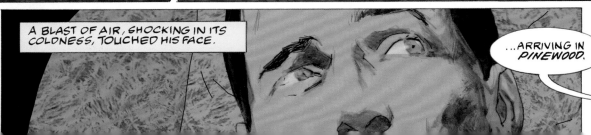

A BLAST OF AIR, SHOCKING IN ITS COLDNESS, TOUCHED HIS FACE.

...ARRIVING IN PINEWOOD.

HEY.. YOU'RE GETTING OFF IN LAKESIDE, RIGHT?

YES, I AM.

HECK, THAT'S A *GOOD* ONE. I THINK SOMETIMES THAT IF I WERE TO PACK IT ALL IN, I'D MOVE TO LAKESIDE. PRETTIEST TOWN I'VE EVER SEEN.

YOU LIVED THERE LONG?

MY FIRST VISIT.

YOU HAVE A PASTY AT MABEL'S FOR ME, YOU HEAR?

UHH... SURE.

TELL ME, WAS I TALKING IN MY SLEEP?

IF YOU WERE, I DIDN'T HEAR YOU.

BACK ON THE BUS!

THE TWO GIRLS WERE FRIENDS AND NOT MUCH OLDER THAN FOURTEEN, SHADOW DECIDED, EAVESDROPPING WITHOUT MEANING TO.

ONE OF THEM KNEW A LOT ABOUT ANIMALS, HELPED OUT AT SOME KIND OF ANIMAL SHELTER.

GOLDIE IS LIKE, SUCH A GOOD DOG. IF ONLY MY DAD WOULD SAY OKAY.

THE OTHER THOUGHT SHE KNEW A GREAT DEAL ABOUT HUMAN SEXUALITY, AND SHADOW LISTENED WITH A HORRIFIED FASCINATION.

SERIOUSLY, ALKA-SELTZER AND ORAL SEX. EVEN BETTER THAN ALTOIDS.

SHADOW STARTED TO TUNE THEM OUT, BLANKED OUT EVERYTHING EXCEPT THE NOISE OF THE ROAD, AND NOW ONLY FRAGMENTS OF CONVERSATION WOULD COME BACK, NOW AND AGAIN.

I MISS SANDY.

I MISS SANDY, TOO.

LAKESIDE!

THE DOORS CLUNKED OPEN AND SHADOW FOLLOWED THE GIRLS OUT INTO THE FLOODLIT PARKING LOT OF A VIDEO STORE AND TANNING SALON.

LAKESIDE'S GREYHOUND STATION.

THE AIR WAS DREADFULLY COLD, BUT IT WAS A FRESH COLD. IT WOKE HIM UP.

MERRY CHRISTMAS.

MERRY CHRISTMAS TO YOU, TOO.

YOU LOOK LIKE SOMEBODY. ARE YOU SOMEBODY'S BROTHER, OR SOMETHING?

YOU ARE SUCH A *SPAZ*, ALISON. EVERYBODY'S SOMEBODY'S BROTHER OR SOMETHING.

THAT WASN'T WHAT I MEANT. I...

OH!

THERE'S OUR RIDE.

YOUNG MAN? ANYTHING I CAN DO FOR YOU?

STORE AIN'T OPEN CHRISTMAS. BUT I COME DOWN TO MEET THE BUS. COULDN'T LIVE WITH MYSELF IF SOME POOR SOUL'D FOUND HIMSELF STRANDED ON CHRISTMAS DAY.

YOU COULD GIVE ME THE NUMBER FOR THE LOCAL TAXI.

I *COULD*, BUT TOM'LL BE IN HIS BED THIS TIME OF NIGHT. WHERE IS IT YOU'RE AIMING TO GO?

502 NORTHRIDGE ROAD.

WELL, THAT'S A TEN-, MEBBE A TWENTY-MINUTE WALK OVER THE BRIDGE AND AROUND.

BUT IT'S NO FUN WHEN IT'S THIS COLD, AND WHEN YOU DON'T KNOW WHERE YOU'RE GOING, IT ALWAYS SEEMS LONGER. EVER NOTICE THAT?

YES. I GUESS IT'S TRUE.

WHAT THE HECK, IT'S CHRISTMAS. I'LL RUN YOU OVER IN TESSIE.

TESSIE?

TESSIE.

AIN'T SHE A BEAUT?

C07764

WHAT MAKE IS SHE?

SHE'S A WENDT PHOENIX.

WENDT WENT UNDER IN '31. HARVEY WENDT, WHO FOUNDED THE COMPANY, WAS A LOCAL BOY. WENT OUT TO CALIFORNIA. KILLED HIMSELF IN, OH... '41... '42...

A GREAT TRAGEDY.

TOMORROW SHE GOES INTO THE GARAGE WHERE SHE'LL STAY UNTIL SPRING. TRUTH IS, I SHOULDN'T BE DRIVING HER RIGHT NOW.

DOESN'T SHE RIDE WELL IN SNOW?

RIDES JUST FINE. IT'S THE SALT THEY PUT ON THE ROADS. RUSTS OUT THESE OLD BEAUTIES.

YOU WANT TO GO STRAIGHT HOME, OR WOULD YOU LIKE THE MOONLIGHT GRAND TOUR OF THE TOWN?

I DON'T WANT TO TROUBLE YOU.

IT'S NO TROUBLE, AND WHERE ARE MY MANNERS? MY NAME IS RICHIE HINZELMANN. 'ROUND HERE, FOLKS JUST CALL ME HINZELMANN. I'D SHAKE HANDS, BUT I NEED BOTH TO DRIVE TESSIE.

MIKE AINSEL. PLEASED TO MEET YOU, HINZELMANN.

SO WE'LL GO 'ROUND THE LAKE. GRAND TOUR.

MAIN STREET WAS A PRETTY STREET, EVEN AT NIGHT. AND IT LOOKED OLD-FASHIONED IN THE BEST SENSE OF THE WORD -- AS IF, FOR A HUNDRED YEARS, PEOPLE HAD BEEN CARING FOR IT.

WE HAVE TWO RESTAURANTS. THERE'S A GERMAN ONE, AND THAT ONE THERE HAS A BIT OF EVERYTHING, POPOVER ON EVERY PLATE.

THERE'S OUR BOOKSTORE. WHAT I SAY IS, A TOWN ISN'T A TOWN WITHOUT A BOOKSTORE. IT MAY CALL ITSELF A TOWN, BUT UNLESS IT'S GOT A BOOKSTORE, IT KNOWS IT'S NOT FOOLIN' A SOUL.

Reader's Corner

AND THERE'S OUR LIBRARY. ISN'T IT A DREAM?

MIRIAM SHULTZ WANTS TO TEAR THE INSIDES OUT AND MODERNIZE, BUT IT'S ON THE REGISTER OF HISTORIC PLACES, AND THERE'S NOT A DAMN THING SHE CAN DO.

HA!

THE TOWN CIRCLED THE LAKE. THEY DROVE AROUND THE SOUTH SIDE.

YOU DO MUCH ICE FISHING, MR. AINSEL?

NEVER.

BEST THING A MAN CAN DO. IT'S NOT THE FISH YOU CATCH, IT'S THE PEACE OF MIND THAT YOU TAKE HOME AT THE END OF THE DAY.

I'LL REMEMBER THAT. CAN YOU WALK ON THE ICE ALREADY?

YOU CAN DRIVE ON IT TOO. THINGS FREEZE HARDER AND FASTER UP HERE IN NORTHERN WISCONSIN.

" I WAS OUT HUNTING ONCE, AND THIS WAS, OH, THIRTY OR FORTY YEARS BACK, AND I SHOT AT A BUCK, MISSED HIM, AND SENT HIM RUNNING OFF THROUGH THE WOODS. FINEST BUCK I EVER DID SEE, TWENTY POINT, BIG AS A SMALL HORSE.

NO LIE, "

"THERE WAS A CLEAN SNOW ON THE GROUND AND I COULD SEE THE BUCK'S HOOFPRINTS. NOW, I'M YOUNGER AND FIESTIER BACK THEN, SO THERE I AM, A DAMN FOOL, RUNNING AFTER HIM.

"AND THERE HE IS, STANDING IN THE LAKE, AND HE'S JUST LOOKING AT ME."

THAT VERY MOMENT, THE SUN GOES BEHIND A CLOUD AND THE FREEZE COMES--TEMPERATURE MUST HAVE FALLEN THIRTY DEGREES IN TEN MINUTES, NOT A WORD OF A LIE.

"AND THAT OLD STAG, HE GETS READY TO RUN AND HE CAN'T MOVE. HE'S FROZEN TO THE ICE.

"ME, I JUST WALK OVER TO HIM SLOWLY. BUT THERE'S NO WAY I CAN BRING MYSELF TO SHOOT A DEFENSELESS CREATURE,

"SO I FIRES OFF ONE SHELL STRAIGHT INTO THE AIR.

B
A
N
G

"WELL, THE NOISE AND THE SHOCK IS ENOUGH TO MAKE THAT BUCK JUST ABOUT JUMP OUT OF HIS SKIN, AND SEEIN' THAT HIS LEGS ARE ICED IN, THAT'S JUST WHAT HE DOES. HE CHARGES BACK INTO THE WOODS, PINK AS A NEWBORN MOUSE, AND SHIVERING, TO BOOT."

" I FELT BAO ENOUGH FOR THAT OLD BUCK THAT I TALKED TO THE LAKESIDE LADIES KNITTING CIRCLE AND THEY KNITTEO HIM AN ALL-OVER ONE-PIECE WOOLEN SUIT, SO HE WOULDN'T FREEZE TO DEATH.

" 'COURSE, THE JOKE WAS ON US, BECAUSE THEY KNITTED HIM A SUIT OF BRIGHT ORANGE, SO N HUNTER EVER SHOT AT IT. HUNTERS IN THESE PARTS WEAR ORANGE AT HUNTING SEASON."

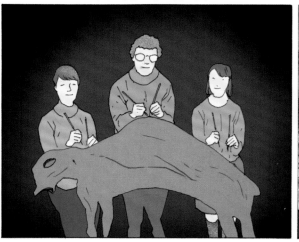

AND IF YOU THINK THERE'S A WORD OF A LIE IN THAT, I CAN PROVE IT TO YOU. I'VE GOT THE ANTLERS ON MY REC ROOM WALL TO THIS DAY.

SHADOW LAUGHED, AND THE OLD MAN SMILED THE SATISFIED SMILE OF A MASTER CRAFTSMAN.

THERE YOU GO, MIKE.

" 502 NORTHRIDGE ROAD."

CHAPTER TWO

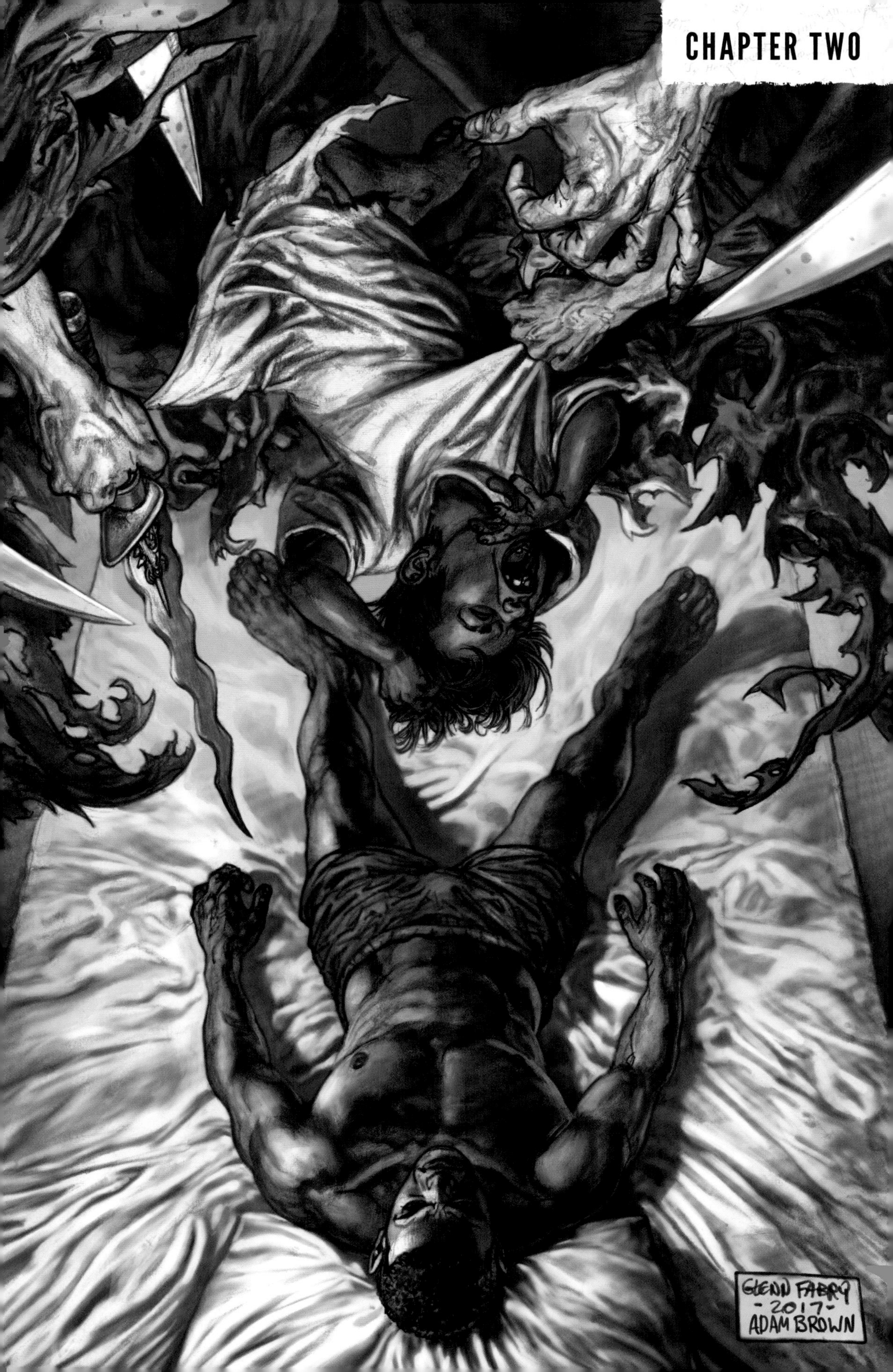
GLENN FABRY
-2017-
ADAM BROWN

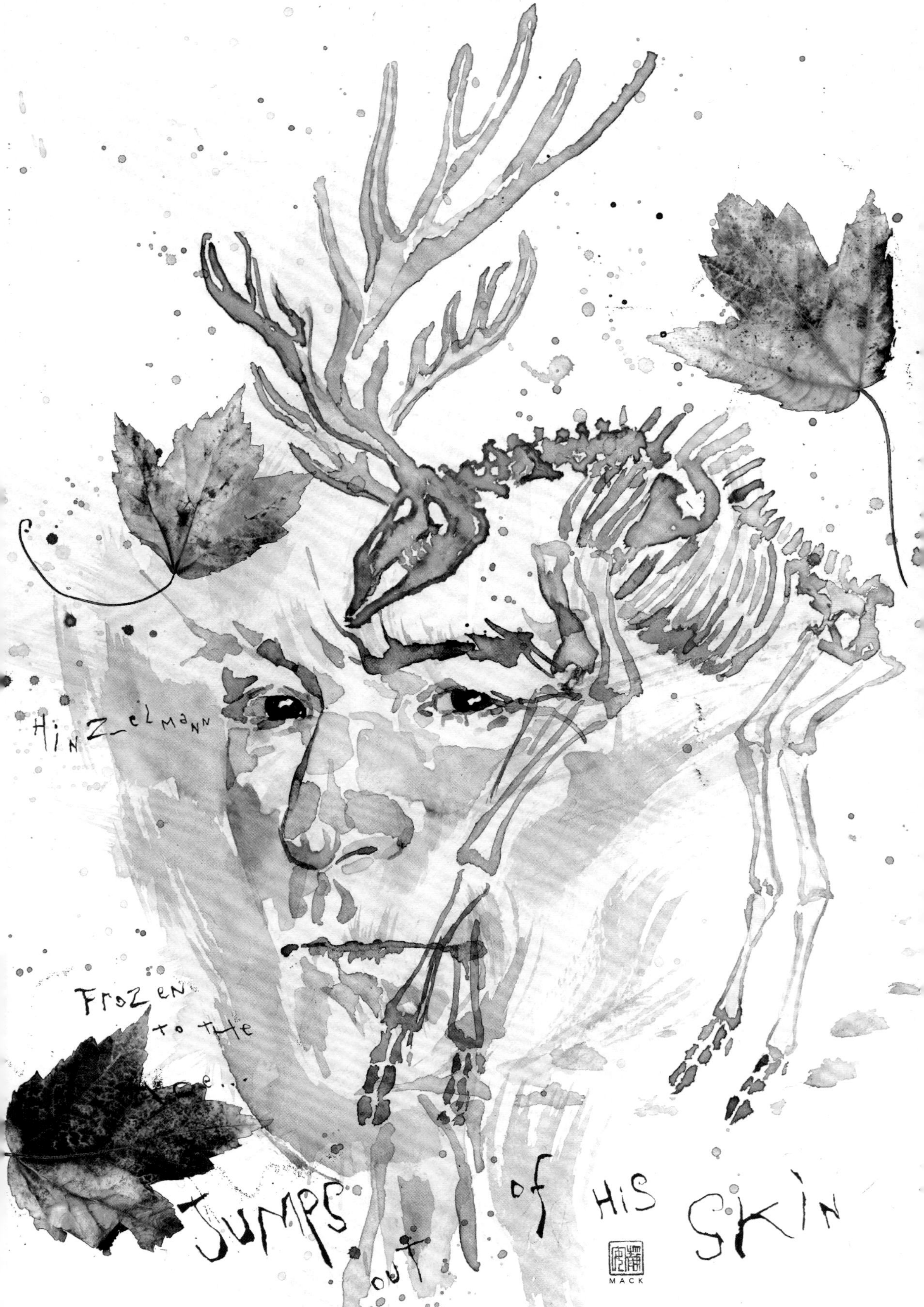
HINZ_ELMANN
FROZEN to THE
JUMPS out of HIS SKIN
MACK

THANK YOU FOR THE RIDE, MR. HINZELMANN. CAN I GIVE YOU ANYTHING TOWARD GAS?

JUST HINZELMANN. AND YOU DON'T OWE ME A PENNY. BUT, TELL YOU WHAT, SOMETIME IN THE NEXT WEEK OR SO, I'LL COME BY AND SELL YOU SOME TICKETS. FOR OUR RAFFLE. CHARITY.

MERRY CHRISTMAS, HINZELMANN.

MERRY CHRISTMAS FROM ME AND FROM TESSIE.

THE ROOM WAS FREEZING. IT SMELLED OF PEOPLE WHO HAD GONE AWAY TO LIVE OTHER LIVES.

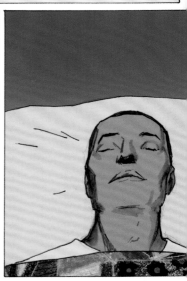

IN THE STILLNESS HE HEARD SOMETHING SNAP LIKE A SHOT. A BRANCH, HE THOUGHT, OR THE ICE.

SHE WAS IN EAGLE POINT,
OUTSIDE HER MOTHER'S
BIG HOUSE. SHE STOOD
IN THE COLD, WHICH SHE
DID NOT FEEL ANYMORE.

SHE WAS STARING IN, WATCHING HER
MOTHER AND ALL HER FAMILY, HOME FOR
CHRISTMAS. OUT IN THE DARKNESS, THAT
WAS WHERE LAURA WAS...

...UNABLE
NOT TO LOOK.

TEARS PRICKLED IN
SHADOW'S EYES AND
HE THOUGHT...

WEDNESDAY.

WITH JUST A THOUGHT, HE
WAS WATCHING FROM A
CORNER IN THE MOTEL 6.
HE FELT LIKE A PEEPING TOM.

HE COULD IMAGINE HUGE BLACK WINGS POUNDING
THROUGH THE NIGHT TOWARD HIM, PRYING JACK-FROST
FINGERS COLDER THAN THE FINGERS OF ANY CORPSE.

IF I'M GOING TO
BE ANYWHERE, IT MIGHT
AS WELL BE HERE.

AND
THEN
HE
SLEPT.

MEANWHILE. A CONVERSATION.

MIZ CROW? MIZ SAMANTHA BLACK CROW?

DO YOU MIND IF WE ASK YOU A FEW QUESTIONS, MA'AM?

YES?

YEAH I DO, ACTUALLY.

THERE'S NO NEED TO TAKE THAT ATTITUDE, MA'AM.

ARE YOU COPS? WHAT ARE YOU?

MY NAME IS TOWN. MY COLLEAGUE HERE IS MISTER ROAD. WE'RE INVESTIGATING THE DISAPPEARANCE OF TWO OF OUR ASSOCIATES.

WHAT ARE THEIR NAMES?

SORRY?

TELL ME THEIR NAMES. I WANT TO KNOW WHAT THEY WERE CALLED, YOUR ASSOCIATES. TELL ME THEIR NAMES AND MAYBE I'LL HELP YOU.

...OKAY. THEIR NAMES WERE MISTER STONE AND MISTER WOOD. NOW, CAN WE ASK *YOU* SOME QUESTIONS?

DO YOU GUYS JUST SEE THINGS AND PICK NAMES? 'OH, YOU BE MISTER SIDEWALK. HE'S MISTER CARPET. SAY HELLO TO MISTER AIRPLANE.'

VERY FUNNY.

FIRST QUESTION: WE NEED TO KNOW IF YOU'VE SEEN THIS MAN. HERE. YOU CAN HOLD THE PHOTOGRAPH.

WHOA. STRAIGHT ON AND PROFILE, WITH NUMBERS ON THE BOTTOM. HE'S CUTE, THOUGH. WHAT DID HE DO?

67

HE WAS THE DRIVER IN A SMALL-TOWN BANK ROBBERY.

HIS TWO COLLEAGUES DECIDED TO KEEP ALL THE LOOT FOR THEMSELVES AND RAN OUT ON HIM.

HE CAME CLOSE TO KILLING THEM WITH HIS BARE HANDS. GOT SIX YEARS, SERVED THREE. GUYS LIKE THAT... LOCK THEM UP AND THROW AWAY THE KEY.

I'VE NEVER HEARD ANYONE SAY THAT IN REAL LIFE, YOU KNOW? NOT OUT LOUD.

SAY WHAT, MIZ CROW?

LOOT. MAYBE IN MOVIES THEY SAY IT. NOT FOR REAL.

THIS ISN'T A MOVIE, MIZ CROW.

BLACK CROW. IT'S MIZ BLACK CROW. MY FRIENDS CALL ME "SAM".

GOT IT, SAM. NOW ABOUT THIS MAN...

BUT YOU AREN'T MY FRIENDS. YOU CAN CALL ME MIZ BLACK CROW.

LISTEN YOU SNOT-NOSED LITTLE...

IT'S OKAY, MISTER ROAD. SAM, HERE--PARDON, MA'AM. I MEAN, MIZ BLACK CROW WANTS TO HELP US. SHE'S A LAW-ABIDING CITIZEN.

MA'AM, WE KNOW YOU HELPED SHADOW. YOU WERE SEEN WITH HIM IN A WHITE HONDA CIVIC. DID HE SAY ANYTHING THAT COULD HELP US IN OUR INVESTIGATION? TWO OF OUR BEST MEN HAVE VANISHED.

I NEVER MET HIM.

YOU MET HIM.

WE'RE NOT STUPID. IT REALLY IS TO YOUR ADVANTAGE TO COOPERATE WITH US.

OTHERWISE YOU'LL HAVE TO INTRODUCE ME TO YOUR FRIENDS, MISTER THUMB-SCREWS AND MISTER PENTOTHAL?

MA'AM, YOU AREN'T MAKING THIS ANY EASIER ON YOURSELF.

GEE, I'M SORRY. NOW, IS THERE ANY-THING ELSE? COS I'M GOING TO CLOSE THE DOOR AND YOU TWO ARE GOING TO GET INTO MISTER CAR AND DRIVE AWAY.

YOUR LACK OF COOPERATION HAS BEEN NOTED MA'AM.

BUH-BYE NOW.

CLICK

10

A WHOLE LIFE IN DARKNESS, SURROUNDED BY FILTH, THAT WAS WHAT SHADOW DREAMED, HIS FIRST NIGHT IN LAKESIDE. A CHILD'S LIFE, LONG AGO, AND FAR AWAY, IN THE LANDS WHERE THE SUN ROSE. BUT THIS LIFE CONTAINED NO SURPRISES, ONLY DIMNESS BY DAY, AND BLINDNESS BY NIGHT.

NOBODY SPOKE TO HIM. HE HEARD HUMAN VOICES, FROM OUTSIDE, BUT HE COULD UNDERSTAND HUMAN SPEECH NO BETTER THAN HE UNDERSTOOD THE YELPS OF DOGS.

HE REMEMBERED ONE NIGHT, HALF A LIFETIME AGO, WHEN ONE OF THE BIG PEOPLE HAD ENTERED, QUIETLY.

SHE HAD NOT CUFFED HIM, OR FED HIM, BUT HAD PICKED HIM UP TO HER BREAST AND EMBRACED HIM.

SHE SMELLED GOOD. SHE HAD MADE COOING NOISES.

HOT DROPS OF WATER HAD FALLEN FROM HER FACE TO HIS. HE HAD BEEN SCARED, AND HAD WAILED LOUDLY IN HIS FEAR.

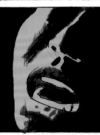

SHE PUT HIM DOWN ON THE STRAW, HURRIEDLY, AND LEFT THE HUT.

HE REMEMBERED THAT MOMENT AND HE TREASURED IT.

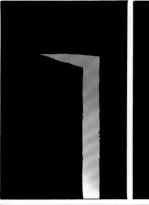

THE BONFIRE LIGHT HURT HIS EYES.

AND NOW HE SAW THE FACES IN THE FIRELIGHT, ALL OF THEM LOOKING AT HIM AS HE WAS LED FROM THE HUT. RAISED IN DARKNESS, HE HAD NEVER SEEN FACES. EVERYTHING WAS SO NEW.

THEY LED HIM TO A SPACE BETWEEN TWO BONFIRES WHERE THE MAN WAITED FOR HIM.

AND WHEN THE FIRST BLADE WAS RAISED IN THE FIRELIGHT...

...WHAT A CHEER WENT UP FROM THE CROWD AND THE CHILD FROM THE DARKNESS BEGAN TO LAUGH WITH THEM, IN DELIGHT....

...AND IN FREEDOM.

AND THEN THE BLADE CAME DOWN.

SHADOW OPENED HIS EYES AND REALIZED THAT HE WAS HUNGRY AND COLD.

HE TRIED TO REMEMBER HIS DREAM, BUT REMEMBERED NOTHING BUT MISERY AND DARKNESS.

HE PUT ON HIS SHOES.

REMEMBERING HIS PROMISE TO HIMSELF TO BUY A WARM WINTER COAT, HE STEPPED OUT ONTO THE WOODEN DECK. THE COLD TOOK HIS BREATH AWAY.

IT COULD NOT BE MUCH ABOVE ZERO, AND IT WOULD NOT BE A PLEASANT WALK TO THE TOWN CENTER, BUT SHADOW WAS A BIG MAN. HE WOULD WALK BRISKLY AND KEEP HIM- SELF WARM. HE SET OFF, HEADING FOR THE BRIDGE.

SOON HE BEGAN TO COUGH AS THE BITTERLY COLD AIR TOUCHED HIS LUNGS. HIS EARS AND FACE AND LIPS HURT, AND THEN HIS FEET.

STEP AFTER STEP AFTER STEP.

THE APARTMENT BUILDING WAS NOT AS FAR AWAY AS HE HAD EXPECTED.

THIS WAS A MISTAKE.

GO HOME.

AND THEN WHAT?

CALL A TAXI ON A DEAD PHONE?

WAIT FOR SPRING?

THERE'S NO FOOD IN THE APARTMENT.

THE WIND WAS NOW HARD AND STEADY AND CONTINUOUS, BLOWING OVER THE LAKE, COMING DOWN FROM THE ARCTIC ACROSS CANADA. HE KEPT REVISING HIS ESTIMATE OF THE TEMPERATURE DOWNWARD AS HE WALKED.

MINUS TEN?

MINUS TWENTY?

HE LOOKED DOWN AT HIS BLACK LEATHER SHOES, AT THE THIN COTTON SOCKS, AND BEGAN, SERIOUSLY, TO WORRY ABOUT FROSTBITE.

THIS WAS BEYOND A JOKE, BEYOND FOOLISHNESS, OVER THE LINE INTO THE TERRITORY OF GENUINE...

JESUS CHRIST! I FUCKED UP BIG TIME.

KEEP WALKING.

A BEATLES SONG STARTED IN HIS HEAD, AND HE ADJUSTED HIS PACE TO MATCH IT. IT WAS ONLY WHEN HE GOT TO THE CHORUS THAT HE REALIZED HE WAS HUMMING......

HELP.

EVERYTHING OKAY HERE?

SHADOW'S FIRST AUTOMATIC INSTINCT WAS TO SAY...

YUP, EVERYTHING'S FINE AND DANDY, OFFICER. NOTHING TO SEE HERE. MOVE ON.

HE WAS THAT FAR INTO THE SENTENCE IN HIS HEAD WHEN HE REALIZED ALL THAT HAD COME OUT WAS...

FREEZING.

YOU GET IN THERE THIS MOMENT AND WARM YOURSELF UP, OKAY?

SHADOW TRIED NOT TO THINK ABOUT THE LAST TIME HE'D BEEN IN THE BACK OF A POLICE CAR.

YOU KNOW, THAT WAS, IF YOU'LL PARDON ME SAYING SO, A REAL STUPID THING TO DO. IT'S MINUS THIRTY OUT THERE. GOD ALONE KNOWS WHAT THE WINDCHILL IS. MINUS SIXTY, MINUS SEVENTY.

THANKS FOR STOPPING. VERY, VERY GRATEFUL.

WOMAN IN RHINELANDER WENT OUT THIS MORNING TO FILL HER BIRD FEEDER IN HER ROBE AND SLIPPERS AND SHE FROZE, LITERALLY FROZE TO THE SIDEWALK. SHE'S IN INTENSIVE CARE NOW. IT WAS ON THE RADIO THIS MORNING.

YOU'RE NEW IN TOWN.

IT WAS ALMOST A QUESTION.

I CAME IN ON THE GREYHOUND LAST NIGHT. FIGURED TODAY I'D BUY MYSELF SOME WARM CLOTHES, FOOD, AND A CAR. WASN'T EXPECTING THIS COLD.

YEAH, IT TOOK ME BY SURPRISE AS WELL.

I'M CHAD MULLIGAN. I'M THE CHIEF OF POLICE HERE IN LAKESIDE.

MIKE AINSEL.

HI, MIKE. SO WHERE WOULD YOU LIKE ME TO TAKE YOU FIRST?

CAN YOU JUST DROP ME OFF IN THE TOWN CENTER?

WOULDN'T HEAR OF IT. I'LL TAKE YOU WHEREVER YOU NEED TO GO... LONG AS YOU DON'T NEED ME TO DRIVE A GET-AWAY CAR FOR YOUR BANK ROBBERY.

HA!

YOU EATEN BREAKFAST YET?

NOT YET.

WELL, THEN-- MABEL'S.

MABEL'S WAS FRAGRANT WITH THE SMELLS OF NEW-BAKED BREAD, OF PASTRY, AND SOUP AND BACON.

HELLO, CHAD. YOU'LL WANT A HOT CHOCOLATE WHILE YOU'RE THINKING.

NO CREAM ON TOP, THOUGH.

MABEL KNOWS ME TOO WELL.

WHAT'LL IT BE, PAL?

HOT CHOCOLATE. AND I'M HAPPY TO HAVE THE WHIPPED CREAM ON TOP.

THAT'S GOOD. LIVE DANGEROUSLY, HON.

ARE YOU GOING TO INTRODUCE ME, CHAD? IS THIS YOUNG MAN A NEW OFFICER?

NOT YET. THIS IS MIKE AINSEL. HE MOVED TO LAKESIDE LAST NIGHT.

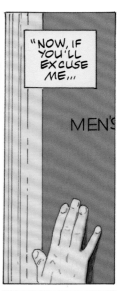

"NOW, IF YOU'LL EXCUSE ME..."

MEN'S

YOU'RE THE NEW MAN IN THE APARTMENT UP ON NORTHRIDGE ROAD. HINZELMANN WAS BY THIS MORNING FOR HIS MORNING PASTY. HE TOLD ME ALL ABOUT YOU. WANT TO LOOK AT THE BREAKFAST MENU?

WHAT'S GOOD?

EVERYTHING'S GOOD. I MAKE IT. BUT THE PASTIES ARE PARTICULARLY GOOD-- WARM AND FILLING, TOO. MY SPECIALTY.

I HAVE NO IDEA WHAT THAT IS, BUT I'LL TRY ONE.

FIRST PASTY I EVER HAD. IT'S REAL GOOD.

THEY'RE A *YOOPIE* THING. MEAT-- POTATOES-- CARROTS-- ONIONS... THE CORNISH MEN WHO CAME OVER TO WORK THE IRON MINES BROUGHT THEM OVER.

YOOPIE?

UPPER PENINSULA OF MICHIGAN. *U.P.* YOOPIE.

THEY GO STRAIGHT TO THE BELLY, I WARN YOU.

OKAY. SO YOU NEED A CAR?

MM-HMFF

RIGHT. I MADE SOME CALLS. THE GUNTHERS' TOYOTA 4RUNNER FOR SALE. UGLY SONOFA-BITCH. PROBABLY PAY YOU TO TAKE IT OUT OF THEIR DRIVEWAY.

IT'S GOT TO BE A GREAT DEAL. I USED THE PHONE IN THE MEN'S ROOM, LEFT A MESSAGE FOR MISSY GUNTHER AT LAKESIDE REALTY.

SO, I FIGURE WE STOP OFF NEXT AT HENNING'S HOME AND FARM, GET YOU A REAL WINTER WARDROBE, SWING BY DAVE'S FINEST FOOD FOR SUPPLIES, THEN I'LL DROP YOU UP BY LAKESIDE REALTY. IF YOU CAN PUT A THOUSAND UP FRONT FOR THE CAR THEY'LL BE HAPPY.

THIS IS VERY GOOD OF YOU, BUT SHOULDN'T YOU BE OUT CATCHING CRIMINALS? NOT HELPING NEW-COMERS?

WE ALL TELL HIM THAT.

IT'S A GOOD TOWN. NOT MUCH TROUBLE. THEY CALL ME OUT WHEN SOMEONE'S LOCKED THEIR KEYS IN THEIR CAR.

"BIGGEST POLICE CASE WE'VE HAD HERE IN FIVE YEARS WAS WHEN DAN SCHWARTZ GOT DRUNK. SHOT UP HIS OWN TRAILER AND WENT ON THE RUN IN HIS WHEELCHAIR HEAD-ING FOR THE INTERSTATE.

"I STILL LAUGH WHENEVER I THINK OF THAT WHEEL-CHAIR OF HIS WITH THE BUMPER STICKER ON THE BACK."

MY JUVENILE DELINQUENT IS SCREWING YOUR HONOR STUDENT

YOU REMEMBER, MABEL?

MM HMMMM~

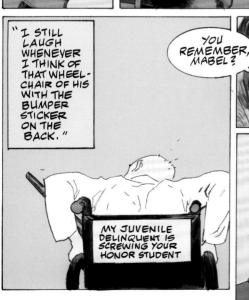

WHAT DID YOU DO?

I TALKED TO HIM. HE GAVE ME THE SHOTGUN. SLEPT IT OFF DOWN AT THE JAIL. DAN'S NOT A BAD GUY, HE WAS JUST DRUNK AND UPSET.

SHADOW PAID FOR HIS BREAKFAST AND, OVER MULLIGAN'S HALF-HEARTED PROTESTS, BOTH HOT CHOCOLATES.

HENNING'S FARM AND HOME -- A WAREHOUSE-SIZED BUILDING ON THE SOUTH SIDE OF TOWN THAT SOLD EVERYTHING FROM TRACTORS TO TOYS -- WAS BUSTLING WITH POST-CHRISTMAS SHOPPERS.

!

FRIEND OF YOURS?

SHE SAT IN FRONT OF ME ON THE BUS INTO TOWN.

THE GIRL AT THE CHECKOUT WAS MOVIE STARLET BEAUTIFUL AND CAPABLE, SHADOW HAD NO DOUBT, OF RINGING UP A TRACTOR SHOULD IT COME THROUGH.

TEN PAIRS OF LONG UNDERWEAR? STOCKING UP, HUH?

HEH

HE HAD NO WISH TO PUT THE CREDIT CARD WEDNESDAY HAD GIVEN HIM TO THE TEST IN FRONT OF CHIEF OF POLICE MULLIGAN, SO HE PAID FOR EVERYTHING IN CASH.

MEN'S DRESSING ROOM

MEN'S DRESSING ROOM

MEN'S DRESSING ROOM

LOOKING GOOD, BIG FELLA.

AT LEAST I'M WARM.

SO, MR. AINSEL, WHAT'S YOUR PROFESSION? AND WILL YOU BE PRACTICING IT IN LAKESIDE?

I WORK FOR MY UNCLE. HE BUYS AND SELLS STUFF. I DO THE HEAVY LIFTING.

I'M FAMILY, SO HE KNOWS I'M NOT GOING TO RIP HIM OFF, AND I'M LEARNING A LITTLE ABOUT THE TRADE UNTIL I FIGURE OUT WHAT I REALLY WANT TO DO.

THE WORDS WERE COMING OUT OF SHADOW WITH CONVICTION, SMOOTH AS A SNAKE. HE KNEW EVERYTHING ABOUT MIKE AINSEL IN THAT MOMENT, AND HE LIKED MIKE AINSEL.

MIKE AINSEL HAD NEVER BEEN INTERROGATED ON A FREIGHT TRAIN BY MR. WOOD AND MR. STONE.

TELEVISIONS DID NOT SPEAK TO HIM.

YOU WANT TO SEE LUCY'S TITS?

MIKE AINSEL DIDN'T HAVE BAD DREAMS, OR BELIEVE THAT THERE WAS A STORM COMING.

HE FILLED HIS SHOPPING BASKET AT DAVE'S FINEST FOODS AS CHAD MULLIGAN INTRODUCED HIM AROUND.

SHADOW GAVE UP TRYING TO REMEMBER NAMES, AND SIMPLY SMILED, SWEATING IN HIS INSULATED LAYERS.

MISSY GUNTHER LAKESIDE REALTY

I KNOW EXACTLY WHO MIKE AINSEL IS.

WHY, THAT NICE MR. BORSON. HIS UNCLE EMERSON, HE'D BEEN BY, WHAT, ABOUT EIGHT WEEKS AGO NOW, AND RENTED THAT APARTMENT, A WHOLE YEAR IN ADVANCE.

ISN'T THE VIEW JUST TO DIE FOR UP THERE?

AND, CHAD, I CAN'T BELIEVE YOU REMEMBERED THAT TOYOTA 4RUNNER.

EXCUSE ME, I'M NEEDED AT THE OFFICE.

TRUTH TO TELL, I WAS RESIGNED TO GIVING IT TO HINZELMANN AS THE YEAR'S KLUNKER.

WELL...

NOT THAT IT'S A *KLUNKER.* IT WAS MY SON'S CAR BEFORE HE WENT OFF TO SCHOOL, *GREEN BAY,* AND...

HE PAINTED IT PURPLE.

COME IN THE KITCHEN.

HOW STONED WOULD YOU HAVE TO BE?

EXCUSE THE *MESS.* THE LITTLE ONES AND THEIR CHRISTMAS TOYS.

NO?

HAVE A SEAT. CARE FOR SOME LEFTOVER TURKEY?

WELL, COFFEE THEN...

HAVE YOU MET YOUR NEIGHBORS YET?

UH... NO.

WELL, THE DOWNSTAIRS FLAT IS TAKEN BY A *COUPLE,* MR. HOLZ AND MR. NEIMAN. TRUTH TO TELL, NOBODY GIVES IT A *SECOND* THOUGHT. THEY'RE IN KEY WEST FOR THE WINTER.

NOW, *NEXT DOOR* TO YOU, MR. AINSEL, THAT'S MARGUERITE OLSEN AND HER LITTLE BOY. A *SWEET* LADY, BUT SHE'S HAD A *HARD* LIFE. WORKS FOR *THE LAKESIDE NEWS.*

NOT THE MOST *EXCITING* NEWSPAPER IN THE WORLD.

TRUTH TO TELL, I THINK THAT'S PROBABLY THE WAY MOST FOLKS LIKE IT.

OH, BUT I *WISH* YOU COULD SEE THE TOWN WHEN THE LILACS, OR THE CHERRY BLOSSOMS ARE OUT. THERE'S *NOTHING* LIKE IT FOR BEAUTY.

NOTHING LIKE IT ANYWHERE IN THE WORLD.

SHADOW GAVE HER A FIVE HUNDRED DOLLAR DEPOSIT, CLIMBED INTO THE CAR, AND STARTED TO BACK OUT OF HER FRONT YARD.

TAP TAP

THIS IS FOR YOU.

I ALMOST FORGOT.

IT'S KIND OF A GAG.

YOU DON'T HAVE TO LOOK AT IT NOW.

CHOCO

PASSPORT

THE ENVELOPE FROM MISSY GUNTHER CONTAINED A 'PASSPORT.' BLUE LAMINATED COVER, AND INSIDE, A PROCLAMATION THAT...

Michael Ainsel
IS A CITIZEN OF
Lakeside.

THE REST OF IT WAS FILLED WITH DISCOUNT COUPONS FOR VARIOUS STORES.

I THINK I MAY LIKE IT HERE.

IF IT EVER WARMS UP.

2 P.M.

?

IH HIHELHAN.

HUH ?

I SAID, IT'S HINZELMANN. YOU KNOW, I DON'T KNOW WHAT THEY DID BEFORE THESE MASKS, I MAY BE AN OLD MAN, BUT I'M NOT GOING TO GRUMBLE ABOUT PROGRESS.

MERRY DAY AFTER CHRISTMAS. I BROUGHT YOU A FEW THINGS.

THAT'S VERY KIND OF YOU.

KIND, NOTHING. I'M GOING TO STICK IT TO YOU NEXT WEEK FOR THE RAFFLE. LAST YEAR WE RAISED SEVENTEEN THOUSAND FOR THE CHILDREN'S HOSPITAL.

WELL, WHY DON'T YOU PUT ME DOWN FOR A TICKET NOW?

IT DON'T START UNTIL THE DAY THE CLUNKER HITS THE ICE. COLD OUT THERE, MUST HAVE DROPPED FIFTY DEGREES LAST NIGHT.

IT HAPPENED REALLY FAST.

WE USED TO PRAY FOR FREEZES LIKE THIS BACK IN THE OLD DAYS.

YOU'D PRAY FOR FREEZES LIKE THIS?

WELL, *YAH*, IT WAS THE ONLY WAY SETTLERS SURVIVED BACK THEN, WEREN'T ENOUGH FOOD FOR EVERYONE IN THE OLD DAYS, NO, *SIR*.

"SO MY GRAMPAW, HE GOT TO THINKING, AND, WHEN A REALLY COLD DAY COME ALONG HE'D TAKE MY GRAMMAW, AND THE KIDS, AND THE HIRED MAN, AND HE'D GO DOWN WITH THEM TO THE CREEK, GIVE 'EM A LITTLE RUM-AND-HERBS DRINK, RECIPE FROM THE OLD COUNTRY...

"THEN HE'D POUR CREEK WATER OVER THEM. 'COURSE THEY'D FREEZE IN SECONDS, STIFF AND BLUE.

" HE'D HAUL THEM TO A TRENCH THEY'D ALREADY DUG AND FILLED WITH STRAW.

" AND HE'D STACK THEM DOWN THERE, LIKE SO MUCH CORDWOOD, AND HE'D PACK STRAW AROUND THEM.

" THEN HE'D COVER THE TRENCH WITH TWO-BY-FOURS TO KEEP THE CRITTERS OUT.

" AND THE NEXT SNOWFALL WOULD COVER IT UP COMPLETELY SAVE FOR THE FLAG HE'D PLANTED TO SHOW HIM WHERE THE TRENCH WAS."

"THEN MY GRAMPAW WOULD NEVER HAVE TO WORRY ABOUT RUNNING OUT OF FOOD OR FUEL.

" AND WHEN HE SAW THAT SPRING WAS COMING HE'D DIG THEM OUT AND SET THEM BY THE FIRE TO THAW.

"NOBODY MINDED EXCEPT THE HIRED MAN, WHO LOST HALF AN EAR TO A FAMILY OF MICE ONE TIME MY GRAMPAW DIDN'T PUSH THOSE TWO-BY-FOURS ALL THE WAY CLOSED. "

OF COURSE, IN THOSE DAYS WE HAD *REAL* WINTERS. THESE PUSSY WINTERS WE GET NOWADAYS, IT DON'T HARDLY GET COLD ENOUGH.

I SEE YOU BOUGHT YOURSELF A VEE-HICLE.

YUP. WHAT DO YOU THINK?

TRUTH TO TELL, I NEVER LIKED THAT *GUNTHER* BOY. I HAD A TROUT STREAM DOWN IN THE WOODS. I MADE LITTLE POOLS AND PLACES WHERE THE TROUT LIKED TO LIVE, AND THAT LITTLE SO-AND-SO THREATENED TO REPORT ME TO THE D.N.R.

NOW HE'S IN GREEN BAY, AND SOON ENOUGH, HE'LL BE BACK HERE. IF THERE WERE ANY JUSTICE IN THE WORLD, HE'D HAVE GONE OFF IN THE WORLD AS A WINTER RUNAWAY.

WINTER RUNAWAY?

MM... WELL, IT AIN'T UNIQUE TO LAKESIDE -- WE'RE A GOOD TOWN, BUT WE'RE NOT PERFECT. SOME WINTERS MAYBE A KID GETS A BIT STIR-CRAZY, WHEN IT GETS SO COLD...

THEY RUN OFF?

I BLAME THE TELEVISION -- SHOWING ALL THE KIDS THINGS THEY'LL NEVER HAVE.

DALLAS AND DYNASTY AND BEVERLY HILLS AND HAWAII FIVE-O, ALL OF THAT NONESENSE.

BIGGEST PROBLEM IN THIS PART OF THE WORLD IS POVERTY. LOGGING'S DEAD. MINING'S DEAD. ONLY A HANDFUL OF HUNTERS DRIVE THIS FAR NORTH AND THEY AREN'T SPENDING THEIR MONEY IN THE TOWNS.

LAKESIDE SEEMS PROSPEROUS, THOUGH.

AND BELIEVE ME, IT TAKES A LOT OF *HARD WORK*. BUT ALL THE WORK ALL THE PEOPLE PUT INTO IT IS WORTHWHILE. NOT THAT MY FAMILY WEREN'T POOR AS KIDS.

ASK ME HOW POOR WE WAS AS KIDS.

HOW POOR *WERE* YOU AS KIDS?

WE WERE SO POOR THAT WE COULDN'T AFFORD A FIRE. COME NEW YEAR'S EVE, MY FATHER WOULD SUCK ON A PEPPERMINT AND WE'D STRETCH OUT OUR HANDS, BASKING IN THE GLOW.

BA DA- BING!

YOU GET TOO BORED UP HERE, YOU JUST COME DOWN TO THE STORE. I'LL SHOW YOU MY COLLECTION OF HAND-TIED FISHING FLIES.

BORE YOU SO MUCH THAT GETTING BACK HERE WILL BE A RELIEF.

I'LL DO THAT. HOW'S TESSIE?

HIBERNATING.

YOU TAKE CARE, MISTER AINSEL.

THE APARTMENT GREW EVER COLDER. SHADOW'S BREATH WAS CLOUDING IN THE AIR.

FOR HEAVEN'S SAKE, SHUT UP AND TURN THAT TELEVISION DOWN.

YES ?

CHAPTER THREE

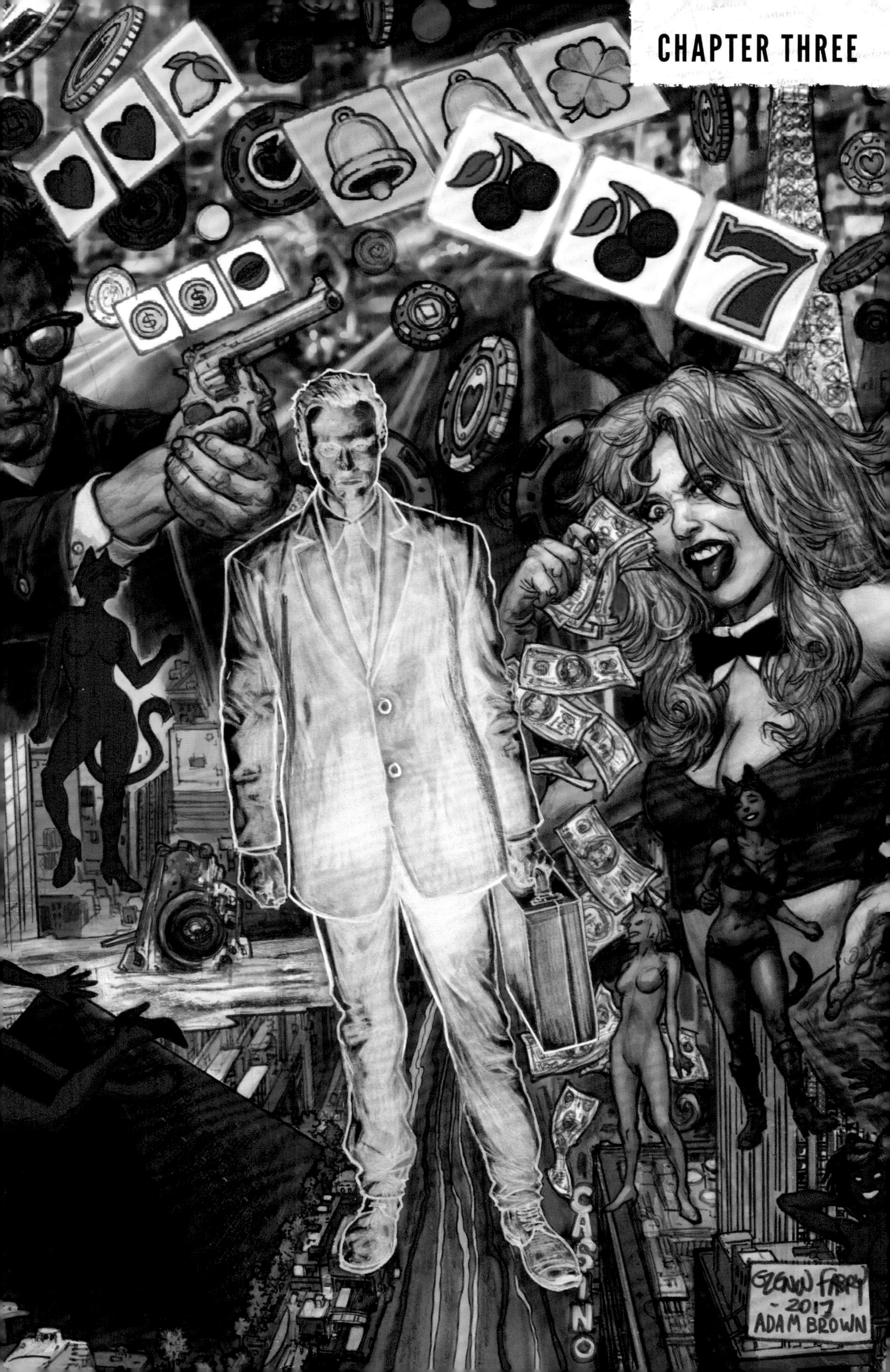
CASINO
GLENN FABRY
-2017-
ADAM BROWN

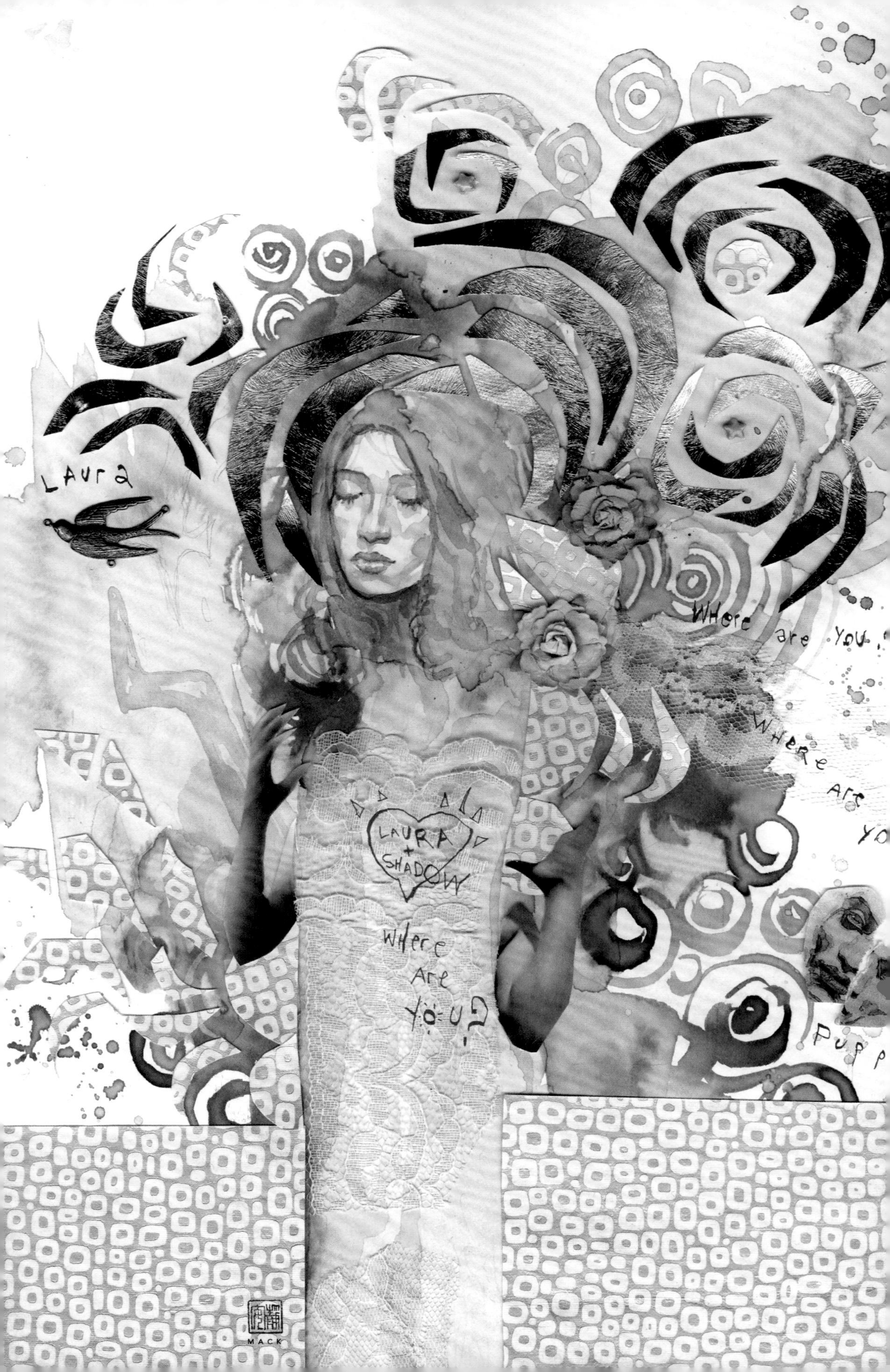
Laura
Where are you
Where are you
LAURA + SHADOW
Where are you?
PUPP
MACK

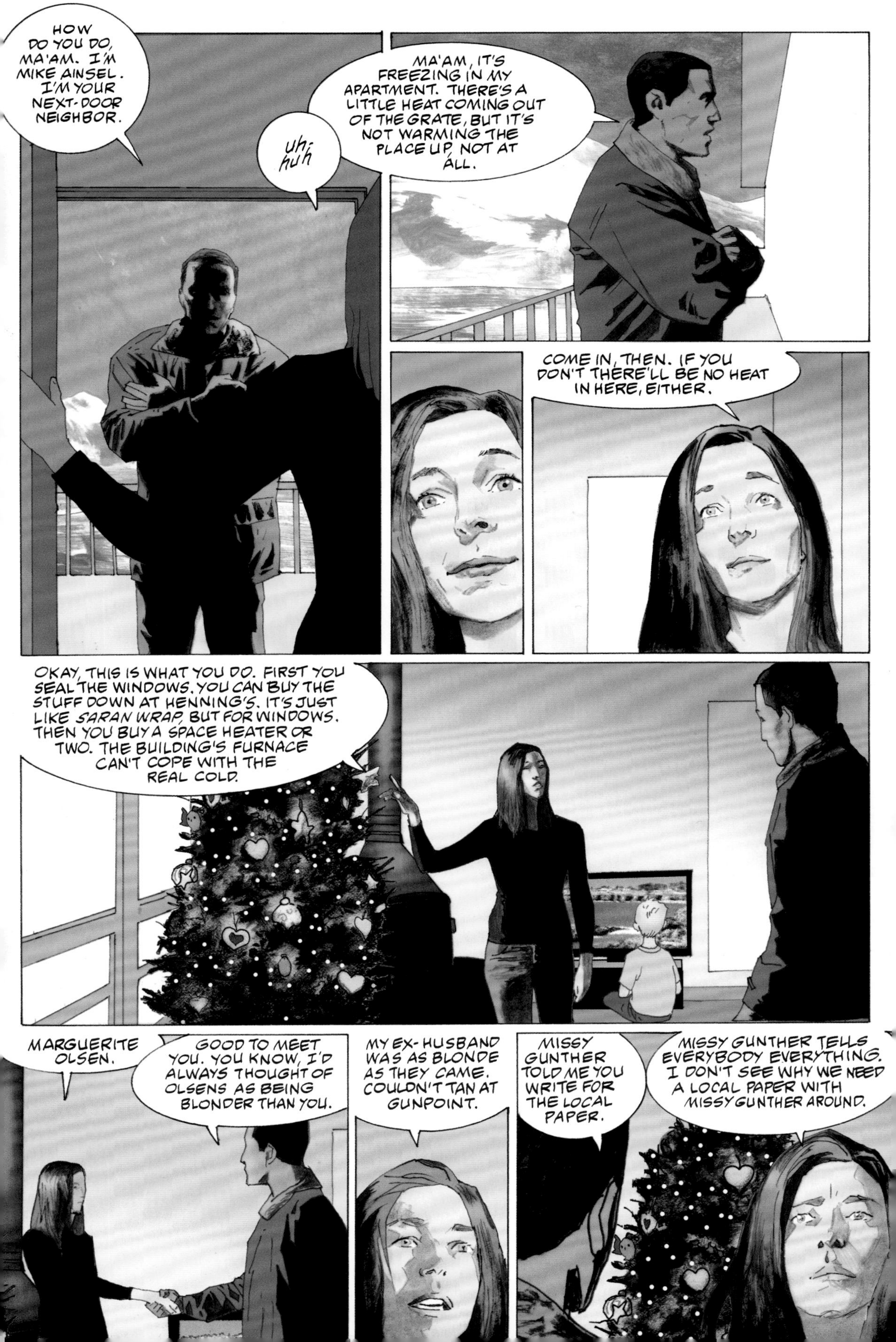
HOW DO YOU DO, MA'AM. I'M MIKE AINSEL. I'M YOUR NEXT-DOOR NEIGHBOR.
UH-HUH
MA'AM, IT'S FREEZING IN MY APARTMENT. THERE'S A LITTLE HEAT COMING OUT OF THE GRATE, BUT IT'S NOT WARMING THE PLACE UP, NOT AT ALL.
COME IN, THEN. IF YOU DON'T THERE'LL BE NO HEAT IN HERE, EITHER.
OKAY, THIS IS WHAT YOU DO. FIRST YOU SEAL THE WINDOWS. YOU CAN BUY THE STUFF DOWN AT HENNING'S. IT'S JUST LIKE SARAN WRAP, BUT FOR WINDOWS. THEN YOU BUY A SPACE HEATER OR TWO. THE BUILDING'S FURNACE CAN'T COPE WITH THE REAL COLD.
MARGUERITE OLSEN.
GOOD TO MEET YOU. YOU KNOW, I'D ALWAYS THOUGHT OF OLSENS AS BEING BLONDER THAN YOU.
MY EX-HUSBAND WAS AS BLONDE AS THEY CAME. COULDN'T TAN AT GUNPOINT.
MISSY GUNTHER TOLD ME YOU WRITE FOR THE LOCAL PAPER.
MISSY GUNTHER TELLS EVERYBODY EVERYTHING. I DON'T SEE WHY WE NEED A LOCAL PAPER WITH MISSY GUNTHER AROUND.

MY EDITOR WRITES MOST OF THE NEWS. I WRITE THE GARDENING COLUMN, THE NATURE COLUMN, AND THE 'NEWS FROM THE COMMUNITY' COLUMN, YOU KNOW, WHO WENT TO DINNER WITH WHO FOR FIFTEEN MILES AROUND?

OR IS IT WHOM?

BEFORE HE COULD STOP HIMSELF...

WHOM. IT'S THE OBJECTIVE CASE.

DEJA VU.

I'VE BEEN HERE BEFORE.

NO. SHE REMINDS ME OF SOMEONE.

ANYWAY, THAT'S HOW YOU HEAT UP YOUR APARTMENT.

THANK YOU. WHEN IT'S WARM YOU AND YOUR LITTLE ONE MUST COME OVER.

HIS NAME'S LEON. GOOD MEETING YOU, MISTER... I'M SORRY...

AINSEL. MIKE AINSEL.

AND WHAT SORT OF NAME IS AINSEL? NORWEGIAN MAYBE?

I'M AFRAID I WAS NEVER VERY KEEN ON FAMILY HISTORY.

I'M YOUR UNCLE BORSON.

ON THAT SIDE, ANYWAY.

BY THE TIME THAT MR. WEDNESDAY ARRIVED, SHADOW HAD PUT CLEAR PLASTIC SHEETING ACROSS THE WINDOWS AND HAD TWO SPACE HEATERS RUNNING. IT WAS PRACTICALLY COZY.

WHAT THE HELL IS THAT PURPLE PIECE OF SHIT YOU'RE DRIVING?

WELL, YOU DROVE OFF WITH MY WHITE PIECE OF SHIT. WHERE IS IT, BY THE WAY?

DULUTH. TRADED IT IN. YOU CAN'T BE TOO CAREFUL.

WHAT AM I DOING HERE? IN LAKESIDE, I MEAN. NOT IN THE WORLD.

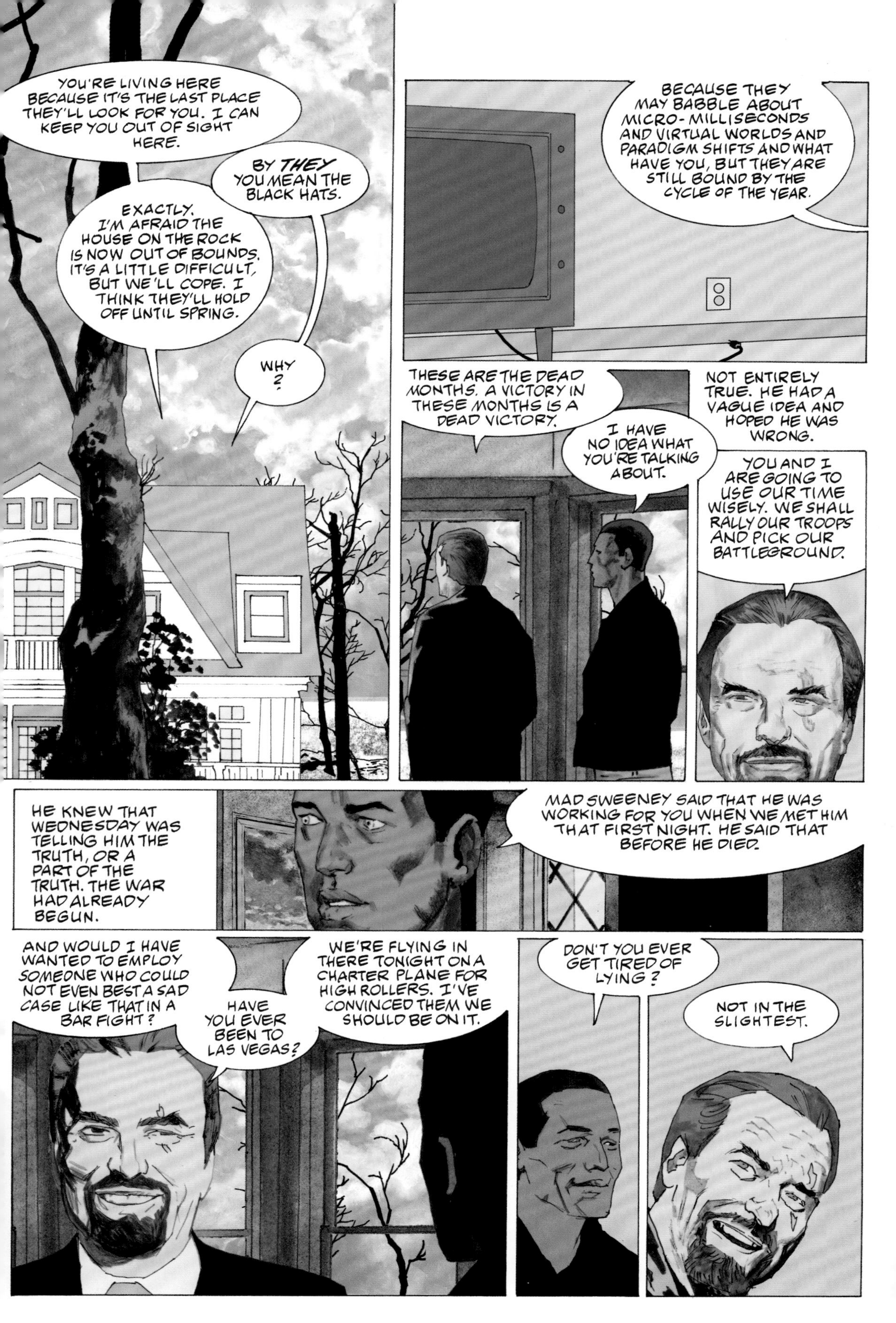
YOU'RE LIVING HERE BECAUSE IT'S THE LAST PLACE THEY'LL LOOK FOR YOU. I CAN KEEP YOU OUT OF SIGHT HERE.
BY *THEY* YOU MEAN THE BLACK HATS.
EXACTLY. I'M AFRAID THE HOUSE ON THE ROCK IS NOW OUT OF BOUNDS. IT'S A LITTLE DIFFICULT, BUT WE'LL COPE. I THINK THEY'LL HOLD OFF UNTIL SPRING.
WHY?
BECAUSE THEY MAY BABBLE ABOUT MICRO-MILLISECONDS AND VIRTUAL WORLDS AND PARADIGM SHIFTS AND WHAT HAVE YOU, BUT THEY ARE STILL BOUND BY THE CYCLE OF THE YEAR.
THESE ARE THE DEAD MONTHS. A VICTORY IN THESE MONTHS IS A DEAD VICTORY.
I HAVE NO IDEA WHAT YOU'RE TALKING ABOUT.
NOT ENTIRELY TRUE. HE HAD A VAGUE IDEA AND HOPED HE WAS WRONG.
YOU AND I ARE GOING TO USE OUR TIME WISELY. WE SHALL RALLY OUR TROOPS AND PICK OUR BATTLEGROUND.
HE KNEW THAT WEDNESDAY WAS TELLING HIM THE TRUTH, OR A PART OF THE TRUTH. THE WAR HAD ALREADY BEGUN.
MAD SWEENEY SAID THAT HE WAS WORKING FOR YOU WHEN WE MET HIM THAT FIRST NIGHT. HE SAID THAT BEFORE HE DIED.
AND WOULD I HAVE WANTED TO EMPLOY SOMEONE WHO COULD NOT EVEN BEST A SAD CASE LIKE THAT IN A BAR FIGHT?
HAVE YOU EVER BEEN TO LAS VEGAS?
WE'RE FLYING IN THERE TONIGHT ON A CHARTER PLANE FOR HIGH ROLLERS. I'VE CONVINCED THEM WE SHOULD BE ON IT.
DON'T YOU EVER GET TIRED OF LYING?
NOT IN THE SLIGHTEST.

...ANYWAY, IT'S TRUE WE ARE PLAYING FOR THE HIGHEST STAKES OF ALL. SO LOCK YOUR DOOR AND TURN OFF THE HEATERS. IT WOULD BE A TERRIBLE THING IF YOU BURNED DOWN YOUR HOUSE IN YOUR ABSENCE.

WHO ARE WE GOING TO SEE IN LAS VEGAS?

WEDNESDAY TOLD HIM.

SHADOW PACKED SOME CLOTHES, AND THEN...

?

LOOK, I KNOW YOU JUST TOLD ME WHO WE'RE GOING TO SEE. BUT I DUNNO, IT'S GONE. WHO ARE WE GOING TO SEE?

WEDNESDAY TOLD HIM AGAIN.

THIS TIME HE ALMOST HAD IT. THE NAME WAS THERE ON THE TIP OF HIS MIND.

HE LET IT GO.

WHO'S DRIVING?

YOU ARE.

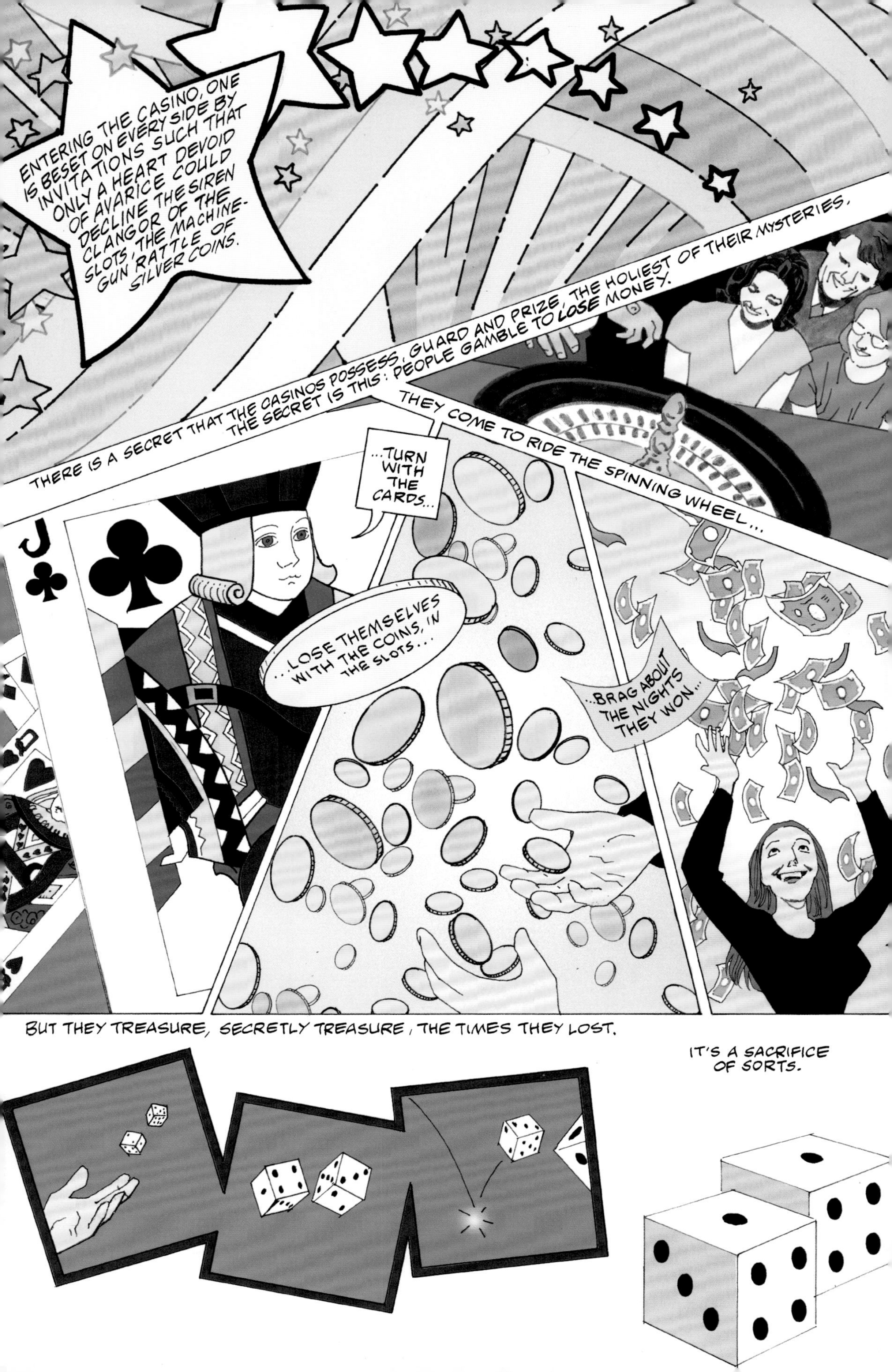
ENTERING THE CASINO, ONE IS BESET ON EVERY SIDE BY INVITATIONS SUCH THAT ONLY A HEART DEVOID OF AVARICE COULD DECLINE THE SIREN CLANGOR OF THE SLOTS, THE MACHINE-GUN RATTLE OF SILVER COINS.
THERE IS A SECRET THAT THE CASINOS POSSESS, GUARD AND PRIZE, THE HOLIEST OF THEIR MYSTERIES.
THE SECRET IS THIS: PEOPLE GAMBLE TO *LOSE* MONEY.
THEY COME TO RIDE THE SPINNING WHEEL...
...TURN WITH THE CARDS...
...LOSE THEMSELVES WITH THE COINS, IN THE SLOTS...
...BRAG ABOUT THE NIGHTS THEY WON...
BUT THEY TREASURE, SECRETLY TREASURE, THE TIMES THEY LOST.
IT'S A SACRIFICE OF SORTS.

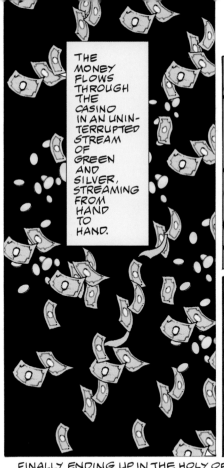

THE MONEY FLOWS THROUGH THE CASINO IN AN UNINTERRUPTED STREAM OF GREEN AND SILVER, STREAMING FROM HAND TO HAND.

FROM GAMBLER TO CROUPIER...

...TO CASHIER...

...TO THE MANAGEMENT...TO SECURITY...

...FINALLY ENDING UP IN THE HOLY OF HOLIES, THE INNERMOST SANCTUM, THE COUNTING ROOM.

AND HERE, UNDER THE GLASSY STARE OF THE CAMERAS THEY CAN SEE, AND THE INSECTILE CAMERAS THEY CANNOT SEE, ARE THE THREE MEN WHO COUNT THE MONEY.

THERE ARE THE GUARDS WHO WATCH AND WHO BRING MONEY AND WHO TAKE IT AWAY.

AND THEN THERE IS ANOTHER PERSON.

HIS CHARCOAL GREY SUIT IS IMMACULATE AND HIS FACE AND DEMEANOR ARE, IN EVERY SENSE, FORGETTABLE.

NONE OF THE OTHER MEN HAS EVEN OBSERVED THAT HE IS THERE.

OR, IF THEY HAVE NOTICED HIM, THEY HAVE FORGOTTEN HIM ON THE INSTANT.

AS THE SHIFT ENDS, THE DOORS ARE OPENED, AND THE MAN IN THE CHARCOAL SUIT FOLLOWS THE GUARDS WITH THE STRONG-BOXES OF MONEY THROUGH THE CARPETED CORRIDORS.

THE MONEY IS WHEELED INTO AN INTERIOR LOADING BAY WHERE IT IS LOADED INTO ARMORED CARS.

AS THE RAMP DOOR SWINGS OPEN, THE MAN IN THE CHARCOAL SUIT SAUNTERS UNNOTICED UP THE RAMP...

...OUT ONTO THE SIDEWALK.

LAS VEGAS HAS BECOME A CHILD'S PICTURE BOOK DREAM OF A CITY-- HERE A STORYBOOK CASTLE, THERE A BLACK PYRAMID BEAMING WHITE LIGHT INTO THE DARKNESS, AS A LANDING BEAM FOR UFOS, AND EVERYWHERE, NEON ORACLES PREDICT HAPPINESS AND LUCK.

THE MAN IN THE CHARCOAL SUIT AMBLES COMFORTABLY ALONG THE SIDEWALK, FEELING THE FLOW OF MONEY THROUGH THE TOWN. IN HIS MIND, THE MOVEMENT OF MONEY FORMS A FINE LATTICEWORK, A THREE-DIMENSIONAL CAT'S CRADLE OF LIGHT AND MOTION.

A TAXI FOLLOWS HIM SLOWLY DOWN THE STREET, KEEPING ITS DISTANCE.

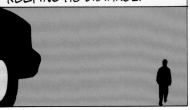

IT'S FOUR IN THE MORNING AND HE FINDS HIMSELF DRAWN TO A HOTEL AND CASINO THAT HAS BEEN OUT OF STYLE FOR THIRTY YEARS.

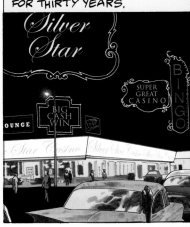

NOBODY RECOGNIZES HIM, BUT THE LOBBY BAR IS TACKY AND QUIET AND SOMEONE'S ABOUT TO DROP SEVERAL MILLION DOLLARS IN A POKER GAME UPSTAIRS.

THE MAN SEATS HIMSELF AND IS IGNORED BY A WAITRESS.

A BIG MAN IN A LIGHT GREY SUIT SITS AT THE MAN IN THE CHARCOAL SUIT'S TABLE.

THE WAITRESS WHO DID NOT NOTICE THE MAN IN THE CHARCOAL SUIT COMES STRAIGHT OVER AND SMILES.

YOU'RE LOOKING A TREAT TONIGHT, M'DEAR. A FINE SIGHT FOR THESE POOR OLD EYES.

AND WHAT CAN I GET FOR YOU GENTLEMEN TODAY?

JACK DANIEL'S FOR MYSELF.

AND A LAPHROAIG AND WATER FOR MY COMPANION.

YOU KNOW, THE FINEST LINE OF POETRY IN THE HISTORY OF THIS WHOLE DAMN COUNTRY WAS SAID BY CANADA BILL JONES IN 1853 IN BATON ROUGE, WHILE HE WAS BEING ROBBED BLIND IN A CROOKED CARD GAME.

GEORGE DeVOL, WHO WAS, LIKE CANADA BILL, NOT AVERSE TO FLEECING THE ODD SUCKER, DREW BILL ASIDE, ASKED HIM IF HE COULDN'T SEE THAT THE GAME WAS CROOKED, AND BILL...

THANK YOU, M'DEAR.

...AND BILL SAID...

I KNOW, BUT IT'S THE ONLY GAME IN TOWN.

THE MAN IN THE CHARCOAL SUIT SAYS SOMETHING IN REPLY.

LOOK, I'M SORRY ABOUT WHAT WENT DOWN IN WISCONSIN, BUT I GOT YOU ALL OUT SAFELY, DIDN'T I? NO ONE WAS HURT.

THE MAN IN THE DARK SUIT SAVORS THE BODY-IN-THE-BOG QUALITY OF THE WHISKY. HE ASKS A QUESTION.

I DON'T KNOW. EVERYONE'S GOT A HARD-ON FOR THE KID I HIRED TO RUN ERRANDS -- I'VE GOT HIM OUTSIDE, WAITING IN THE TAXI. ARE YOU STILL IN?

SHE'S NOT BEEN SEEN FOR TWO HUNDRED YEARS. IF SHE'S NOT DEAD, SHE'S TAKEN HERSELF OUT OF THE PICTURE.

LOOK, YOU BE THERE WHEN WE NEED YOU AND I'LL TAKE CARE OF YOU. WHADDAYA WANT? SOMA? I'VE GOT THE REAL STUFF.

OF COURSE I AM. WHAT DO YOU EXPECT? BUT LOOK AT IT THIS WAY...

...IT'S THE ONLY GAME IN TOWN.

YOU DOING OKAY? IS YOUR FRIEND COMING BACK?

THE MAN EXPLAINS THAT HIS FRIEND WON'T BE COMING BACK AND THUS SHE WON'T BE PAID FOR HER TIME.

AND THEN SEEING THE HURT IN HER EYES, AND TAKING PITY, HE EXAMINES THE GOLDEN THREADS IN HIS MIND, FOLLOWS THE MONEY.

HE TELLS HER THAT IF SHE'S OUTSIDE TREASURE ISLAND AT 6:00 a.m. SHE'LL MEET AN ONCOLOGIST WHO WILL HAVE JUST WON $40,000 AND WILL NEED SOMEONE TO HELP HIM SPEND IT BEFORE HE GETS BACK ON THE PLANE. THE WORDS EVAPORATE IN HER MIND, BUT LEAVE HER HAPPY.

AND IT OCCURS TO HER THAT WHEN SHE GETS OFF HER SHIFT, SHE'S GOING TO DRIVE OVER TO TREASURE ISLAND.

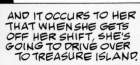

BUT SHE WOULD NEVER BE ABLE TO TELL YOU WHY.

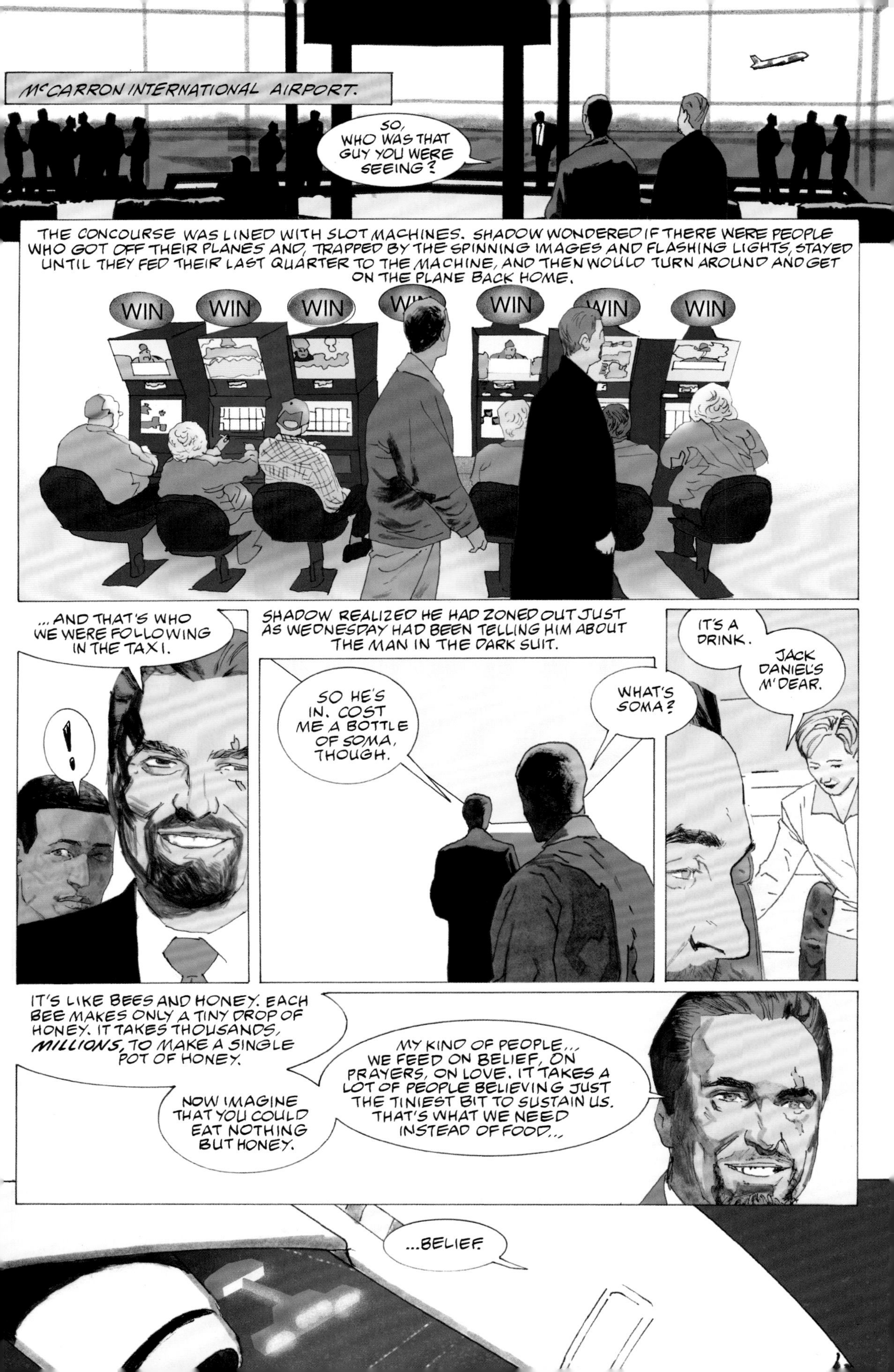
McCARRON INTERNATIONAL AIRPORT.
SO, WHO WAS THAT GUY YOU WERE SEEING?
THE CONCOURSE WAS LINED WITH SLOT MACHINES. SHADOW WONDERED IF THERE WERE PEOPLE WHO GOT OFF THEIR PLANES AND, TRAPPED BY THE SPINNING IMAGES AND FLASHING LIGHTS, STAYED UNTIL THEY FED THEIR LAST QUARTER TO THE MACHINE, AND THEN WOULD TURN AROUND AND GET ON THE PLANE BACK HOME.
WIN
WIN
WIN
WIN
WIN
WIN
...AND THAT'S WHO WE WERE FOLLOWING IN THE TAXI.
!
SHADOW REALIZED HE HAD ZONED OUT JUST AS WEDNESDAY HAD BEEN TELLING HIM ABOUT THE MAN IN THE DARK SUIT.
SO HE'S IN. COST ME A BOTTLE OF SOMA, THOUGH.
WHAT'S SOMA?
IT'S A DRINK.
JACK DANIEL'S M'DEAR.
IT'S LIKE BEES AND HONEY. EACH BEE MAKES ONLY A TINY DROP OF HONEY. IT TAKES THOUSANDS, MILLIONS, TO MAKE A SINGLE POT OF HONEY.
NOW IMAGINE THAT YOU COULD EAT NOTHING BUT HONEY.
MY KIND OF PEOPLE... WE FEED ON BELIEF, ON PRAYERS, ON LOVE. IT TAKES A LOT OF PEOPLE BELIEVING JUST THE TINIEST BIT TO SUSTAIN US. THAT'S WHAT WE NEED INSTEAD OF FOOD...
...BELIEF.

MY WIFE...

...THE DEAD ONE.

LAURA. SHE DOESN'T WANT TO BE DEAD. SHE TOLD ME. AFTER SHE GOT ME AWAY FROM THE GUYS ON THE TRAIN. ALIVE. NOT ONE OF THE WALKING DEAD. IS IT POSSIBLE?

WEDNESDAY SAID NOTHING FOR A LONG TIME.

?

THEN, STARING AHEAD OF HIM AS HE SPOKE...

I KNOW A CHARM THAT CAN LIFT THE GRIEF FROM THE HEART OF THE GRIEVER.

" NINE NIGHTS I HUNG ON THE BARE TREE, MY SIDE PIERCED WITH A SPEAR'S POINT, I SWAYED AND BLEW IN THE COLD WINDS AND THE HOT WINDS, A SACRIFICE OF MYSELF, TO MYSELF, AND THE WORLDS OPENED TO ME.

"THESE ARE THE CHARMS I LEARNED.

"I KNOW A CHARM THAT CAN HEAL WITH A TOUCH.

"I KNOW A CHARM THAT CAN TAKE WARRIORS THROUGH THE TUMULT UNSCATHED AND UNHURT.

"I KNOW A CHARM TO FREE MYSELF FROM ALL BONDS AND LOCKS."

"I CAN QUENCH A FIRE SIMPLY BY LOOKING AT IT.

"I CAN SING THE STORM TO SLEEP FOR LONG ENOUGH TO BRING A SHIP TO SHORE.

"I LEARNED TO DISPEL WITCHES, TO SPIN THEM AROUND IN THE SKIES SO THAT THEY WILL NEVER FIND THEIR WAY BACK TO THEIR OWN DOORS AGAIN.

"I KNOW A CHARM TO TURN ASIDE THE WEAPONS OF AN ENEMY."

WEDNESDAY SPOKE AS IF HE WERE RECITING THE WORDS OF A RELIGIOUS RITUAL.

"I CAN MAKE PEOPLE BELIEVE MY DREAMS.

"I KNOW THE NAMES OF ALL THE GODS."

AND I KNOW THE GREATEST CHARM OF ALL, AND THAT CHARM I CAN TELL TO NO MAN. FOR A SECRET THAT NO ONE KNOWS BUT YOU IS THE MOST POWERFUL CHARM OF ALL.

SHADOW COULD FEEL HIS SKIN CRAWL. IT WAS AS IF HE HAD JUST SEEN A DOOR OPEN TO ANOTHER PLACE, SOMEWHERE WORLDS AWAY WHERE HANGED MEN BLEW IN THE WIND AT EVERY CROSSROADS, WHERE WITCHES SHRIEKED OVERHEAD IN THE NIGHT.

ALL WEDNESDAY SAID WAS...

LAURA...

I CAN'T MAKE HER LIVE AGAIN. I DON'T EVEN KNOW WHY SHE ISN'T DEAD AS SHE OUGHT TO BE.

I THINK I DID IT. IT WAS *MY* FAULT. MAD SWEENEY GAVE ME A GOLDEN COIN WHEN HE SHOWED ME THAT TRICK. BUT IT WAS THE WRONG COIN, SOMETHING MORE POWERFUL THAN WHAT HE THOUGHT HE WAS GIVING ME.

" I PASSED IT ON TO LAURA. "

THAT COULD DO IT. AND NO, I CAN'T HELP YOU. WHAT YOU DO IN YOUR OWN TIME IS YOUR OWN AFFAIR, OF COURSE.

WHAT DOES *THAT* MEAN ?

IT MEANS THAT I CAN'T STOP YOU FROM HUNTING EAGLE STONES OR THUNDERBIRDS.

BUT I WOULD INFINITELY PREFER THAT YOU SPEND YOUR DAYS QUIETLY IN LAKESIDE, OUT OF SIGHT, AND I HOPE, OUT OF *MIND*.

WHEN THINGS GET HAIRY, WE'LL NEED ALL HANDS TO THE WHEEL.

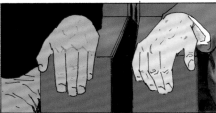

HE LOOKED OLD AND FRAGILE AS HE SAID THIS, AND SHADOW WANTED TO PUT HIS HAND OVER WEDNESDAY'S GRAY HAND TO TELL HIM EVERYTHING WOULD BE OKAY. BUT THERE WERE MEN IN BLACK TRAINS OUT THERE, AND A FAT KID IN A STRETCH LIMO.

HE DID NOT TOUCH WEDNESDAY.

HE DID NOT SAY ANYTHING.

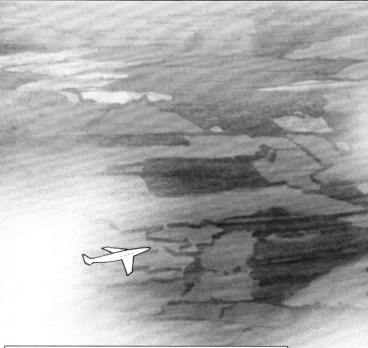

LATER, HE WONDERED IF THAT GESTURE COULD HAVE AVERTED ANY OF THE HARM THAT WAS TO COME. HE KNEW IT COULDN'T. BUT STILL, AFTERWARD, HE WISHED THAT JUST FOR A MOMENT ON THAT SLOW FLIGHT HOME, HE HAD TOUCHED WEDNESDAY'S HAND.

11 THE BRIEF WINTER DAYLIGHT WAS ALREADY FADING WHEN WEDNESDAY DROPPED SHADOW OUTSIDE HIS APARTMENT.

YOU CAN KEEP OUT OF SIGHT HERE. I PULLED IN A BIG FAVOR TO TO KEEP YOU SAFE HERE. IN A CITY, THEY'D GET YOUR SCENT IN MINUTES, SO DON'T GET INTO ANY TROUBLE.

WHEN ARE YOU COMING BACK?

SOON.

WEDNESDAY GUNNED THE LINCOLN'S ENGINE AND DROVE OFF INTO THE FRIGID NIGHT.

FOR THREE DAYS THE THERMOMETER NEVER MADE IT PAST THE ZERO MARK. SHADOW WONDERED HOW PEOPLE HAD SURVIVED IN THE DAYS BEFORE ELECTRICITY AND THERMAL MASKS.

SOMETIMES THEY DIDN'T, AND THEY DIED. LEAKY CHIMNEYS AND BADLY VENTILATED STOVES KILLED AS MANY PEOPLE AS THE COLD.

BUT THOSE DAYS WERE HARD.

"THE WORST OF ALL WAS THE MADNESS. HAS TO DO WITH THE SUNLIGHT, HOW THERE ISN'T ENOUGH OF IT IN WINTER. FOLK JUST WENT STIR-CRAZY.

"LAKESIDE HAD IT EASY. BUT SOME OF THE OTHER TOWNS AROUND HERE HAD IT HARD.

TWENTY MILES SOUTH OF HERE, IN JIBWAY, THEY FOUND A WOMAN WALKING MOTHER-NAKED WITH A DEAD BABE AT HER BREAST, AND SHE'D NOT SUFFER THEM TO TAKE IT FROM HER."

BAD BUSINESS.

YOU WANT A VIDEO CARD?

BLOCKBUSTER COMING. WE'LL BE OUT OF BUSINESS.

NO THANKS.

HE DIDN'T TELL HINZELMANN THAT HE'D UNPLUGGED THE TELEVISION EVER SINCE IT HAD STARTED TALKING TO HIM.

SO, HOW MANY DO YOU WANT?

OF WHAT?

KLUNKER TICKETS.

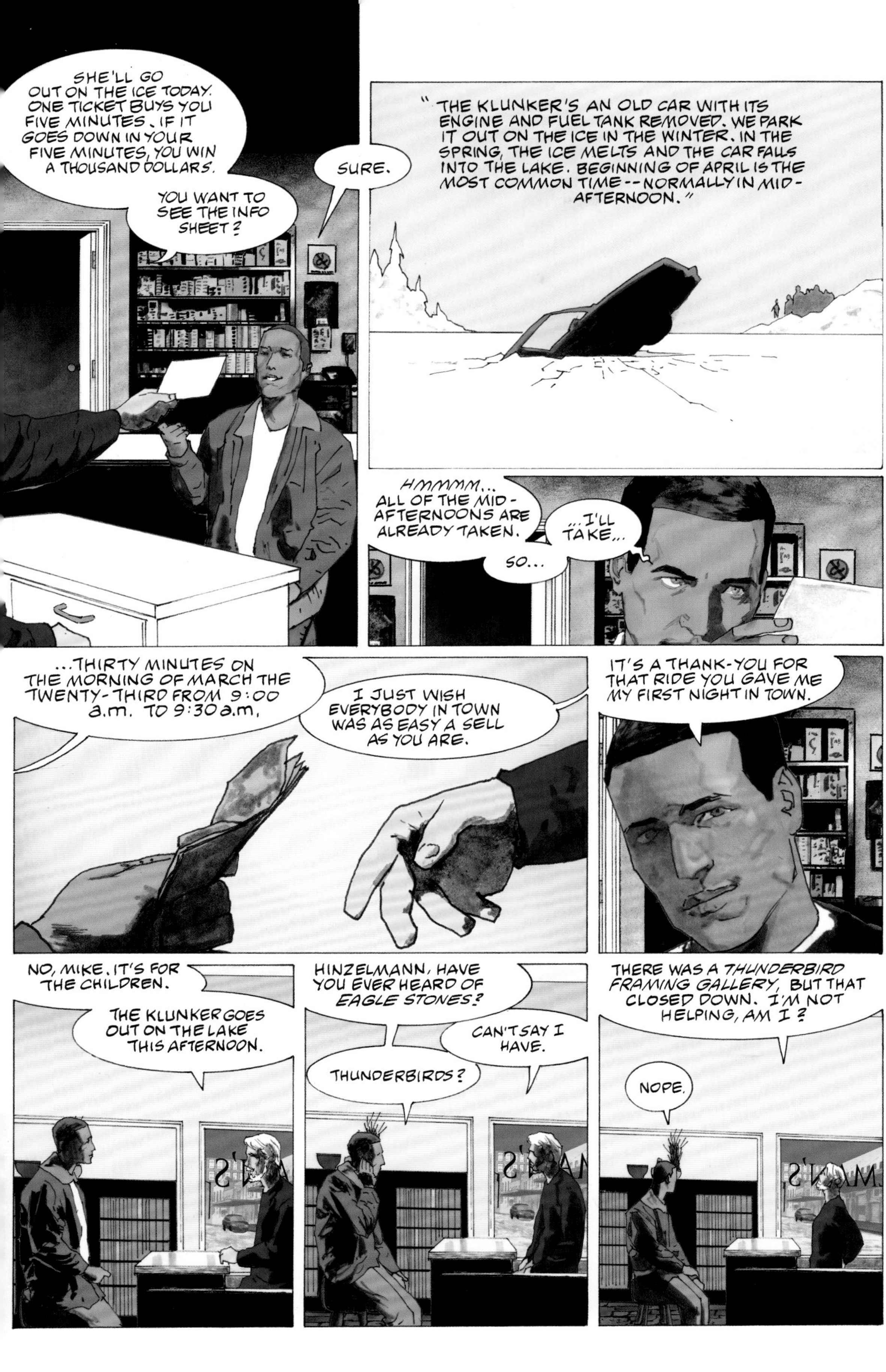
SHE'LL GO OUT ON THE ICE TODAY. ONE TICKET BUYS YOU FIVE MINUTES. IF IT GOES DOWN IN YOUR FIVE MINUTES, YOU WIN A THOUSAND DOLLARS.
YOU WANT TO SEE THE INFO SHEET?
SURE.
"THE KLUNKER'S AN OLD CAR WITH ITS ENGINE AND FUEL TANK REMOVED. WE PARK IT OUT ON THE ICE IN THE WINTER. IN THE SPRING, THE ICE MELTS AND THE CAR FALLS INTO THE LAKE. BEGINNING OF APRIL IS THE MOST COMMON TIME--NORMALLY IN MID-AFTERNOON."
HMMMM... ALL OF THE MID-AFTERNOONS ARE ALREADY TAKEN.
SO...
...I'LL TAKE...
...THIRTY MINUTES ON THE MORNING OF MARCH THE TWENTY-THIRD FROM 9:00 a.m. TO 9:30 a.m.
I JUST WISH EVERYBODY IN TOWN WAS AS EASY A SELL AS YOU ARE.
IT'S A THANK-YOU FOR THAT RIDE YOU GAVE ME MY FIRST NIGHT IN TOWN.
NO, MIKE. IT'S FOR THE CHILDREN.
THE KLUNKER GOES OUT ON THE LAKE THIS AFTERNOON.
HINZELMANN, HAVE YOU EVER HEARD OF EAGLE STONES?
CAN'T SAY I HAVE.
THUNDERBIRDS?
THERE WAS A THUNDERBIRD FRAMING GALLERY, BUT THAT CLOSED DOWN. I'M NOT HELPING, AM I?
NOPE.

"TELL YOU WHAT. WHY DON'T YOU GO LOOK AT THE LIBRARY. GOOD PEOPLE THERE AND THERE'S A BOOK SALE ON THIS WEEK."

SHOULD HAVE THOUGHT OF THE LIBRARY MYSELF.

SHADOW HAD KNOWN A MAN IN PRISON WHO HAD BEEN IMPRISONED FOR STEALING LIBRARY BOOKS.

HALF A MILLION DOLLARS WORTH OF BOOKS.

JESUS. WHY DID YOU TAKE THEM?

I *WANTED* THEM. AND THEY NEVER FOUND THE GARAGE IN SAN CLEMENTE WITH THE *REALLY* GOOD STUFF IN IT.

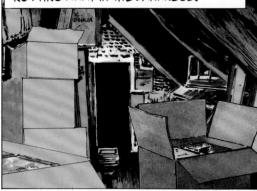

THE MAN HAD DIED IN PRISON AND NOW SHADOW FOUND HIMSELF THINKING OF ALL THOSE RARE AND BEAUTIFUL BOOKS ROTTING AWAY IN THE DARKNESS.

NATIVE AMERICAN BELIEFS AND TRADITIONS WAS ON A SINGLE SHELF IN ONE CASTLE-LIKE TURRET.

HE LEARNED THAT THUNDERBIRDS WERE MYTHICAL GIGANTIC BIRDS WHO LIVED ON MOUNTAINTOPS, WHO BROUGHT THE LIGHTNING AND FLAPPED THEIR WINGS TO MAKE THE THUNDER.

HE COULD FIND NO MENTION OF THE EAGLE STONES AT ALL.

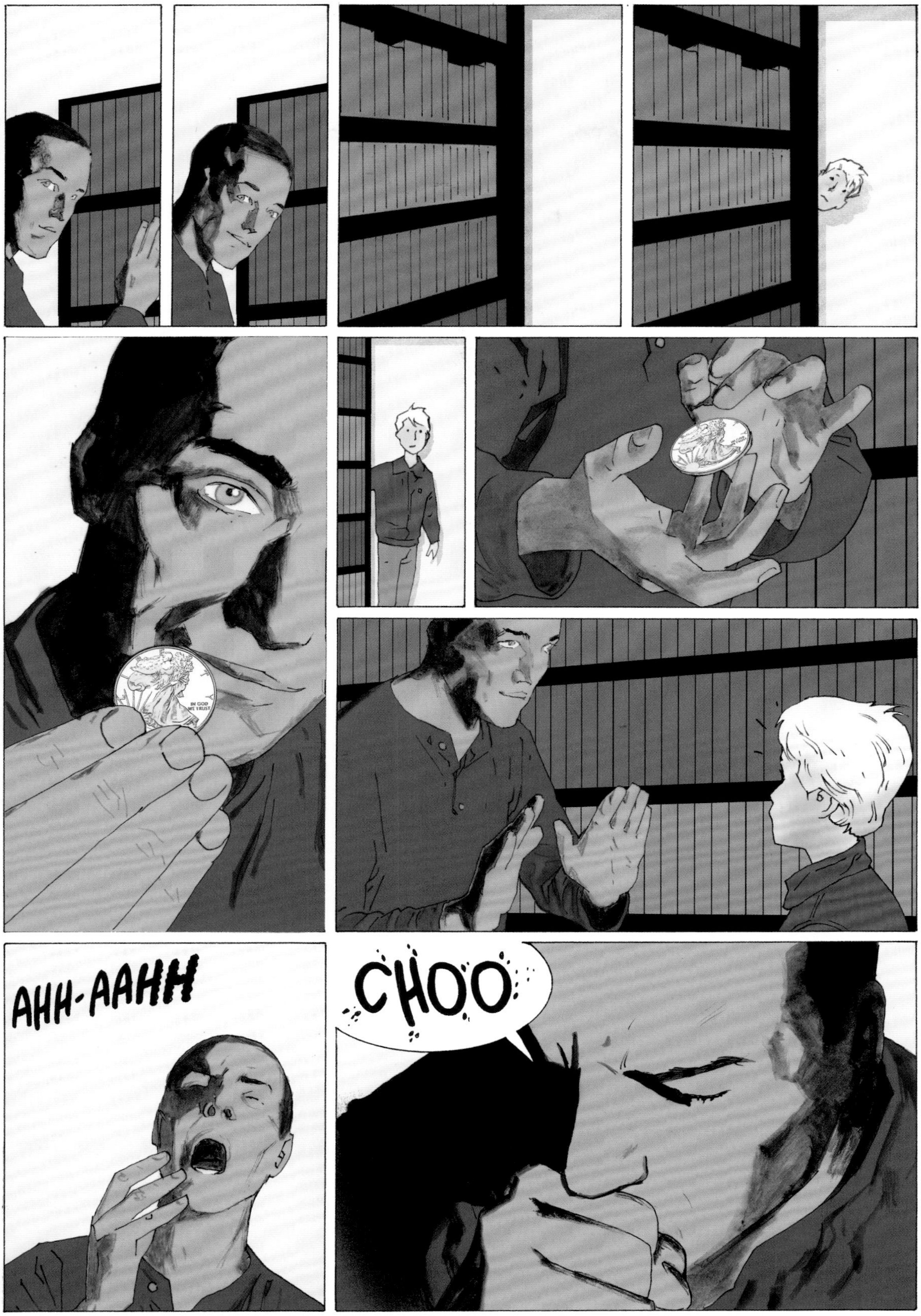

IN GOD WE TRUST
AHH-AAHH
CHOO

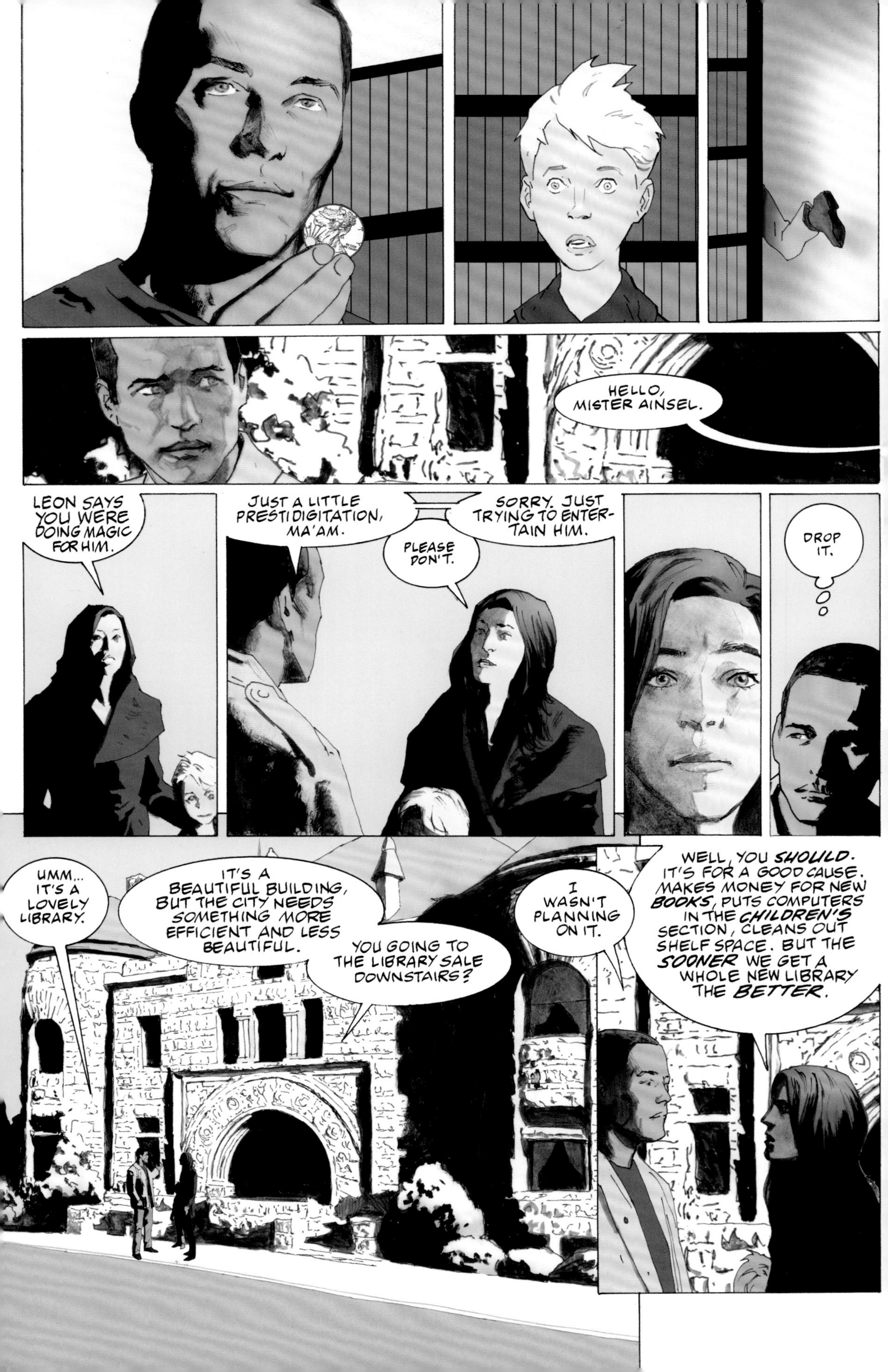
HELLO, MISTER AINSEL.
LEON SAYS YOU WERE DOING MAGIC FOR HIM.
JUST A LITTLE PRESTIDIGITATION, MA'AM.
PLEASE DON'T.
SORRY. JUST TRYING TO ENTERTAIN HIM.
DROP IT.
UMM... IT'S A LOVELY LIBRARY.
IT'S A BEAUTIFUL BUILDING, BUT THE CITY NEEDS SOMETHING MORE EFFICIENT AND LESS BEAUTIFUL.
YOU GOING TO THE LIBRARY SALE DOWNSTAIRS?
I WASN'T PLANNING ON IT.
WELL, YOU SHOULD. IT'S FOR A GOOD CAUSE. MAKES MONEY FOR NEW BOOKS, PUTS COMPUTERS IN THE CHILDREN'S SECTION, CLEANS OUT SHELF SPACE. BUT THE SOONER WE GET A WHOLE NEW LIBRARY THE BETTER.

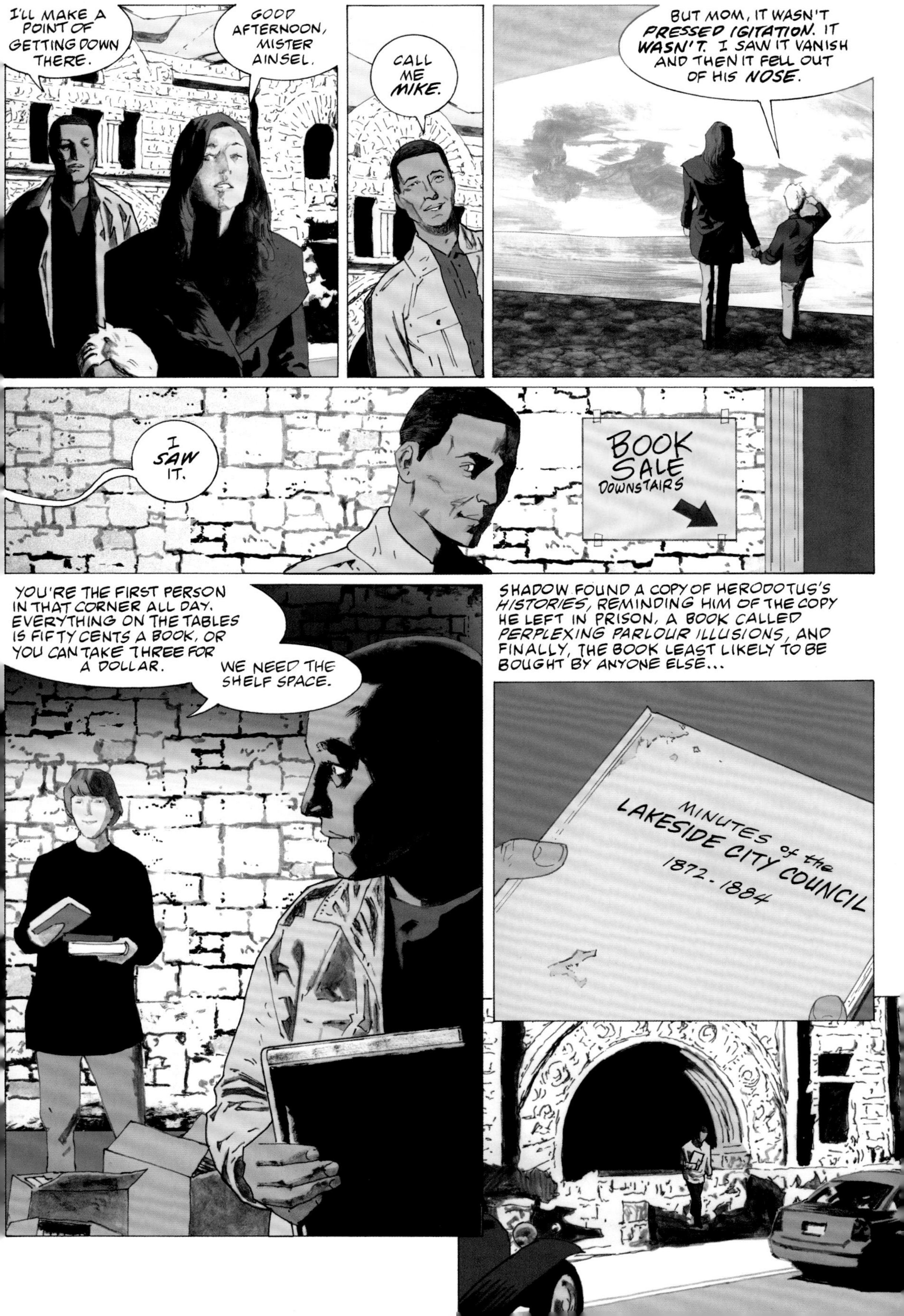
I'LL MAKE A POINT OF GETTING DOWN THERE.
GOOD AFTERNOON, MISTER AINSEL.
CALL ME MIKE.
BUT MOM, IT WASN'T PRESSED IGITATION. IT WASN'T. I SAW IT VANISH AND THEN IT FELL OUT OF HIS NOSE.
I SAW IT.
BOOK SALE DOWNSTAIRS
YOU'RE THE FIRST PERSON IN THAT CORNER ALL DAY. EVERYTHING ON THE TABLES IS FIFTY CENTS A BOOK, OR YOU CAN TAKE THREE FOR A DOLLAR.
WE NEED THE SHELF SPACE.
SHADOW FOUND A COPY OF HERODOTUS'S HISTORIES, REMINDING HIM OF THE COPY HE LEFT IN PRISON, A BOOK CALLED PERPLEXING PARLOUR ILLUSIONS, AND FINALLY, THE BOOK LEAST LIKELY TO BE BOUGHT BY ANYONE ELSE...
MINUTES of the LAKESIDE CITY COUNCIL 1872-1884

FROM THE LIBRARY STEPS SHADOW HAD A CLEAR VIEW OF THE LAKE. THERE WERE MEN ON THE ICE NEAR THE BRIDGE, PUSHING A DARK GREEN CAR INTO THE CENTER OF THE LAKE.

MARCH THE TWENTY-THIRD. 9:00 A.M. TO 9:30 A.M.

HE WONDERED IF THE LAKE OR THE KLUNKER COULD HEAR HIM-- AND IF THEY WOULD PAY ATTENTION TO HIM, EVEN IF THEY COULD.

THE WIND BLEW BITTER AGAINST HIS FACE.

CHAPTER FOUR

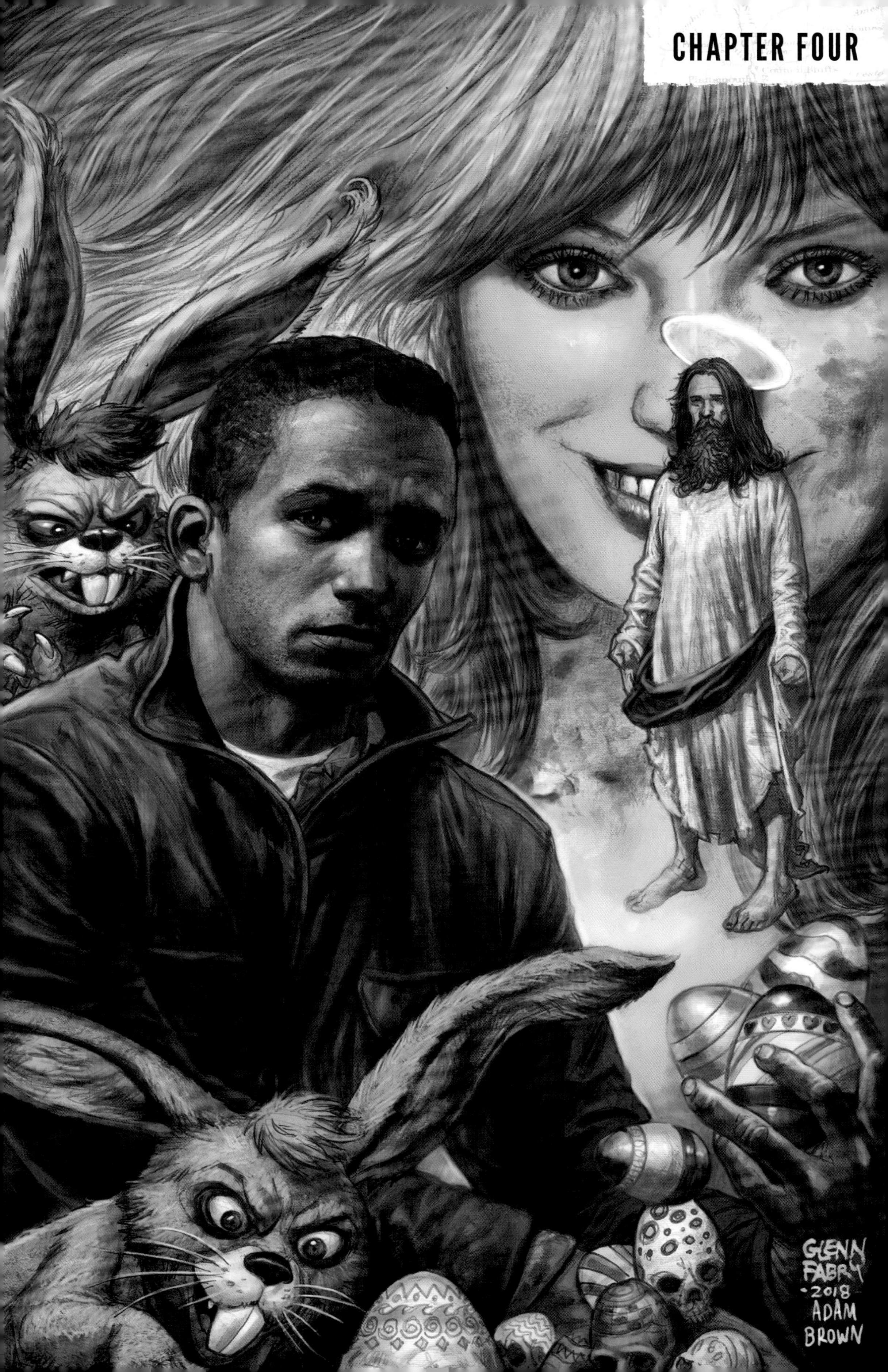
GLENN FABRY
-2018
ADAM
BROWN

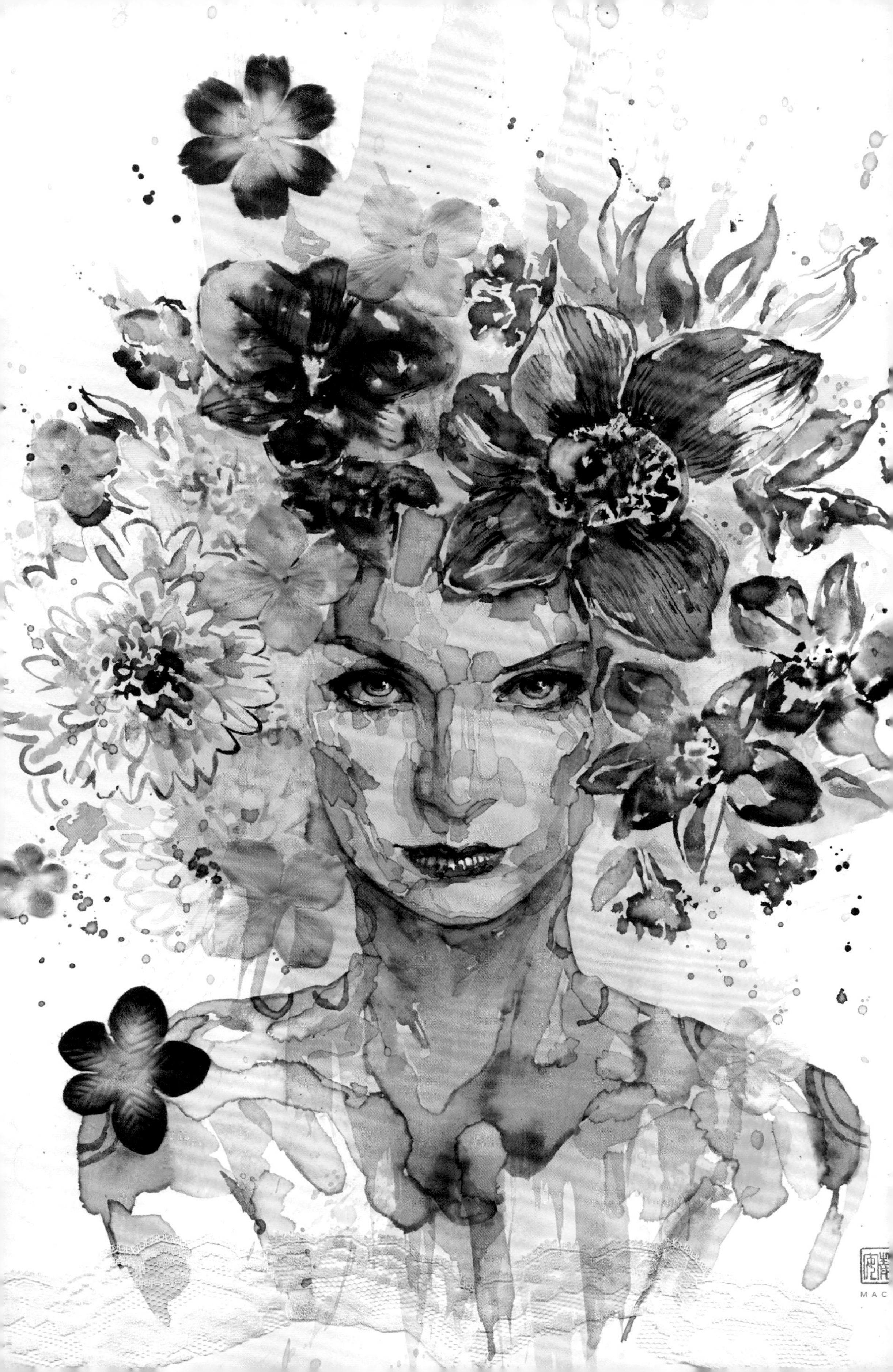
MAC

SHADOW'S HEART BEGAN TO POUND WHEN HE SAW THE POLICE CAR WAITING OUTSIDE HIS APARTMENT, WITH OFFICER CHAD MULLIGAN IN THE FRONT SEAT.

SOMETHING PARTICULAR I CAN DO FOR YOU, CHIEF?

NOT A DAMN THING, PAL. THOUGHT I'D STOP BY AND SEE HOW YOU WERE SETTLING IN. HOW'S THE GUNTHER PURPLEMOBILE DOING?

IT'S GOOD. RUNNING FINE.

I SAW MY NEXT-DOOR NEIGHBOR IN THE LIBRARY, MIZ OLSEN. I WAS WONDERING...

WHAT CRAWLED UP HER BUTT AND DIED?

IF YOU WANT TO PUT IT LIKE THAT.

LONG STORY. YOU WANT TO RIDE ALONG FOR A SPELL, AND I'LL TELL YOU ALL ABOUT IT?

OKAY.

DARREN OLSEN MET MARGIE AT UW STEVENS POINT AND HE BROUGHT HER BACK NORTH TO LAKESIDE. SHE WAS A JOURNALISM MAJOR. HE WAS STUDYING, SHIT, HOTEL MANAGEMENT, SOMETHING LIKE THAT.

"THEY HAD TWO BOYS. AT THAT TIME *SANDY* WAS ELEVEN. THE LITTLE ONE--*LEON*, IS IT?-- WAS JUST A BABE IN ARMS."

WHEN THEY GOT HERE, JAWS DROPPED. SHE WAS SO BEAUTIFUL ...

THAT HAIR ...

"DARREN MANAGED THE MOTEL AMERICA OVER IN CAMDEN. EXCEPT NOBODY WANTED TO STOP IN CAMDEN AND EVENTUALLY THE MOTEL CLOSED.

"DARREN OLSEN COULDN'T FIND THE COURAGE TO TELL MARGIE THAT HE'D LOST HIS JOB. SO HE'D DRIVE OFF EARLY IN THE MORNING, COME HOME LATE IN THE EVENING."

WHAT WAS HE DOING ?

" COULDN'T SAY FOR CERTAIN. GUESS HE STARTED OUT AS A JOB HUNTER. PRETTY SOON HE WAS DRINKING THE TIME AWAY. HE EMPTIED OUT THEIR JOINT ACCOUNT IN ABOUT TEN WEEKS. IT WAS ONLY A MATTER OF TIME TILL MARGIE FIGURED IT OUT."

"SO, MARGIE KICKS HIM OUT, SUES FOR DIVORCE.

"VICIOUS CUSTODY BATTLE."

"SHE GOT THE KIDS. DARREN GOT VISITATION RIGHTS AND PRECIOUS LITTLE ELSE."

THEY LOST THE HOUSE. SHE MOVED INTO THE APARTMENTS, DARREN LEFT TOWN, CAME BACK EVERY FEW MONTHS TO MAKE EVERYBODY MISERABLE.

MOST OF US STARTED WISHING HE'D NEVER COME BACK AT ALL.

THIS WENT ON FOR A FEW YEARS. HE'D COME BACK, SPEND MONEY ON THE KIDS, LEAVE MARGIE IN TEARS.

"SO, LAST YEAR HE CAME OUT, SAID HE WANTED TO TAKE THE BOYS TO FLORIDA FOR CHRISTMAS, VISIT THEIR GRANDPARENTS. MARGIE TOLD HIM TO GET LOST. IT GOT PRETTY UNPLEASANT. AT ONE POINT, I HAD TO GO OVER THERE.

" DOMESTIC DISPUTE.

" BY THE TIME I GOT THERE, DARREN WAS STANDING IN THE FRONT YARD SHOUTING STUFF, THE BOYS WERE BARELY HOLDING IT TOGETHER. MARGIE WAS CRYING.

"I TOLD DARREN HE WAS SHAPING UP FOR A NIGHT IN THE CELLS. THOUGHT FOR A MOMENT HE WAS GOING TO HIT ME, BUT HE WAS SOBER ENOUGH NOT TO DO THAT.

"NEXT DAY, HE LEFT TOWN. "

"TWO WEEKS LATER, SANDY VANISHED.

"DIDN'T GET ON THE SCHOOL BUS, TOLD HIS BEST FRIEND THAT HE'D BE SEEING HIS DAD SOON, THAT DARREN WAS BRINGING AN ESPECIALLY COOL GIFT FOR HAVING MISSED CHRISTMAS IN FLORIDA.

"NOBODY'S SEEN HIM SINCE.

"NON-CUSTODIAL KIDNAPPINGS ARE THE HARDEST.

"IT'S TOUGH TO FIND A KID WHO DOESN'T WANT TO BE FOUND, Y' SEE? "

SHADOW DID SEE. HE SAW SOMETHING ELSE AS WELL. CHAD MULLIGAN WAS IN LOVE WITH MARGUERITE OLSEN HIMSELF.

I WONDER IF HE KNOWS HOW OBVIOUS IT IS?

HUP. THERE WE GO.

MULLIGAN PULLED OUT, LIGHTS FLASHING, AND PULLED OVER SOME TEENAGERS DOING SIXTY. HE DIDN'T TICKET THEM.

JUST PUT THE FEAR OF GOD IN THEM.

THAT EVENING SHADOW SAT AT THE KITCHEN TABLE TRYING TO FIGURE OUT A TRICK HE HAD FOUND IN *PERPLEXING PARLOUR ILLUSIONS*, BUT THE INSTRUCTIONS WERE INFURIATING, UNHELPFUL AND VAGUE.

HE SIGHED, DROPPED THE COINS IN HIS POCKET, AND FLIPPED OPEN THE *MINUTES OF THE LAKESIDE COUNCIL 1872-1884.*

THE TYPE WAS SO SMALL AS TO BE ALMOST UNREADABLE. HE LOOKED AT THE COUNCIL PHOTOGRAPHS THEREIN, SURPRISED THAT SO MANY LOOKED PECULIARLY FAMILIAR.

THE SECRETARY OF THE 1882 CITY COUNCIL WAS A *PATRICK MULLIGAN.*

SHAVE HIM AND HE'D BE A DEAD RINGER FOR CHAD MULLIGAN.

I DON'T SEE HINZELMANN'S PIONEER GRANDFATHER IN THE PHOTOGRAPHS. MAYBE HE WASN'T CITY COUNCIL MATERIAL.

DIDN'T I SEE A REFERENCE TO A HINZELMANN IN THE TEXT?

BUT THAT REFERENCE ELUDED HIM WHEN HE LEAFED BACK FOR IT, AND THE TINY TYPE MADE HIS EYES ACHE. HE REALIZED HIS HEAD WAS NODDING.

BE FOOLISH TO FALL ASLEEP ON THE COUCH. BEDROOM JUST A FEW FEET AWAY.

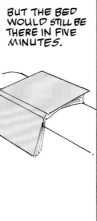

BUT THE BED WOULD STILL BE THERE IN FIVE MINUTES.

HE WAS NOT GOING TO GO TO SLEEP ...

... JUST REST HIS EYES.

DARKNESS ROARED. HE STOOD ON AN OPEN PLAIN. BESIDE HIM WAS THE PLACE FROM WHICH HE HAD ONCE EMERGED, FROM WHICH THE EARTH HAD SQUEEZED HIM. STARS WERE STILL FALLING FROM THE SKY.

EACH STAR THAT TOUCHED THE RED EARTH BECAME A MAN OR A WOMAN, AND THE MEN HAD LONG BLACK HAIR AND HIGH CHEEKBONES. THE WOMEN ALL LOOKED LIKE MARGUERITE OLSEN.

THESE WERE THE STAR PEOPLE. THEY LOOKED AT HIM WITH DARK, PROUD EYES.

TELL ME ABOUT THE THUNDERBIRDS, PLEASE. IT'S NOT FOR ME. IT'S FOR MY WIFE.

ONE BY ONE THEY TURNED THEIR BACKS ON HIM AND THEY WERE GONE, ONE WITH THE LANDSCAPE.

BUT THE LAST OF THEM, BEFORE SHE TURNED AWAY, POINTED INTO THE WINE-COLORED SKY.

"ASK THEM YOURSELF."

SUMMER LIGHTNING FLICKERED MOMENTARILY, ILLUMINATING THE LANDSCAPE FROM HORIZON TO HORIZON.

THERE WERE HIGH ROCKS NEAR HIM, PEAKS AND SPIRES OF SANDSTONE, AND SHADOW BEGAN TO CLIMB THE NEAREST.

HE GRABBED AT A HAND-HOLD, AND FELT IT SLICE INTO HIS HAND.

IT'S **BONE**, NOT STONE. IT'S OLD DRY BONE.

EACH OF THE BONES WAS DRY AND BALL-LIKE AND HE IMAGINED THEY MIGHT BE THE OLD *EGGS* OF SOME DREADFUL BIRD.

BUT ANOTHER FLARE OF LIGHTNING TOLD HIM DIFFERENTLY.

SOMEWHERE, BIRDS WERE CALLING. RAIN SPATTERED HIS FACE.

HE WAS HUNDREDS OF FEET ABOVE THE GROUND. OVERHEAD, THE BIRDS CIRCLED THE SPIRE.

THEY MUST BE TWENTY FEET FROM WINGTIP TO WING-TIP.

THEY WERE HUGE, GRACEFUL, AWFUL BIRDS, AND THE BEATS OF THEIR WINGS CRASHED LIKE THUNDER ON THE NIGHT AIR.

THEN ONE HUGE BIRD SWUNG OUT OF ITS GLIDE TOWARD HIM AND HE PUSHED HIMSELF INTO A CREVICE OF SKULLS, FEELING REVULSION AND TERROR AND AWE.

ONE HAND-SIZED TALON SANK INTO HIS ARM AND HE REACHED OUT AND TRIED TO GRASP A FEATHER FROM ITS WING.

IF HE RETURNED TO HIS TRIBE WITHOUT A THUNDERBIRD FEATHER HE WOULD BE DISGRACED. HE WOULD NEVER BE A MAN.

BUT THE BIRD PULLED UP SO THAT HE COULD NOT GRASP EVEN ONE FEATHER.

SHADOW CONTINUED TO CLIMB, PULLING HIMSELF UP. BONE POPPED AND CRUSHED UNDER HIS BARE FEET, CUTTING THEM PAINFULLY.

HE STOOD AT LAST ON THE TOP OF THE SPIRE, THE GREAT BIRDS CIRCLING HIM SLOWLY. HE HEARD A VOICE, THE VOICE OF THE BUFFALO MAN, CALLING TO HIM ON THE WIND, TELLING HIM WHO THE SKULLS BELONGED TO.

THE TOWER BEGAN TO TUMBLE, THE BIGGEST BIRD PLUMMETED DOWN TOWARD HIM...

...AND SHADOW WAS FALLING, TUMBLING DOWN THE TOWER OF SKULLS.

WHAT THE ALMIGHTY FLYING FUCK DO YOU THINK YOU'RE PLAYING AT?

WEDNESDAY...? I WAS ASLEEP.

WHAT DO YOU THINK IS THE FUCKING POINT OF STASHING YOU IN A HIDING PLACE LIKE LAKESIDE, IF YOU'RE GOING TO RAISE SUCH A RUCKUS THAT NOT EVEN A DEAD MAN COULD MISS IT?

I DREAMED OF THUNDERBIRDS, AND A TOWER OF SKULLS...

I KNOW. EVERYBODY KNOWS. CHRIST ALMIGHTY. WHAT'S THE POINT OF HIDING YOU IF YOU'RE GOING TO FUCKING ADVERTISE.

SHADOW SAID NOTHING.

I'LL BE THERE IN THE MORNING. WE'RE GOING TO SAN FRANCISCO.

THE LINE WENT DEAD.

HE COULD HEAR SOMEONE CRYING, ONLY THE THICKNESS OF A WALL AWAY. IT WAS MARQUERITE OLSEN, AND HER SOBBING WAS INSISTENT AND LOW AND HEARTBREAKING.

OUTSIDE, THE WIND HOWLED AND WAILED AS IF IT, TOO, WAS SEEKING FOR A LOST CHILD, AND HE SLEPT NO MORE THAT NIGHT.

SAN FRANCISCO IN JANUARY. IT WAS LATE IN THE AFTERNOON AND UNSEASONABLY WARM. SHADOW, WHO HAD NOT BEEN HERE SINCE HE WAS A BOY, WAS ASTONISHED AT HOW FAMILIAR IT WAS, HOW VERY MUCH IT DIDN'T FEEL LIKE ANYWHERE ELSE.

IT'S HARD TO BELIEVE THAT THIS IS IN THE SAME COUNTRY AS LAKESIDE.

IT'S NOT. SAN FRANCISCO ISN'T IN THE SAME COUNTRY AS LAKESIDE ANY MORE THAN NEW ORLEANS IS IN THE SAME COUNTRY AS NEW YORK.

WEDNESDAY'S ANGER SEEMED TO HAVE DISSIPATED, OR PERHAPS TO HAVE BEEN INVESTED FOR THE FUTURE.

BE NICE TO THE LADY WE ARE VISITING.

BUT NOT *TOO* NICE.

I'LL BE COOL.

:ARF:

!

BUY DOG FOOD WITH IT.

LET ME PUT IT BLUNTLY. YOU MUST BE VERY CAUTIOUS AROUND THE LADY WE ARE VISITING. SHE MIGHT TAKE A FANCY TO YOU, AND THAT WOULD BE BAD.

IS SHE YOUR GIRLFRIEND OR SOMETHING?

NOT FOR ALL THE LITTLE PLASTIC TOYS IN CHINA.

HELLO, YOU OLD FRAUD.

YOU LOOK *DIVINE.*

HOW THE HELL *ELSE* SHOULD I LOOK?

ANYWAY, YOU'RE A LIAR. NEW ORLEANS WAS *SUCH* A MISTAKE -- I PUT ON, WHAT? -- THIRTY POUNDS THERE?

I SWEAR.

THE TOPS OF MY THIGHS RUB TOGETHER NOW WHEN I WALK.

HE'S *BLUSHING!* WEDNESDAY, MY SWEET, YOU BROUGHT ME A *BLUSHER.* HOW PERFECTLY WONDERFUL OF YOU.

SHADOW COULD SMELL HER PERFUME FROM WHERE HE WAS STANDING, AN INTOXICATING MIXTURE OF JASMINE AND HONEYSUCKLE, OF SWEET MILK AND FEMALE SKIN.

THIS IS SHADOW. SHADOW, SAY HELLO TO EASTER.

HELLO.

SO, HOW'S TRICKS?

EVERYTHING'S FINE. HOW ABOUT YOU, YOU OLD **WOLF?**

I WAS HOPING TO ENLIST YOUR ASSISTANCE.

WASTING YOUR TIME. DON'T EVEN BOTHER.

SHADOW...

PLEASE SIT DOWN HERE AND HELP YOURSELF TO SOME OF THIS FOOD.

EGGS, ROAST CHICKEN, CHICKEN CURRY, CHICKEN SALAD.

AND OVER HERE IS LAPIN, RABBIT ACTUALLY, BUT COLD RABBIT IS A DELIGHT.

AND IN THAT BOWL OVER THERE IS JUGGED HARE.

IT'S ALL GOOD.

WELL, WHY DON'T I JUST FILL A PLATE FOR YOU?

ARE YOU EATING?

I AM AT YOUR DISPOSAL, MY DEAR.

YOU ARE SO FULL OF SHIT IT'S A WONDER YOUR EYES DON'T TURN BROWN. HELP YOURSELF.

"SHADOW." THAT'S A SWEET NAME, WHY DO THEY CALL YOU "SHADOW"?

WHEN I WAS A KID MY MOTHER AND I LIVED IN A BUNCH OF U.S. EMBASSIES. SHE WAS, WELL, LIKE A SECRETARY. WE WENT FROM CITY TO CITY, ALL OVER NORTHERN EUROPE. THEN SHE GOT SICK.

WE CAME BACK TO THE STATES. I NEVER KNEW WHAT TO SAY TO THE OTHER KIDS, SO I'D JUST FIND ADULTS AND FOLLOW THEM AROUND. I NEEDED THE COMPANY, I GUESS. I WAS A SMALL KID.

YOU GREW.

YES... I GREW.

IS THIS THE BOY WHO'S GOT EVERYBODY SO UPSET?

YOU HEARD?

I KEEP MY EARS PRICKED UP.

YOU KEEP OUT OF THEIR WAY. THERE ARE TOO MANY SECRET SOCIETIES OUT THERE, AND THEY HAVE NO LOYALTIES AND NO LOVE. COMMERCIAL, INDEPENDENT, GOVERNMENT--THEY'RE ALL IN THE SAME BOAT.

HEY, OLD WOLF-- HOW DO YOU KNOW THE C.I.A. WASN'T INVOLVED IN THE KENNEDY ASSASINATION?

I'VE HEARD IT.

BUT THE SPOOK SHOW, THE ONES YOU MET, THEY'RE SOMETHING ELSE, THEY EXIST BECAUSE EVERYONE *KNOWS* THEY MUST EXIST.

SHADOW'S A GOOD NAME.

I WANT A MOCHACCINO. COME ON.

WHAT ABOUT THE FOOD? YOU CAN'T JUST LEAVE IT HERE.

LET IT FEED THEM.

REMEMBER, *I'M* RICH. I'M DOING JUST PEACHY. WHY SHOULD I HELP *YOU*?

YOU'RE ONE OF US. YOU'RE AS FORGOTTEN AND UNLOVED AS ANY OF US, IT'S PRETTY CLEAR WHOSE SIDE YOU SHOULD BE ON.

I'M TELLING YOU, I'M DOING *FINE*. ON MY FESTIVAL DAYS THEY STILL FEAST ON EGGS AND RABBITS, AND CANDY, TO REPRESENT REBIRTH AND COPULATION, MORE AND MORE EVERY YEAR, THEY DO IT IN *MY* NAME, OLD WOLF.

YES, MILLIONS STILL PRACTICE ALL THE RITES OF YOUR FESTIVAL, EVEN DOWN TO HUNTING FOR HIDDEN EGGS. BUT HOW MANY OF THEM KNOW WHO YOU ARE, EH?

EXCUSE ME, MISS?

YES ?

MY FRIEND AND I WERE DISAGREEING OVER WHAT THE WORD 'EASTER' MEANS. WOULD YOU HAPPEN TO KNOW?

I DON'T KNOW ABOUT ANY OF THAT CHRISTIAN STUFF. I'M A PAGAN.

I THINK IT'S LIKE LATIN, OR SOMETHING FOR CHRIST HAS RISEN, MAYBE...

REALLY?

YEAH, SURE. EASTER. JUST LIKE THE SUN RISES IN THE EAST, YOU KNOW.

THE RISEN SON, OF COURSE. A MOST LOGICAL SUPPOSITION, AND TELL ME, AS A PAGAN WHO DO YOU WORSHIP?

WORSHIP?

THAT'S RIGHT. TO WHOM DO YOU PRAY AT DAWN AND DUSK?

THE FEMALE PRINCIPLE. IT'S AN EMPOWERMENT THING.

INDEED, AND THIS FEMALE PRINCIPLE OF YOURS-- DOES SHE HAVE A NAME?

SHE'S THE GODDESS WITHIN US ALL. SHE DOESN'T NEED A NAME.

AH! SO, DO YOU HAVE MIGHTY BACCHANALS IN HER HONOR? DO YOU STEP NAKED INTO THE SEA FOAM CHANTING ECSTATICALLY TO YOUR NAMELESS GODDESS WHILE THE WAVES LICK YOUR THIGHS LIKE THE TONGUES OF A THOUSAND LEOPARDS?

YOU'RE MAKING FUN OF ME. WE DON'T DO ANY OF THAT STUFF.

ANY MORE COFFEES?

NO?

THERE IS ONE WHO 'DOES NOT HAVE THE FAITH AND WILL NOT HAVE THE FUN.'

CHESTERTON.

PAGAN INDEED.

SO, SHALL WE GO OUT INTO THE STREET, EASTER, MY DEAR, AND REPEAT THE EXERCISE? FIND OUT HOW MANY PASSERSBY KNOW THAT THEIR EASTER FESTIVAL TAKES ITS NAME FROM *EOSTRE OF THE DAWN?*

LET'S SEE... *I* HAVE IT.

WE SHALL ASK A HUNDRED PEOPLE. FOR EVERY ONE THAT KNOWS THE TRUTH, YOU MAY CUT OFF ONE OF MY FINGERS--AND THEN, MY TOES; FOR EVERY TWENTY WHO DON'T KNOW, YOU SPEND A NIGHT MAKING LOVE TO ME.

" AND THE ODDS ARE CERTAINLY IN YOUR FAVOR HERE -- THIS *IS* SAN FRANCISCO, AFTER ALL. THERE ARE HEATHENS AND PAGANS AND WICCANS APLENTY HERE."

WE *COULD* TRY IT, BUT I WOULD END UP WITH TEN FINGERS, TEN TOES, AND FIVE NIGHTS IN YOUR BED.

SO DON'T TELL ME THEY WORSHIP YOU AND KEEP YOUR FESTIVAL DAY.

YOUR NAME HAS NO MEANING TO THEM. NONE AT ALL.

I KNOW THAT. I'M NOT A FOOL.

NO. YOU'RE NOT.

I'M SORRY. WE *NEED* YOU. WE NEED YOUR ENERGY, YOUR POWER. WILL YOU FIGHT BESIDE US WHEN THE STORM COMES?

YES.

WEDNESDAY CALLED THE WAITRESS OVER AND PAID FOR THEIR COFFEES, COUNTING OUT THE MONEY CAREFULLY AND FOLDING IT OVER WITH THE CHECK.

MA'AM? EXCUSE ME. I THINK YOU *DROPPED* THIS...

UH... NO, I DON'T THINK SO.

I SAW IT FALL, MA'AM. YOU SHOULD COUNT THEM.

JESUS. YOU'RE *RIGHT*. I'M SORRY.

OUTSIDE, THE LIGHT WAS JUST STARTING TO FADE. EASTER NODDED TO WEDNESDAY, THEN SHE TOUCHED SHADOW'S HAND.

WHAT DID YOU DREAM ABOUT LAST NIGHT?

AND DO YOU KNOW WHOSE SKULLS THEY WERE?

THUNDERBIRDS. A MOUNTAIN OF SKULLS.

" THERE WAS A VOICE IN MY DREAM. IT SAID THEY WERE MINE. OLD SKULLS OF MINE. THOUSANDS AND *THOUSANDS* OF THEM. "

EASTER LOOKED AT WEDNESDAY AND *SMILED* HER BRIGHT SMILE.

I THINK THIS ONE'S A KEEPER.

THEN SHE PATTED SHADOW'S ARM AND WALKED AWAY.

SHADOW TRIED NOT TO THINK OF HER THIGHS RUBBING TOGETHER AS SHE WALKED.

IN THE TAXI ON THE WAY TO THE AIRPORT.

WHAT THE HELL WAS THAT BUSINESS WITH THE TEN DOLLARS ABOUT?

YOU SHORT-CHANGED HER. IT COMES OUT OF HER WAGES IF SHE'S SHORT.

WHAT THE HELL DO YOU CARE?

WELL, I WOULDN'T WANT ANYONE TO DO IT TO ME. SHE HADN'T DONE ANYTHING WRONG.

NO?

WHEN SHE WAS SEVEN YEARS OLD SHE SHUT A KITTEN IN A CLOSET. SHE LISTENED TO IT MEW FOR SEVERAL DAYS. WHEN IT CEASED TO MEW, SHE PUT IT IN A SHOEBOX AND BURIED IT IN THE BACKYARD. SHE CONSISTENTLY STEALS FROM EVERYWHERE SHE WORKS. SHE,...

I GET IT.

SHE ALSO HAS A SYMPTOMATIC GONORRHEA. SHE SUSPECTS SHE MIGHT BE INFECTED, BUT DOES NOTHING ABOUT IT. WHEN HER LAST BOY-FRIEND ACCUSED HER OF GIVING HIM A DISEASE, SHE SAID SHE WAS HURT, OFFENDED--AND REFUSED TO SEE HIM AGAIN.

THIS ISN'T NECESSARY. I SAID I GET THE IDEA. YOU COULD DO THIS TO ANYONE, COULDN'T YOU? TELL ME BAD THINGS ABOUT THEM.

OF COURSE THEY ALL DO THE SAME THINGS. THEY MAY *THINK* THEIR SINS ARE ORIGINAL, BUT FOR THE MOST PART, THEY ARE PETTY AND REPETITIVE.

AND THAT MAKES IT OKAY FOR YOU TO STEAL TEN BUCKS FROM HER?

WHAT THE HELL *ELSE* CAN I DO?

"THEY DON'T SACRIFICE RAMS OR BULLS TO ME, THEY DON'T SEND ME THE SOULS OF KILLERS AND SLAVES, GALLOWS-HUNG AND RAVEN-PICKED."

THEY MADE ME.

THEY FORGOT ME.

NOW I TAKE A LITTLE BACK FROM THEM. ISN'T THAT FAIR?

MY MOM USED TO SAY, "LIFE ISN'T FAIR."

YOU STIFFED THAT GIRL FOR TEN BUCKS, I SLIPPED HER TEN BUCKS. IT WAS THE RIGHT THING TO DO AND I DID IT.

MAY YOUR CHOICES ALWAYS BE SO CLEAR.

FOR ONCE, HE SOUNDED TOTALLY SINCERE, AND SHADOW THOUGHT...

IT'S TRUE WHAT THEY SAY. "IF YOU CAN FAKE SINCERITY, YOU'VE GOT IT MADE."

THE COLD SNAP WAS EASING WHEN WEDNESDAY DROPPED SHADOW OFF, IN THE SMALL HOURS OF THE MORNING.

IT WAS 9:30 a.m. WHEN CHIEF OF POLICE CHAD MULLIGAN KNOCKED ON SHADOW'S DOOR AND ASKED...

DO YOU KNOW A GIRL NAMED ALISON McGOVERN?

I DON'T THINK SO.

THIS IS HER PICTURE.

OH, YEAH... OKAY, SHE WAS ON THE BUS WHEN I CAME INTO TOWN.

WHERE WERE YOU YESTERDAY, MISTER AINSEL?

SHADOW FELT HIS WORLD BEGIN TO SPIN AWAY FROM HIM. HE KNEW HE HAD NOTHING TO FEEL GUILTY ABOUT.

YOU'RE A PAROLE-VIOLATING FELON LIVING UNDER AN ASSUMED NAME.

SAN FRANCISCO. HELPING MY UNCLE.

YOU GOT ANY WAY OF PROVING THAT? TICKET STUBS? ANYTHING LIKE THAT?

I STILL HAVE MY BOARDING PASS STUBS.

WHAT'S GOING ON?

MMM

ALISON McGOVERN'S VANISHED. SHE HELPED OUT AT THE LAKESIDE HUMANE SOCIETY, FEED ANIMALS, WALK DOGS. THE MANAGER SAID ALISON NEVER SHOWED UP YESTERDAY AFTER SCHOOL.

YUP. PARENTS CALLED US LAST NIGHT. SILLY KID USED TO HITCH-HIKE OUT THERE. HER PARENTS TOLD HER NOT TO, BUT THIS ISN'T THE KIND OF PLACE WHERE THINGS HAPPEN.

VANISHED.

YOU CAN HONESTLY SAY YOU DIDN'T KIDNAP HER, ANYTHING LIKE THAT?

I WAS IN SAN FRANCISCO.

AND I WOULDN'T DO THAT SHIT.

THAT'S WHAT I FIGURED, PAL. SO, YOU WANT TO COME HELP US LOOK FOR HER?

ME?

YES, YOU.

WE'VE HAD THE K-9 GUYS OUT THIS MORNING. NOTHING SO FAR. I JUST HOPE SHE TURNS UP IN THE TWIN CITIES WITH SOME DOPEY BOYFRIEND.

I THINK IT'S POSSIBLE. YOU WANT TO JOIN THE HUNTING PARTY?

YOU THINK IT'S LIKELY?

I'LL COME.

CHAPTER FIVE

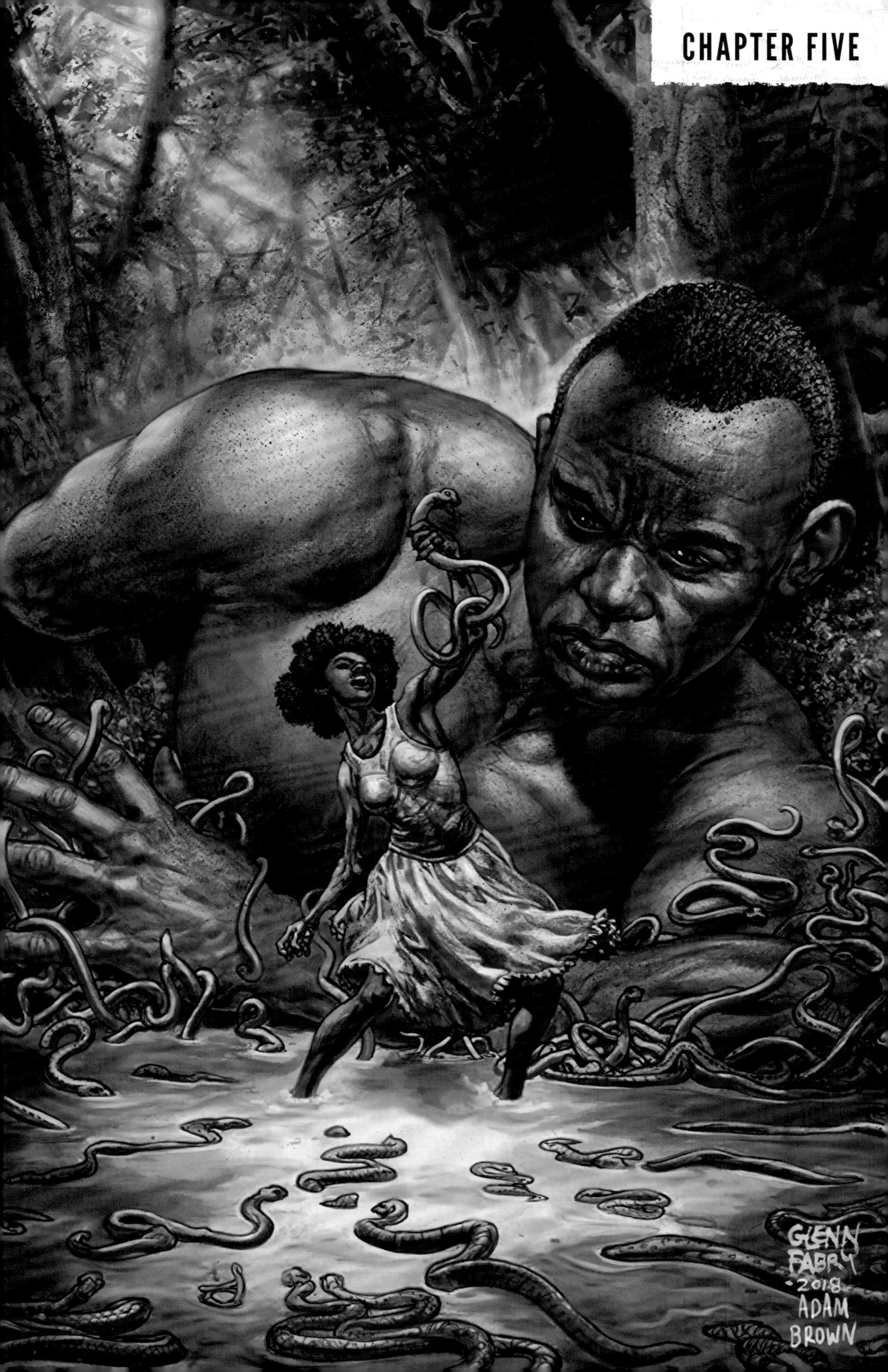
GLENN FABRY ·2018· ADAM BROWN

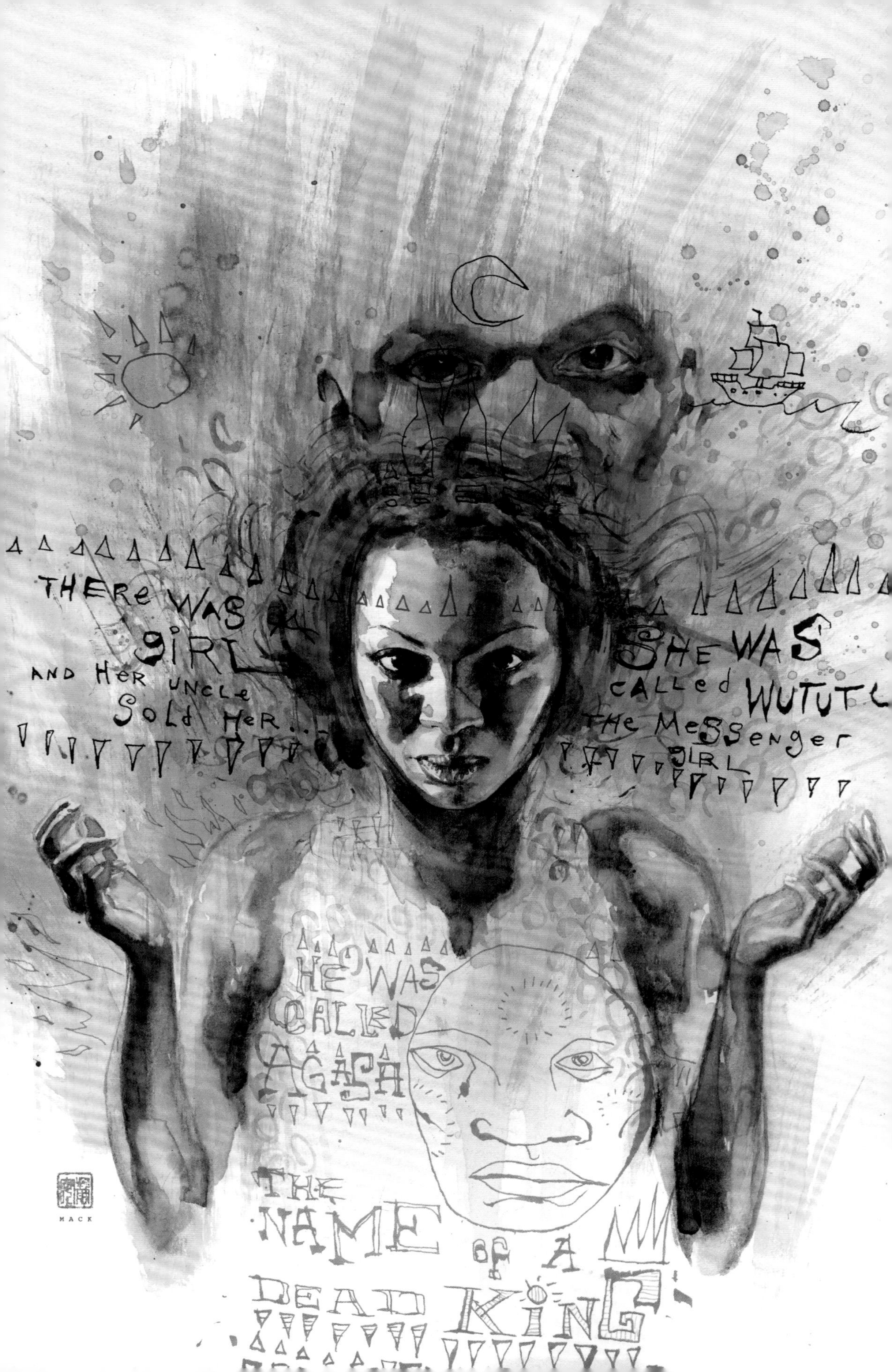
THERE WAS
GIRL
AND HER UNCLE
SOLD HER...
SHE WAS
CALLED WUTUT
THE MESSENGER
GIRL
HE WAS
CALLED
AGASA
THE
NAME OF A
DEAD KING
MACK

THERE WERE TWO DOZEN MEN AND WOMEN WAITING AT THE FIRE STATION.

REMEMBER, WE HAVE A SHORT DAYLIGHT PERIOD. IF, GOD FORBID, YOU FIND ALISON'S BODY, YOU ARE NOT, I REPEAT, *NOT* TO DISTURB ANYTHING, JUST TO RADIO BACK FOR HELP.

COUNTY ROAD W

HINZELMANN, SHADOW, AND A MAN NAMED BROGAN WALKED ALONG A FROZEN CREEK.

ON THE ONE HAND, I HOPE WE FIND HER. ON THE OTHER, IF SHE'S GOING TO BE FOUND, I'D BE VERY GRATEFUL IF IT WAS SOMEONE ELSE WHO GOT TO FIND HER AND NOT US.

KNOW WHAT I MEAN?

I DO.

THE THREE MEN DID NOT TALK MUCH. THEY WERE LOOKING FOR...

RED SNOW-SUIT.

GREEN GLOVES.

BLUE HAT.

"WHITE BODY."

MISSING

AT LUNCHTIME THEY SAT WITH THE REST OF THE SEARCH PARTY ON A COMMANDEERED SCHOOL BUS. HINZELMANN TOLD THEM A STORY ABOUT HIS GRANDFATHER'S TRUMPET.

HE TRIED PLAYING IT DURING A COLD SNAP, AND IT WAS SO COLD OUTSIDE BY THE BARN WHERE HE'D GONE TO PRACTICE, THAT NO MUSIC CAME OUT.

THEN, AFTER HE CAME INSIDE, HE PUT THE TRUMPET DOWN BY THE WOODSTOVE TO THAW. WELL, THE FAMILY'RE ALL IN BED THAT NIGHT AND SUDDENLY THE UNFROZEN TUNES STARTED COMING OUT OF THAT TRUMPET.

SCARED MY GRANDMOTHER SO MUCH SHE NEARLY HAD KITTENS.

THE AFTERNOON WAS ENDLESS, UNFRUITFUL, AND DEPRESSING.

WHEN IT WAS TOO DARK TO CONTINUE, MULLIGAN RADIOED TO THEM TO CALL IT OFF FOR THE EVENING.

THE SEARCHERS WERE EXHAUSTED AND DISPIRITED.

The BUCK Stops Here

YOU SHOULDN'T THINK BADLY OF THE TOWN BECAUSE OF THIS. IT IS A GOOD TOWN.

LAKESIDE IS THE BEST TOWN IN THE NORTH WOODS.

YOU KNOW HOW MANY PEOPLE ARE UNEMPLOYED IN LAKESIDE? *LESS THAN TWENTY.* WE MAY NOT BE RICH, BUT AT LEAST EVERYONE'S WORKING.

IT'S NOT LIKE THE MINING TOWNS UP IN THE NORTHEAST--MOST OF THEM ARE GHOST TOWNS BY NOW. YOU KNOW WHAT THE BIGGEST CAUSE OF UNNATURAL DEATH IS AMONG FARMERS IN THE MIDWEST?

SUICIDE?

YEAH, THAT'S IT.

THEN THERE ARE THE COMPANY TOWNS, WHERE EVERYTHING IS HUNKY-DORY UNTIL 3M STOPS MANUFACTURING CD CASES, OR WHATEVER, AND SUDDENLY NOBODY CAN PAY THEIR MORTGAGE.

I'M SORRY, I DIDN'T CATCH YOUR NAME.

AINSEL. MIKE AINSEL.

I'M CALLIE KNOPH. DOLLY'S SISTER. SO WHAT I'M SAYING IS THAT LAKE-SIDE IS A LUCKY TOWN.

WE'VE GOT A LITTLE OF EVERYTHING HERE.

FARM.

LIGHT INDUSTRY.

CRAFTS.

GOOD SCHOOLS.

TOURISM.

IT'S LIKE LISTENING TO A SALES-MAN, A GOOD SALESMAN WHO BELIEVES IN THE PRODUCT. BUT STILL...

...A SALESMAN.

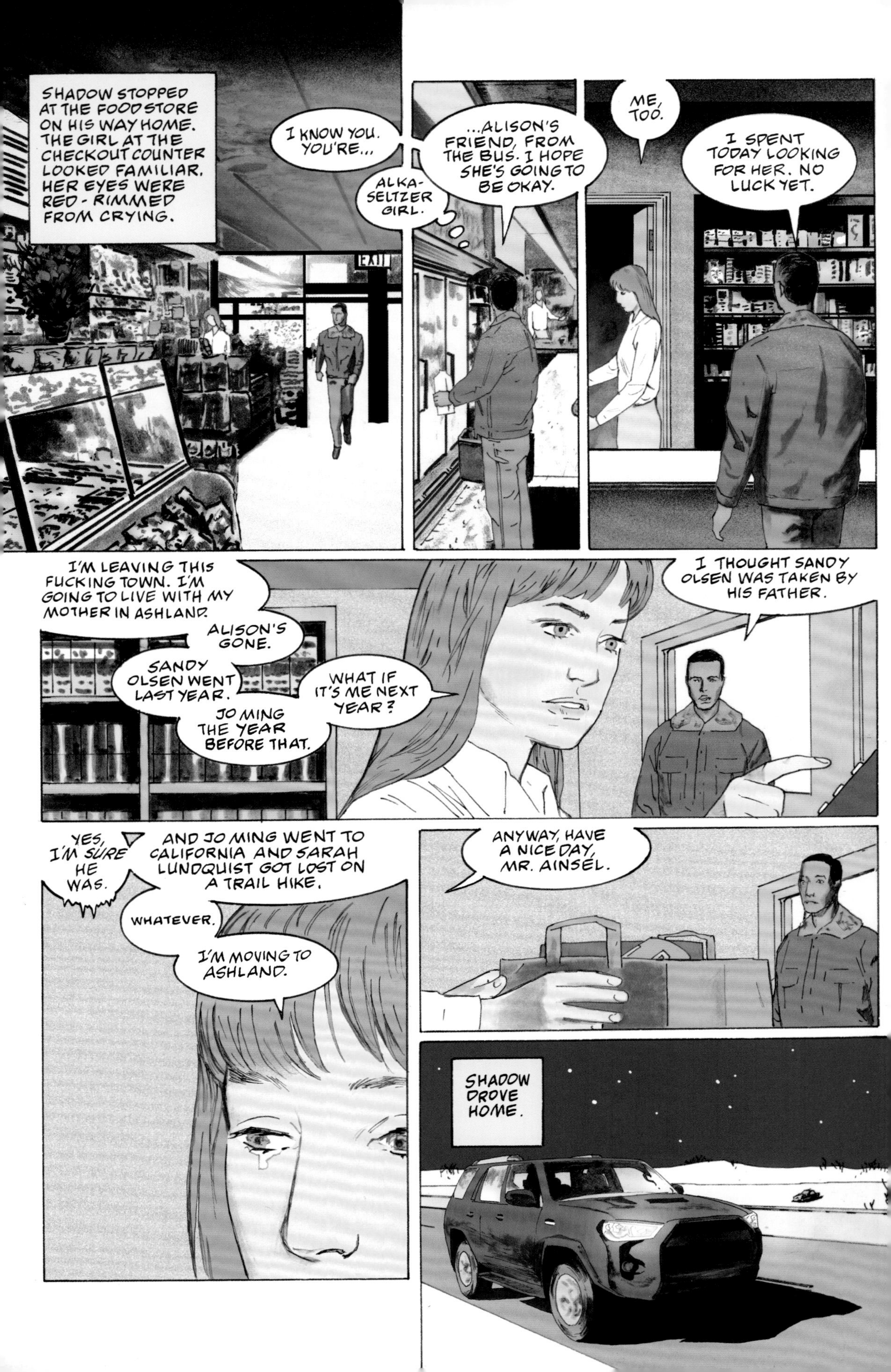
SHADOW STOPPED AT THE FOOD STORE ON HIS WAY HOME. THE GIRL AT THE CHECKOUT COUNTER LOOKED FAMILIAR. HER EYES WERE RED-RIMMED FROM CRYING.
EXIT
I KNOW YOU. YOU'RE...
ALKA-SELTZER GIRL.
...ALISON'S FRIEND, FROM THE BUS. I HOPE SHE'S GOING TO BE OKAY.
ME, TOO.
I SPENT TODAY LOOKING FOR HER. NO LUCK YET.
I'M LEAVING THIS FUCKING TOWN. I'M GOING TO LIVE WITH MY MOTHER IN ASHLAND.
ALISON'S GONE.
SANDY OLSEN WENT LAST YEAR.
JO MING THE YEAR BEFORE THAT.
WHAT IF IT'S ME NEXT YEAR?
I THOUGHT SANDY OLSEN WAS TAKEN BY HIS FATHER.
YES, I'M SURE HE WAS.
AND JO MING WENT TO CALIFORNIA AND SARAH LUNDQUIST GOT LOST ON A TRAIL HIKE.
WHATEVER.
I'M MOVING TO ASHLAND.
ANYWAY, HAVE A NICE DAY, MR. AINSEL.
SHADOW DROVE HOME.

There was a girl and her uncle sold her—

THAT IS THE TALE; THE REST IS DETAIL.

THERE ARE STORIES THAT ARE TRUE IN WHICH EACH INDIVIDUAL'S TALE IS UNIQUE AND TRAGIC, AND THE WORST OF IT IS THAT WE HAVE HEARD IT BEFORE AND CAN NOT ALLOW OURSELVES TO FEEL IT TOO DEEPLY.

WE BUILD A SHELL AROUND IT LIKE AN OYSTER WITH A PAINFUL PARTICLE OF GRIT, COATING IT WITH SMOOTH PEARL LAYERS IN ORDER TO COPE.

"THIS HOW IS WE FUNCTION, DAY IN, DAY OUT, IMMUNE TO OTHERS' PAIN. IF IT WERE TO TOUCH US, IT WOULD CRIPPLE US OR MAKE SAINTS OF US; FOR THE MOST PART IT DOES NOT.

"THERE ARE ACCOUNTS WHICH, IF WE OPEN OUR HEARTS TO THEM, WILL CUT US TOO DEEPLY.

"LOOK-- HERE IS A GOOD MAN. HE IS FAITHFUL TO HIS WIFE, ADORES HIS CHILDREN, CARES ABOUT HIS COUNTRY, DOES HIS JOB AS BEST HE CAN.

"SO, EFFICIENTLY AND GOOD-NATUREDLY, HE EXTERMINATES JEWS.

"OUR MAN SUPERVISES THE DETAIL TAKING THE BODIES TO THE OVENS; AND IF THERE IS ANYTHING HE FEELS BAD ABOUT, IT IS THAT HE STILL ALLOWS THE GASSING OF VERMIN TO AFFECT HIM.

"WERE HE A TRULY GOOD MAN, HE KNOWS HE WOULD FEEL NOTHING BUT JOY AS THE EARTH IS CLEANSED OF ITS PESTS."

LEAVE HIM; HE CUTS TOO DEEP. HE IS TOO CLOSE TO US AND IT HURTS.

There was a girl and her uncle sold her.

PUT LIKE THAT AND IT SEEMS SO SIMPLE.

JOHN DONNE

NO MAN IS AN ISLAND.

JOHN DONNE WAS WRONG. IF WE WERE NOT ISLANDS, WE WOULD BE LOST IN EACH OTHERS' TRAGEDIES. WE NEED INDIVIDUAL STORIES.

"WITHOUT INDIVIDUALS WE SEE ONLY NUMBERS: A THOUSAND DEAD. A HUNDRED THOUSAND DEAD.

""CASUALTIES MAY RISE TO A MILLION.""

"LOOK, SEE THE CHILD'S SWOLLEN BELLY. WILL IT MAKE IT EASIER FOR YOU TO KNOW HIS NAME, HIS DREAMS, HIS FEARS?

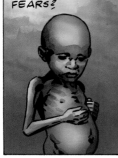

"AND IF IT DOES, ARE WE NOT DOING A DISSERVICE TO THE THOUSAND OTHER CHILDREN TOUCHED BY THE SAME FAMINE...?

"A THOUSAND OTHER LIVES WHO WILL SOON BE FOOD FOR THE FLIES' OWN MYRIAD SQUIRMING CHILDREN?

"WE DRAW LINES AROUND THESE MOMENTS OF PAIN. THEY ARE COVERED WITH A SMOOTH NACREOUS LAYER TO LET THEM SLIP PEARL-LIKE FROM OUR SOULS WITHOUT REAL PAIN.

"FICTION ALLOWS US TO LOOK OUT THROUGH OTHER EYES, TO DIE VICARIOUSLY AND UNHARMED.

"AND IN THE WORLD BEYOND THE TALE WE TURN THE PAGE OR CLOSE THE BOOK, AND WE RESUME OUR LIVES.

"A LIFE WHICH IS LIKE ANY OTHER, UNLIKE ANY OTHER.

AND THE SIMPLE TRUTH IS THIS..."

"THERE WAS A GIRL AND HER UNCLE SOLD HER.

"THERE WAS A WAR IN THAT PLACE. IT WAS A SMALL WAR, ALMOST AN ARGUMENT. ONE VILLAGE WON THE ARGUMENT, ONE LOST IT.

"LIFE AS A COMMODITY, PEOPLE AS POSSESSIONS, ENSLAVEMENT HAD BEEN PART OF THE CULTURE FOR THOUSANDS OF YEARS.

"THERE WAS NOTHING UNUSUAL ABOUT THEIR UNCLE SELLING THE TWINS, ALTHOUGH TWINS WERE CONSIDERED MAGICAL BEINGS, AND THEIR UNCLE WAS SCARED OF THEM. THEY WERE TWELVE YEARS OLD.

"SHE WAS CALLED WUTUTU, THE MESSENGER GIRL.

"HE WAS CALLED AGASU, THE NAME OF A DEAD KING.

"BECAUSE THEY WERE TWINS, MALE AND FEMALE, THEY WERE TOLD MANY THINGS ABOUT THE GODS. THEY LISTENED TO THE THINGS THEY WERE TOLD, AND THEY REMEMBERED.

"THEIR UNCLE WAS A FAT AND LAZY MAN. IF HE WERE RICH, PERHAPS HE WOULD HAVE SOLD ONE OF HIS CATTLE INSTEAD OF THE CHILDREN. BUT HE DID NOT.

"HE SOLD THE TWINS.

"ENOUGH OF HIM: HE SHALL NOT ENTER FURTHER INTO THIS NARRATIVE.

"WE FOLLOW THE TWINS."

"THEY WERE MARCHED, WITH SEVERAL OTHER SLAVES, TAKEN OR SOLD IN THE WAR, FOR A DOZEN MILES TO A SMALL OUTPOST.

" HERE THEY WERE BOUGHT, ALONG WITH THIRTEEN OTHERS, BY SIX MEN WITH SPEARS AND KNIVES.

"THE MEN WITH SPEARS MARCHED THEM TO THE WEST, TOWARD THE SEA. "

WHAT WILL HAPPEN TO US?

I DO NOT KNOW.

THEY WILL SELL US TO THE WHITE DEVILS, WHO WILL TAKE US TO THEIR HOME ACROSS THE WATER.

AND WHAT WILL THEY DO TO US THERE?

IT IS POSSIBLE THEY WILL *EAT* US. THAT IS WHY THEY NEED *SO* MANY SLAVES. IT IS BECAUSE THEY ARE ALWAYS HUNGRY.

" WUTUTU BEGAN TO CRY. "

DO NOT CRY, MY SISTER. THEY WILL NOT EAT YOU. I SHALL PROTECT YOU.

"WUTUTU WAS NOT WORRIED ABOUT THE WHITE DEVILS EATING HER. SHE CRIED BECAUSE SHE WAS SCARED THEY WOULD EAT HER BROTHER.

"... AND SHE WAS NOT CERTAIN SHE COULD PROTECT HIM. "

"THEY REACHED A TRADING POST AND WERE PLACED IN A HUT. IT SOON BECAME VERY CROWDED AS MEN ARRIVED FROM FAR AWAY, BRINGING THEIR OWN STRINGS OF SLAVES.

"IN THE MORNING OF THE TENTH DAY THEY WERE MARCHED TO THE HARBOR AND WUTUTU SAW THE SHIP THAT WAS TO TAKE THEM AWAY.

"HER FIRST THOUGHT WAS HOW *BIG* A SHIP IT WAS...

"... HER SECOND THAT IT WAS *TOO SMALL* FOR ALL OF THEM TO FIT INSIDE. IT SAT LIGHTLY ON THE WATER.

"THE SHIP'S BOAT CAME BACK AND FORTH, FERRYING THE CAPTIVES TO THE SHIP.

"THE MEN AND THE WOMEN AND THE CHILDREN WERE SEPARATED.

"WUTUTU WAS PUT IN WITH THE CHILDREN, NOT CHAINED, MERELY LOCKED IN.

"AGASU WAS FORCED IN WITH THE MEN, IN CHAINS. IT STANK UNDER THAT DECK. THE SMELL OF FEAR, DIARRHEA, AND DEATH, OF FEVER AND MADNESS AND HATE.

"THE SHIP SET SAIL. NOW IT SAT HEAVY IN THE WATER."

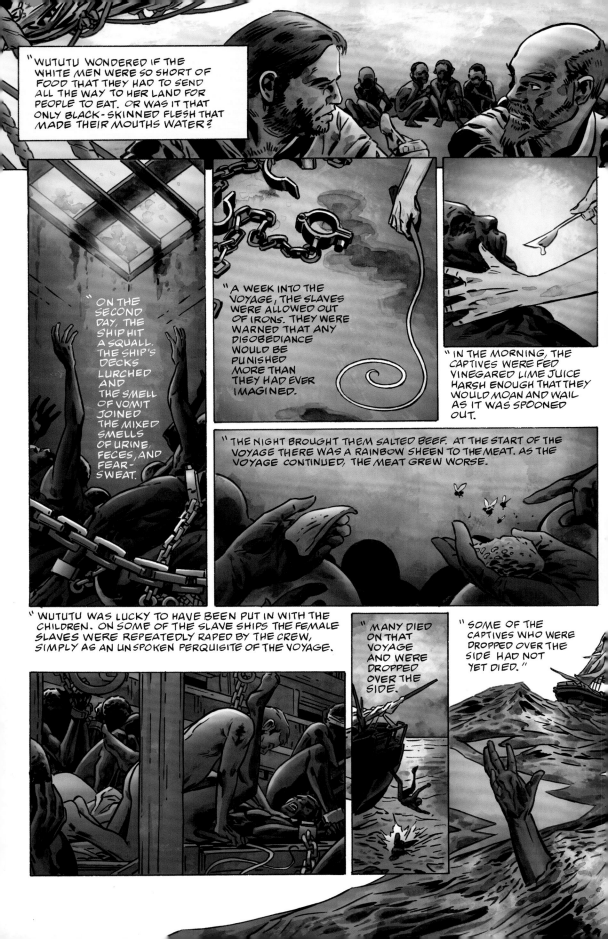

"WUTUTU WONDERED IF THE WHITE MEN WERE SO SHORT OF FOOD THAT THEY HAD TO SEND ALL THE WAY TO HER LAND FOR PEOPLE TO EAT. OR WAS IT THAT ONLY BLACK-SKINNED FLESH THAT MADE THEIR MOUTHS WATER?

" ON THE SECOND DAY, THE SHIP HIT A SQUALL. THE SHIP'S DECKS LURCHED AND THE SMELL OF VOMIT JOINED THE MIXED SMELLS OF URINE, FECES, AND FEAR-SWEAT.

" A WEEK INTO THE VOYAGE, THE SLAVES WERE ALLOWED OUT OF IRONS. THEY WERE WARNED THAT ANY DISOBEDIANCE WOULD BE PUNISHED MORE THAN THEY HAD EVER IMAGINED.

" IN THE MORNING, THE CAPTIVES WERE FED VINEGARED LIME JUICE HARSH ENOUGH THAT THEY WOULD MOAN AND WAIL AS IT WAS SPOONED OUT.

" THE NIGHT BROUGHT THEM SALTED BEEF. AT THE START OF THE VOYAGE THERE WAS A RAINBOW SHEEN TO THE MEAT. AS THE VOYAGE CONTINUED, THE MEAT GREW WORSE.

" WUTUTU WAS LUCKY TO HAVE BEEN PUT IN WITH THE CHILDREN. ON SOME OF THE SLAVE SHIPS THE FEMALE SLAVES WERE REPEATEDLY RAPED BY THE CREW, SIMPLY AS AN UNSPOKEN PERQUISITE OF THE VOYAGE.

" MANY DIED ON THAT VOYAGE AND WERE DROPPED OVER THE SIDE.

" SOME OF THE CAPTIVES WHO WERE DROPPED OVER THE SIDE HAD NOT YET DIED. "

IN THE EVENING WHEN THEY COULD, WUTUTU AND AGASU WOULD HUDDLE TOGETHER TALKING, AND WUTUTU WOULD TELL AGASU THE STORIES THEIR MOTHER HAD TOLD THEM, LIKE THOSE OF ELEGBA, THE TRICKIEST OF THE GODS, WHO WAS GREAT MAWU'S EYES AND EARS IN THE WORLD, WHO TOOK MESSAGES TO MAWU AND BROUGHT BACK MAWU'S REPLIES.

"IN THE EVENINGS THE SAILORS WOULD MAKE THE SLAVES SING AND DANCE FOR THEM.

"ONE NIGHT WUTUTU CAUGHT ONE OF THE BLACK GUARDS STARING AT HER."

WHY DO YOU SERVE THE WHITE DEVILS?

IF YOU WERE OLDER, I WOULD MAKE YOU SCREAM WITH HAPPINESS FROM MY PENIS.

PERHAPS I WILL DO IT TONIGHT. I SEE HOW WELL YOU DANCE.

IF YOU PUT IT IN ME DOWN THERE I WILL BITE IT OFF. I AM A WITCH GIRL, AND I HAVE VERY SHARP TEETH DOWN THERE.

!

"THE WORDS HAD COME OUT OF HER MOUTH, BUT THEY HAD NOT BEEN HER WORDS. IT WAS ELEGBA OF THE CLEVER WAYS AND THE IRON-HARD ERECTION WHO HAD RIDDEN HER FOR A MOMENT. THAT NIGHT SHE GAVE THANKS TO ELEGBA."

"SEVERAL OF THE CAPTIVES REFUSED TO EAT. THEY WERE WHIPPED UNTIL THEY PUT FOOD INTO THEIR MOUTHS, ALTHOUGH THE WHIPPING WAS SEVERE ENOUGH THAT TWO MEN DIED OF IT.

IT WAS A LONG JOURNEY AND A BAD ONE FOR THE CAPTIVES.

" THEY MADE HARBOR ON A PLEASANT, BALMY DAY IN BRIDGETOWN, BARBADOS.

" THE CAPTIVES WERE TAKEN TO THE MARKET SQUARE. THE SQUARE WAS FILLED WITH RED-FACED MEN, SHOUTING, INSPECTING, APPRAISING. A BIG MAN FORCED OPEN AGASU'S MOUTH, LOOKED AT HIS TEETH, FELT HIS ARM MUSCLES.

" HE NODDED TO TWO OTHER MEN WHO HAULED AGASU AWAY."

AGASU.

"HE DID NOT FIGHT THEM. HE CALLED TO WUTUTU..."

BE BRAVE.

" HER VISION BLURRED WITH TEARS. TOGETHER, THEY WERE TWINS, MAGICAL, POWERFUL. APART, THEY WERE TWO CHILDREN IN PAIN. SHE NEVER SAW HIM AGAIN BUT ONCE, AND NEVER IN LIFE.

" THIS IS WHAT HAPPENED TO AGASU. FIRST, THEY TOOK HIM TO A SEASONING FARM, WHERE THEY WHIPPED HIM DAILY FOR THINGS HE DID AND DIDN'T DO. THEY TAUGHT HIM A SMATTERING OF ENGLISH AND GAVE HIM THE NAME OF INKYJACK FOR THE DARKNESS OF HIS SKIN."

" WHEN HE RAN AWAY, THEY HUNTED HIM DOWN WITH DOGS AND BROUGHT HIM BACK.

" THEY CUT OFF A TOE WITH A CHISEL TO TEACH HIM A LESSON HE WOULD NOT FORGET.

" WHEN HE REFUSED TO EAT, HIS FRONT TEETH WERE BROKEN AND THIN GRUEL WAS FORCED INTO HIS MOUTH.

" WHEN INKYJACK WAS SIXTEEN, HE WAS SOLD TO A SUGAR PLANTATION ON ST. DOMINGUE. THEY CALLED HIM *HYACINTH*, THE BIG, BROKEN-TOOTHED SLAVE.

" HYACINTH LEARNED SOME FRENCH AND SOME TEACHINGS OF THE CATHOLIC CHURCH. EACH DAY HE CUT SUGAR CANE BEFORE THE SUN ROSE UNTIL WELL AFTER THE SUN SET.

" HE WENT WITH THE OTHER SLAVES, IN THE SMALL HOURS OF THE NIGHT, TO THE WOODS. ALTHOUGH IT WAS FORBIDDEN TO DANCE THE *CALINDA*, TO SING TO *DAMBALLA-WEDO*, THE SERPENT-GOD. HE SANG TO *ELEGBA*, TO *OGU*, *SHANGO*, *ZAKA*, AND MANY OTHERS, ALL THE GODS THE CAPTIVES HAD BROUGHT WITH THEM TO THE ISLAND, BROUGHT IN THEIR MINDS, AND THEIR SECRET HEARTS. "

" THE SLAVES ON THE SUGAR PLANTA-
TIONS OF ST. DOMINGUE RARELY
LIVED MORE THAN A DECADE.

" THE FREE TIME THEY WERE GIVEN -- TWO HOURS IN THE HEAT
OF NOON, AND FIVE HOURS IN THE DARK OF NIGHT WAS THE
ONLY TIME THEY HAD TO GROW THE FOOD THEY WOULD EAT.

" EVEN SO,
THEY WOULD TAKE
THAT TIME TOGETHER
AND DANCE AND SING AND
WORSHIP THE GODS OF
DAHOMEY AND THE CONGO
PUT DOWN THICK ROOTS THERE,
LUSH AND DEEP AND THEY
PROMISED FREEDOM TO
THOSE WHO WORSHIPPED
THEM AT NIGHT IN
THE GROVES.

" HYACINTH WAS TWENTY-FIVE WHEN A
SPIDER BIT THE BACK OF HIS RIGHT HAND.

" THE
BITE
BECAME
INFECTED
AND SOON
HIS
WHOLE
ARM
THROBBED
AND
BURNED.

" THEY HEATED THE BLADE OF
A MACHETE. THEY CUT OFF
HIS ARM WITH A SAW AND
CAUTERIZED IT WITH THE
BURNING BLADE.

" HE LAY IN A FEVER FOR A WEEK.

" THEN HE RETURNED TO WORK

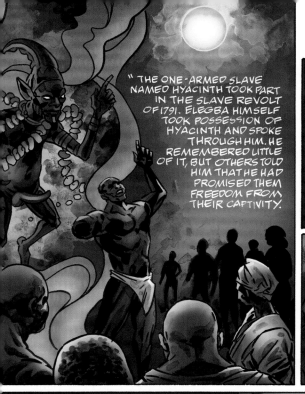

" THE ONE-ARMED SLAVE NAMED HYACINTH TOOK PART IN THE SLAVE REVOLT OF 1791. ELEGBA HIMSELF TOOK POSSESSION OF HYACINTH AND SPOKE THROUGH HIM. HE REMEMBERED LITTLE OF IT, BUT OTHERS TOLD HIM THAT HE HAD PROMISED THEM FREEDOM FROM THEIR CAPTIVITY.

"A PIG WAS KILLED AND THE MEN AND WOMEN OF THAT PLANTATION DRANK THE HOT BLOOD, BINDING THEMSELVES INTO A BROTHERHOOD. THEY SWORE THAT THEY WERE AN ARMY OF FREEDOM."

IF WE DIE IN BATTLE WITH THE WHITES, WE WILL BE REBORN IN AFRICA, IN OUR HOMES, IN OUR OWN TRIBES.

NOW THEY CALLED AGASU BY THE NAME OF BIG ONE-ARM. HE FOUGHT, HE WORSHIPPED, HE SACRIFICED, HE PLANNED, AND HE KEPT FIGHTING. THEY FOUGHT FOR TWELVE YEARS, A MADDENING BLOODY STRUGGLE WITH THE PLANTATION OWNERS. THEY FOUGHT, AND THEY KEPT FIGHTING, AND IMPOSSIBLY...

...THEY WON.

" ON JANUARY THE FIRST, 1804, THE INDEPENDENCE OF ST. DOMINGUE, SOON TO BE KNOWN AS THE REPUBLIC OF HAITI, WAS DECLARED.

" ONE-ARM DID NOT LIVE TO SEE IT. HE HAD DIED IN AUGUST OF 1802, BAYONETED BY A FRENCH SOLDIER.

" AT THE PRECISE MOMENT OF HIS DEATH, HIS SISTER FELT THE BAYONET SLIDE BETWEEN HER RIBS AND SCREAMED. "

"HER TWIN DAUGHTERS WOKE AND BEGAN TO HOWL. HER NEW BABIES WERE CREAM- AND COFFEE-COLORED...

".. NOT LIKE THE BLACK CHILDREN SHE HAD BORNE WHEN LITTLE MORE THAN A CHILD HERSELF AND WHO HAD BEEN SOLD AWAY.

" SINCE HER BROTHER HAD BEEN TAKEN FROM HER SHE HAD WEPT ONLY ONCE. SHE HAD SEEN THE FOOD FOR THE SLAVE CHILDREN AND THE DOGS POURED INTO THE SAME TROUGH. SHE SAW IT EVERY DAY-- AND IT BROKE HER HEART.

" THE YEARS OF PAIN HAD TAKEN THEIR TOLL AND SHE WAS NO LONGER BEAUTIFUL.

" ELEVEN YEARS EARLIER HER RIGHT ARM HAD WITHERED. THE FLESH SEEMED TO MELT FROM THE BONE. NONE OF THE WHITE PEOPLE KNEW WHAT TO MAKE OF IT.

" AFTER THIS SHE BECAME A HOUSE-SLAVE.

" THE CASTERTON FAMILY, WHO OWNED THE PLANTATION, CALLED HER DAISY, BUT MRS. CASTERTON FOUND THE WITHERED ARM UNSETTLING AND SO SHE WAS SOLD TO THE LAVERE FAMILY OUT OF NEW ORLEANS.

" SHE WAS NOW KNOWN AS SUKEY.

" IN NEW ORLEANS, THE WOMEN CAME TO HER TO BUY LOVE CHARMS AND FETISHES. THE LAVERES TURNED A BLIND EYE TO IT.

" PERHAPS THEY LIKED THE PRESTIGE OF HAVING A SLAVE WHO WAS FEARED AND RESPECTED. THEY WOULD NOT, HOWEVER, SELL HER HER FREEDOM."

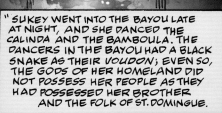

"SUKEY WENT INTO THE BAYOU LATE AT NIGHT, AND SHE DANCED THE CALINDA AND THE BAMBOULA. THE DANCERS IN THE BAYOU HAD A BLACK SNAKE AS THEIR *VOUDON*; EVEN SO, THE GODS OF HER HOMELAND DID NOT POSSESS HER PEOPLE AS THEY HAD POSSESSED HER BROTHER AND THE FOLK OF ST. DOMINGUE."

"SHE LISTENED WHEN THE WHITE FOLK SPOKE OF THE REVOLT IN ST. DOMINGUE AND HOW IT WAS DOOMED TO FAIL."

THINK OF IT. A CANNIBAL LAND.

"AND THEN SHE OBSERVED THAT THEY NO LONGER TALKED OF IT.

"THE YOUNGEST LAVERE CHILD UNABLE TO SAY SUKEY HAD CALLED HER:

ZOUZOU

... AND THE NAME HAD STUCK.

"NOW THE YEAR WAS 1821, AND SUKEY WAS IN HER MID-FIFTIES. SHE LOOKED MUCH OLDER.

"SHE KNEW MORE OF THE SECRETS THAN OLD SANITÉ DEDE, WHO SOLD CANDIES, MORE THAN MARIE SALOPPÉ, WHO CALLED HERSELF THE *VOODOO QUEEN*.

"THE YOUNG WOMAN WHO CAME TO HER STYLED HERSELF *THE WIDOW PARIS*. SHE HAD AFRICAN BLOOD IN HER, AND EUROPEAN BLOOD, AND INDIAN. HER MISSING HUSBAND, JACQUES, WAS THREE-QUARTERS WHITE AS THESE THINGS ARE CALCULATED."

MY JACQUES, IS HE DEAD?

"MAMA ZOUZOU CONSULTED THE BONES."

HE IS WITH A WHITE WOMAN, SOMEWHERE NORTH OF HERE. HE IS ALIVE.

" THIS WAS NOT MAGIC. IT WAS COMMON KNOWLEDGE IN NEW ORLEANS JUST WITH WHOM JACQUES HAD RUN OFF WITH. MAMA ZOUZOU WAS SURPRISED THE WIDOW PARIS DID NOT ALREADY KNOW THIS.

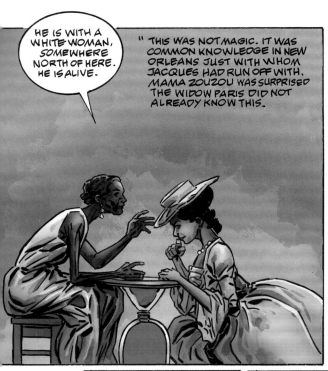

"PERHAPS SHE HAD ANOTHER REASON FOR COMING.

" THE WIDOW CAME TO SEE THE OLD SLAVE WOMAN ONE OR TWO TIMES A WEEK. AFTER A MONTH, SHE BROUGHT GIFTS.

" HAIR RIBBONS. A SEED CAKE.

" A BLACK ROOSTER.

MAMA ZOUZOU, IT IS TIME FOR YOU TO TEACH ME WHAT YOU KNOW.

" THE WIDOW PARIS HAD CONFESSED THAT SHE HAD BEEN BORN WITH WEBBED TOES, WHICH MEANT SHE WAS A TWIN AND SHE HAD KILLED HER TWIN IN THE WOMB. WHAT CHOICE DID MAMA ZOUZOU HAVE ?"

YES.

" SHE TAUGHT THE GIRL THAT TWO NUTMEGS HUNG ABOUT THE NECK UNTIL THE STRING BREAKS WILL CURE HEART MURMURS, WHILE A PIGEON, CUT OPEN AND LAID OUT ON A PATIENT'S HEAD, WILL DRAW A FEVER, THAT DRIED SNAKE POWDER PLACED IN FACE POWDER WILL CAUSE BLINDNESS AND THAT AN ENEMY WILL DROWN HERSELF IF A PIECE OF HER UNDERWEAR IS PLACED UNDER A BRICK AT MIDNIGHT.

" MAMA ZOUZOU SHOWED HER THE WORLD WONDER ROOT, DRAGON'S BLOOD, VALERIAN, AND FIVE-FINGER GRASS.

" SHE SHOWED HER HOW TO BREW WASTEAWAY TEA. "

"ALL THESE THINGS MAMA ZOUZOU SHOWED THE WIDOW PARIS. SHE DID HER BEST TO TEACH THE DEEP KNOWLEDGE, TO TELL HER OF ELEGBA, OF MAWU, OF THE VOUDON SERPENT. BUT THE WIDOW PARIS WAS INTERESTED ONLY IN THE PRACTICALITIES."

"IT WAS DISAPPOINTING TO THE OLD WOMAN SO MAMA ZOUZOU COMPLAINED TO HER CONFIDANT, CLEMINTINE."

SHE DOES NOT WANT TO *KNOW!*

THEN DO NOT TEACH HER.

I TEACH HER, BUT SHE DOES NOT SEE WHAT IS VALUABLE. I GIVE HER DIAMONDS, BUT SHE CARES ONLY FOR PRETTY THINGS. I GIVE HER CLARET AND SHE DRINKS RIVER WATER.

THEN WHY DO YOU PERSIST?

"MAMA ZOUZOU SHRUGS. SHE CANNOT ANSWER.

"SHE COULD SAY THAT SHE TEACHES BECAUSE SHE IS GRATEFUL TO BE ALIVE, AND SHE IS: SHE HAS SEEN TOO MANY DIE.

"SHE COULD SAY SHE DREAMS THAT ONE DAY THE SLAVES WILL RISE, AS THEY ROSE (AND WERE DEFEATED) IN LAPLACE.

"BUT SHE KNOWS IN HER HEART THAT WITHOUT THE GODS OF AFRICA, THEY WILL NEVER OVERCOME THEIR WHITE CAPTORS, WILL NEVER RETURN TO THEIR HOMELANDS."

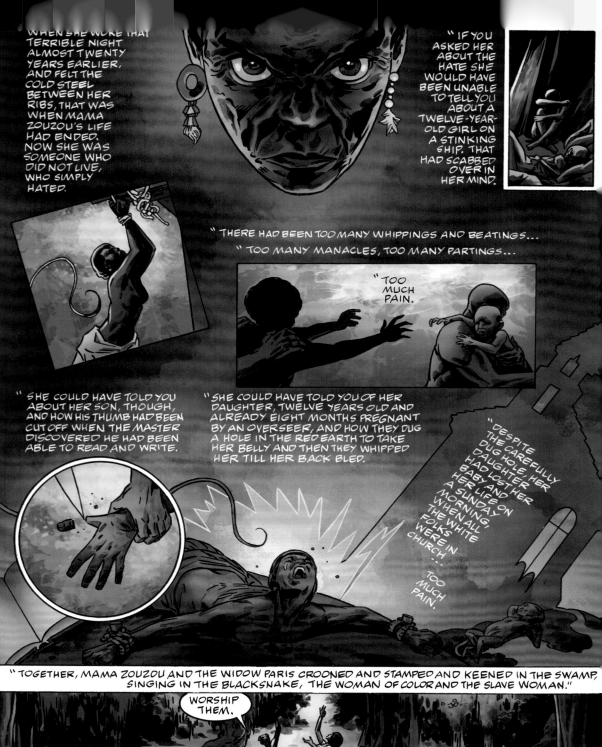

WHEN SHE WOKE THAT TERRIBLE NIGHT ALMOST TWENTY YEARS EARLIER, AND FELT THE COLD STEEL BETWEEN HER RIBS, THAT WAS WHEN MAMA ZOUZOU'S LIFE HAD ENDED. NOW SHE WAS SOMEONE WHO DID NOT LIVE, WHO SIMPLY HATED.

"IF YOU ASKED HER ABOUT THE HATE SHE WOULD HAVE BEEN UNABLE TO TELL YOU ABOUT A TWELVE-YEAR-OLD GIRL ON A STINKING SHIP. THAT HAD SCABBED OVER IN HER MIND.

"THERE HAD BEEN TOO MANY WHIPPINGS AND BEATINGS...

"TOO MANY MANACLES, TOO MANY PARTINGS...

"TOO MUCH PAIN.

"SHE COULD HAVE TOLD YOU ABOUT HER SON, THOUGH, AND HOW HIS THUMB HAD BEEN CUT OFF WHEN THE MASTER DISCOVERED HE HAD BEEN ABLE TO READ AND WRITE.

"SHE COULD HAVE TOLD YOU OF HER DAUGHTER, TWELVE YEARS OLD AND ALREADY EIGHT MONTHS PREGNANT BY AN OVERSEER, AND HOW THEY DUG A HOLE IN THE RED EARTH TO TAKE HER BELLY AND THEN THEY WHIPPED HER TILL HER BACK BLED.

"DESPITE THE CAREFULLY DUG HOLE, HER DAUGHTER HAD LOST HER BABY AND HER LIFE ON A SUNDAY MORNING, WHEN ALL THE WHITE FOLKS WERE IN CHURCH...

"TOO MUCH PAIN.

"TOGETHER, MAMA ZOUZOU AND THE WIDOW PARIS CROONED AND STAMPED AND KEENED IN THE SWAMP, SINGING IN THE BLACKSNAKE, THE WOMAN OF COLOR AND THE SLAVE WOMAN."

WORSHIP THEM.

"THE WIDOW PARIS'S HUS-BAND, JACQUES, HAD TOLD MARIE ABOUT THE GODS OF ST. DOMINQUE, BUT SHE DID NOT CARE. POWER CAME FROM RITUALS, NOT FROM THE GODS."

THERE IS MORE TO IT THAN JUST, YOU PROSPER, YOUR ENEMIES FAIL.

"MANY OF THE WORDS OF THE CEREMONIES, WORDS SHE KNEW ONCE, HAD FLED FROM HER MEMORY. SHE TOLD PRETTY MARIE LAVEAU THAT..."

THE WORDS DO NOT MATTER...

...ONLY THE TUNES.

"AND THERE, SINGING AND TAPPING IN THE BLACKSNAKES, IN THE SWAMP, SHE HAS AN ODD VISION.

AND THE BEATS.

" SHE SEES THE BEATS OF THE SONGS, THE CALINDA BEAT, A BAMBOULA BEAT, ALL THE RHYTHMS OF EQUATORICAL AFRICA SPREADING SLOWLY ACROSS THIS MIDNIGHT LAND, UNTIL THE WHOLE COUNTRY SHIVERS AND SWINGS TO THE BEATS OF THE OLD GODS.

"SHE TURNS TO PRETTY MARIE AND SEES HERSELF THROUGH MARIE'S EYES, A BLACK-SKINNED OLD WOMAN, HER BONY ARM HANGING LIMPLY BY HER SIDE, HER EYES THE EYES OF ONE WHO HAS SEEN HER CHILDREN FIGHT IN THE TROUGH FOR FOOD FROM THE DOGS.

" SHE KNEW THEN FOR THE FIRST TIME THE FEAR AND REVULSION THE YOUNGER WOMAN HAD FOR HER.

"THEN SHE LAUGHED AND PICKED UP A BLACK-SNAKE AS THICK AS A SHIP'S ROPE."

"AND THEN, IN THE MOONLIGHT, THE SECOND SIGHT POSSESSED HER FOR A FINAL TIME, AND SHE SAW HER BROTHER, AGASU, NOT THE TWELVE-YEAR OLD BOY SHE HAD LAST SEEN SO LONG AGO, BUT A HUGE *MAN*, GRINNING WITH BROKEN TEETH, HIS BACK LINED WITH DEEP SCARS."

HERE. HERE WILL BE OUR *VOUDON*.

STAY STAY A WHILE.

I WILL BE THERE. I WILL BE WITH YOU SOON!

"AND MARIE PARIS THOUGHT THE OLD WOMAN WAS SPEAKING TO HER."

CHAPTER SIX

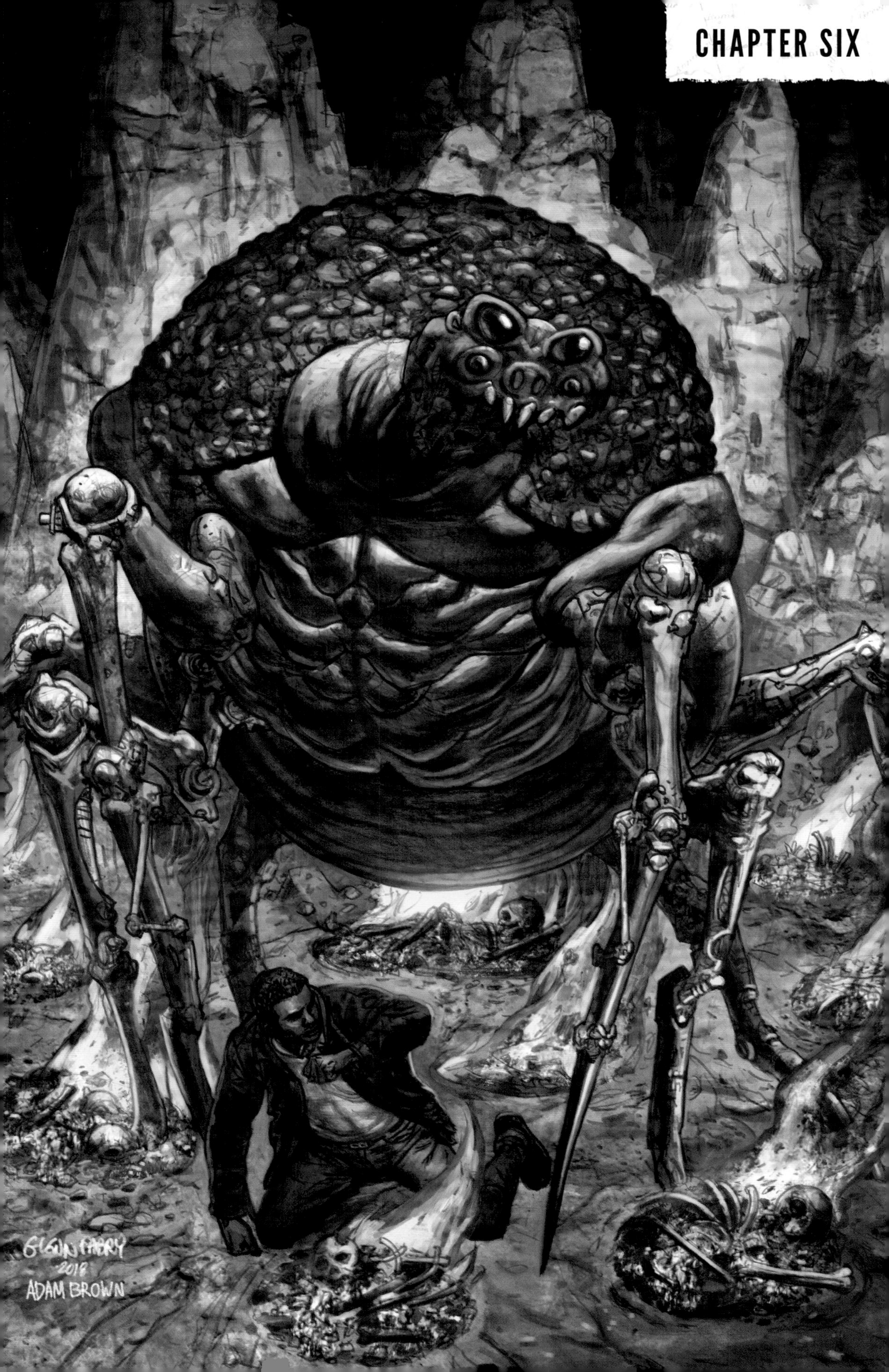
2018
ADAM BROWN

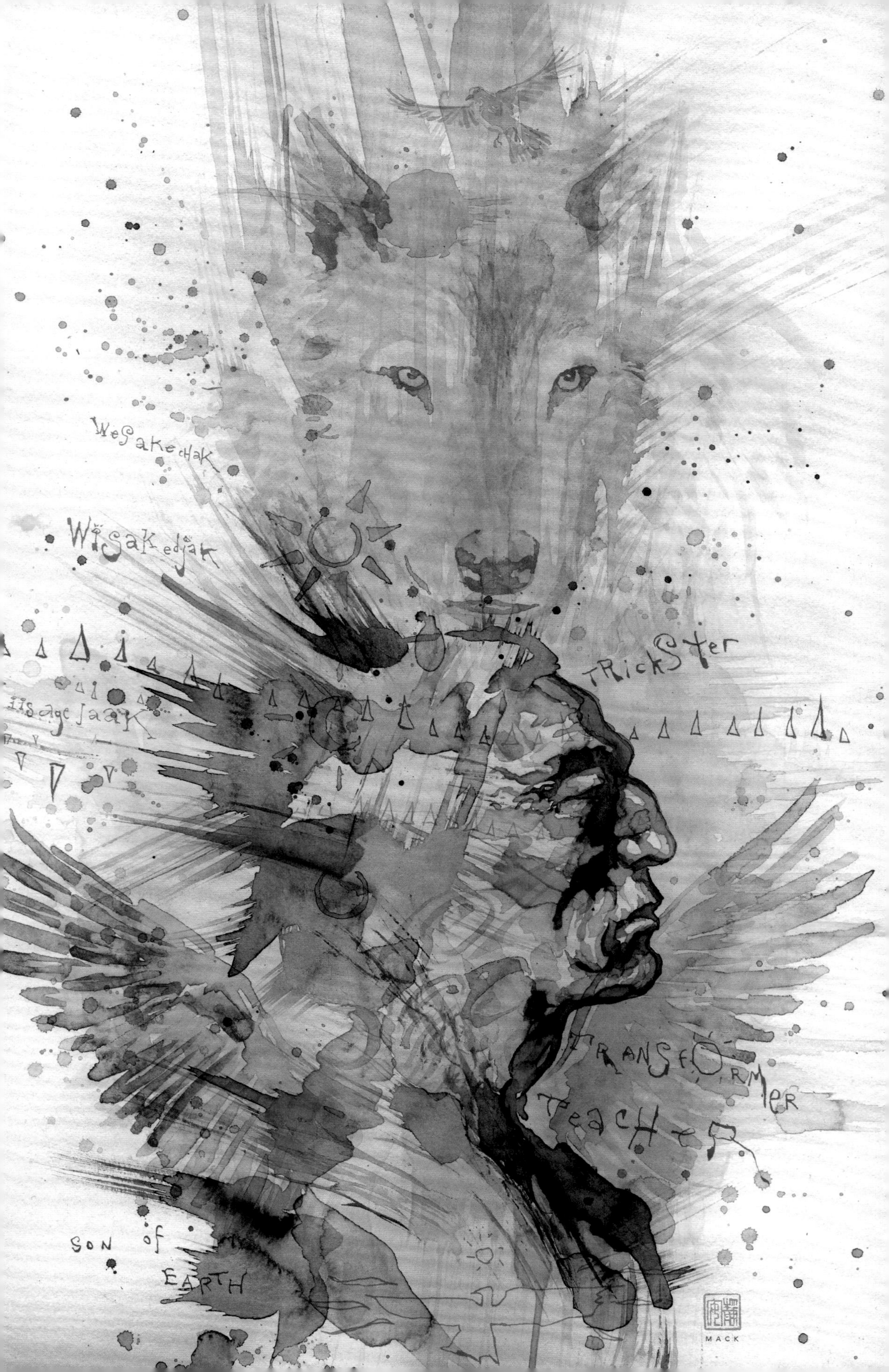
Wesakechak
Wisakedjak
Trickster
Transformer
Teacher
Son of
Earth
MACK

SHADOW DROVE WEST, ACROSS WISCONSIN AND MINNESOTA AND INTO NORTH DAKOTA. THEN INTO SOUTH DAKOTA AND RESERVATION COUNTRY.

WEDNESDAY HAD TRADED IN THE LINCOLN, TOWN CAR FOR A LUMBERING AND ANCIENT WINNEBAGO WHICH SMELLED OF MALE CAT.

MT RUSHM
350 MIL

NOW *THAT* IS A HOLY PLACE.

I KNOW IT USED TO BE SACRED TO THE INDIANS.

IT'S A HOLY PLACE. THAT'S THE AMERICAN WAY--THEY NEED TO GIVE PEOPLE AN EXCUSE TO COME AND WORSHIP.

"THUS, MISTER GUTZON BORGLUM'S TREMENDOUS PRESIDENTIAL FACES. ONCE THEY WERE CARVED, PERMISSION WAS GRANTED FOR PEOPLE TO DRIVE OUT IN MULTITUDES TO SEE SOMETHING IN THE FLESH THEY'VE ALREADY SEEN ON A THOUSAND POSTCARDS.

I KNEW A GUY FROM THE MUSCLE FARM, YEARS BACK. HE SAID THAT THE DAKOTA INDIANS, THE YOUNG MEN CLIMB UP THE MOUNTAIN, THEN FORM DEATH-DEFYING HUMAN CHAINS OFF THE HEADS.

" JUST SO THAT THE GUY AT THE END OF THE CHAIN CAN PISS ON THE PRESIDENT'S NOSE. "

OH, FINE! VERY FINE! IS ANY SPECIFIC PRESIDENT THE BUTT OF THEIR IRE?

HE DIDN'T SAY.

MILES VANISHED BENEATH THE WHEELS OF THE WINNEBAGO. SHADOW BEGAN TO IMAGINE THAT HE WAS STAYING STILL WHILE THE AMERICAN LANDSCAPE MOVED PAST THEM AT A STEADY SIXTY-SEVEN MILES PER HOUR.

A GIRL VANISHED FROM LAKESIDE LAST WEEK WHEN WE WERE IN SAN FRANCISCO.

MM?

KID NAMED ALISON McGOVERN. NOT THE FIRST KID TO VANISH THERE. THEY GO IN WINTERTIME.

IT IS A TRAGEDY, IS IT NOT?

THE LITTLE FACES ON THE MILK CARTONS. "HAVE YOU SEEN ME?" THEY ASK. A DEEPLY EXISTENTIAL QUESTION AT THE BEST OF TIMES.

PULL OFF AT THE NEXT EXIT.

WHY DID YOU PICK LAKESIDE?

I TOLD YOU. IT'S A NICE QUIET PLACE TO HIDE YOU AWAY. YOU'RE UNDER THE RADAR THERE.

WHY?

BECAUSE. MAKE A LEFT HERE.

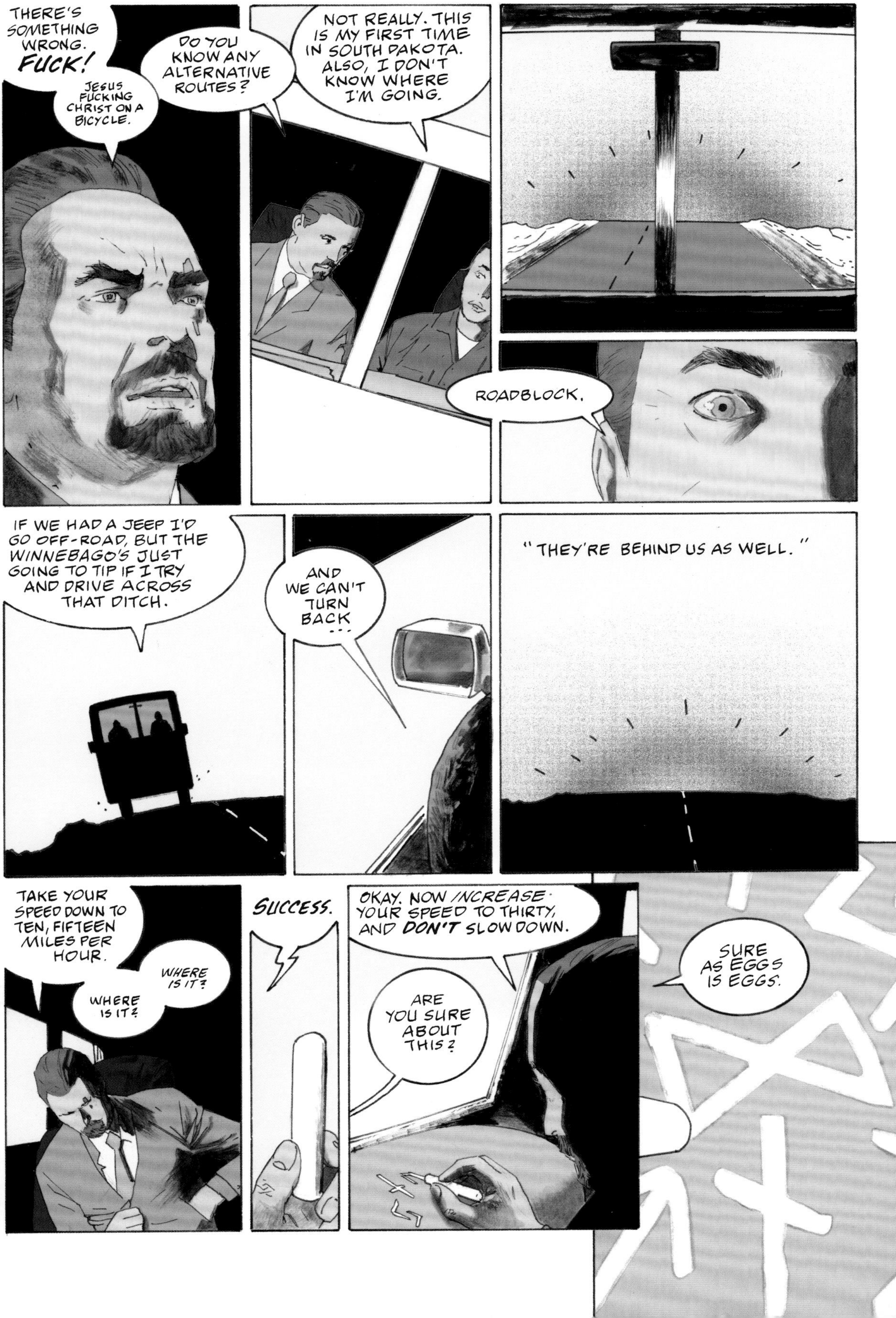
THERE'S SOMETHING WRONG. FUCK!
JESUS FUCKING CHRIST ON A BICYCLE.
DO YOU KNOW ANY ALTERNATIVE ROUTES?
NOT REALLY. THIS IS MY FIRST TIME IN SOUTH DAKOTA. ALSO, I DON'T KNOW WHERE I'M GOING.
ROADBLOCK.
IF WE HAD A JEEP I'D GO OFF-ROAD, BUT THE WINNEBAGO'S JUST GOING TO TIP IF I TRY AND DRIVE ACROSS THAT DITCH.
AND WE CAN'T TURN BACK...
"THEY'RE BEHIND US AS WELL."
TAKE YOUR SPEED DOWN TO TEN, FIFTEEN MILES PER HOUR.
WHERE IS IT?
WHERE IS IT?
SUCCESS.
OKAY. NOW INCREASE YOUR SPEED TO THIRTY, AND DON'T SLOW DOWN.
ARE YOU SURE ABOUT THIS?
SURE AS EGGS IS EGGS.

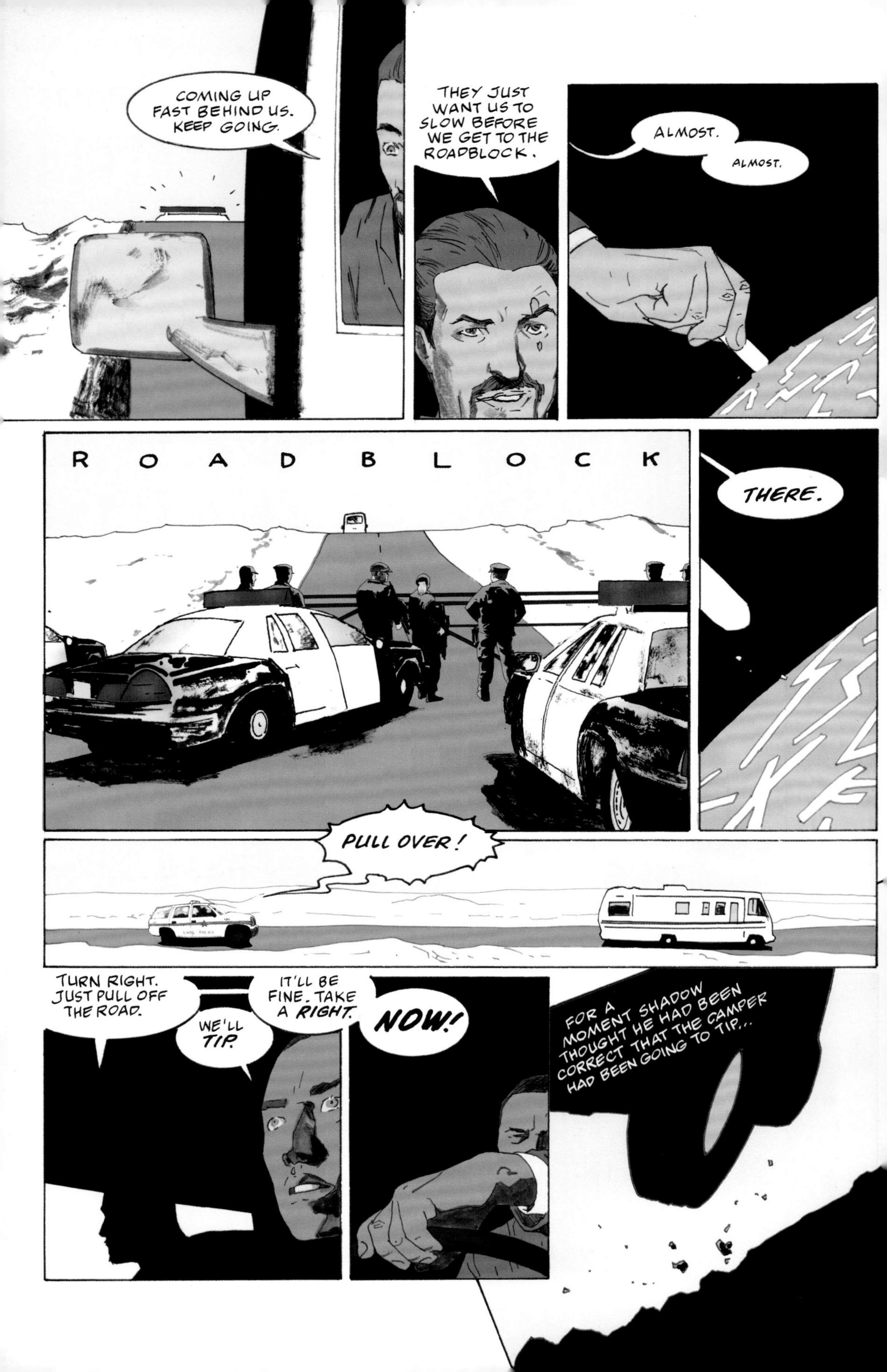
COMING UP FAST BEHIND US. KEEP GOING.
THEY JUST WANT US TO SLOW BEFORE WE GET TO THE ROADBLOCK.
ALMOST.
ALMOST.
R O A D B L O C K
THERE.
PULL OVER!
TURN RIGHT. JUST PULL OFF THE ROAD.
WE'LL TIP.
IT'LL BE FINE. TAKE A RIGHT.
NOW!
FOR A MOMENT SHADOW THOUGHT HE HAD BEEN CORRECT THAT THE CAMPER HAD BEEN GOING TO TIP...

... AND THEN THE WORLD THROUGH THE WINDSHIELD DISSOLVED AND SHIMMERED AND THE CLOUDS AND THE SNOW AND THE DAY WERE G O N E

PARK HERE. WE CAN WALK THE REST OF THE WAY.

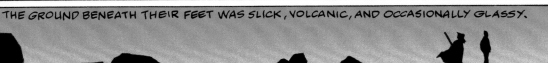

THE GROUND BENEATH THEIR FEET WAS SLICK, VOLCANIC, AND OCCASIONALLY GLASSY.

WHY DON'T YOU ARGUE, EXPLAIN THAT IT'S ALL IMPOSSIBLE? WHY THE HELL DO YOU TAKE IT ALL SO FUCKING CALMLY?

BECAUSE YOU'RE NOT PAYING ME TO ASK QUESTIONS. ANYWAY, NOTHING'S REALLY SURPRISED ME SINCE LAURA.

SINCE SHE CAME BACK FROM THE DEAD?

SINCE I LEARNED SHE WAS SCREWING ROBBIE.

?!

WHAT THE HELL IS THAT?

IT LOOKED LIKE A MECHANICAL SPIDER, BLUE METAL, GLITTERING L.E.D. LIGHTS, AND IT WAS THE SIZE OF A TRACTOR.

SHHHH

BEYOND THE THING WAS AN ASSORTMENT OF BONES, EACH WITH A LITTLE FLAME BESIDE IT.

KEEP YOUR DISTANCE.

SHADOW TOOK AN EXTRA STEP TO THE SIDE, WHICH WAS A MISTAKE ON THAT GLASSY PATH.

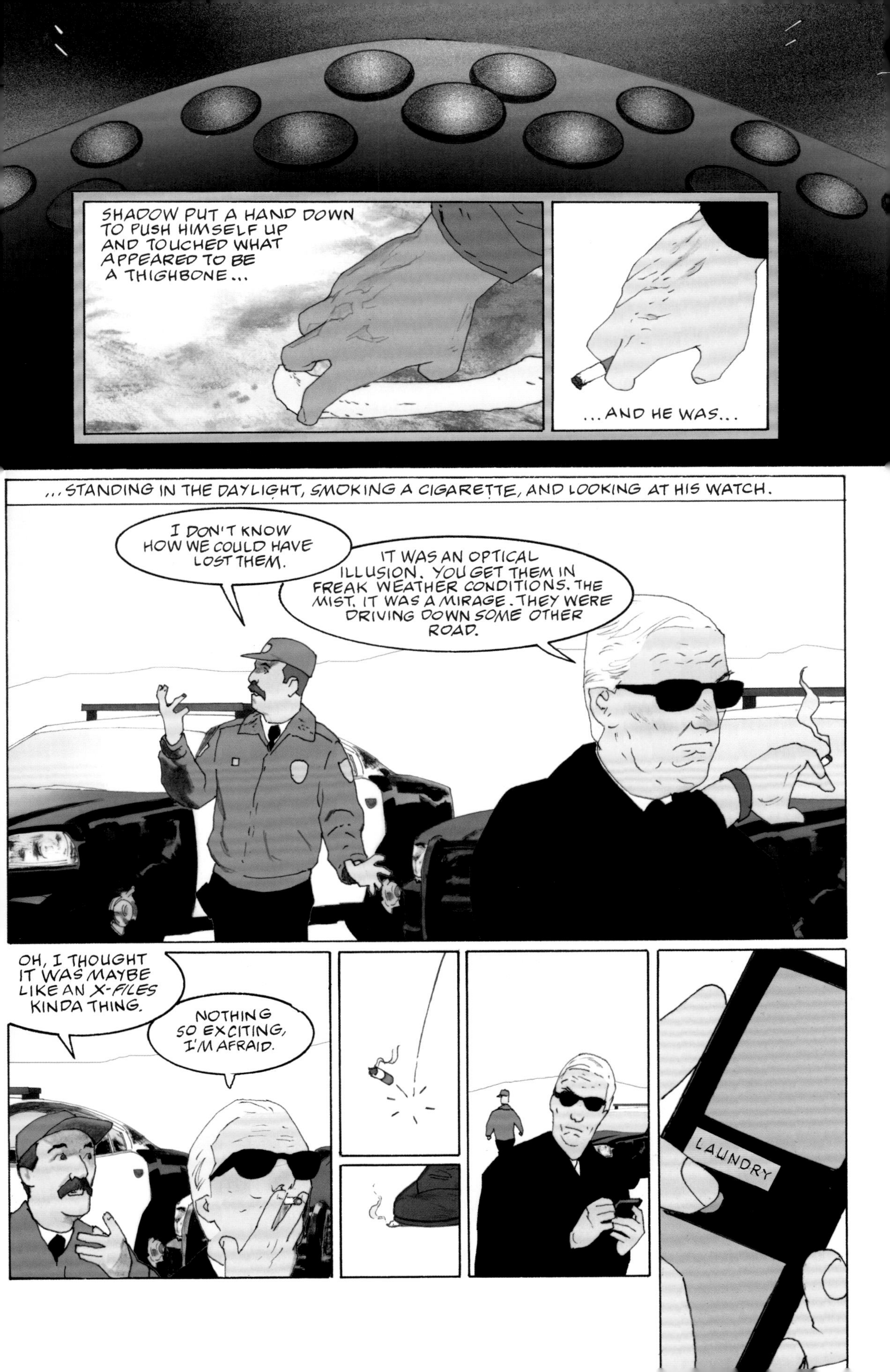
SHADOW PUT A HAND DOWN TO PUSH HIMSELF UP AND TOUCHED WHAT APPEARED TO BE A THIGHBONE...
...AND HE WAS...
...STANDING IN THE DAYLIGHT, SMOKING A CIGARETTE, AND LOOKING AT HIS WATCH.
I DON'T KNOW HOW WE COULD HAVE LOST THEM.
IT WAS AN OPTICAL ILLUSION. YOU GET THEM IN FREAK WEATHER CONDITIONS. THE MIST. IT WAS A MIRAGE. THEY WERE DRIVING DOWN SOME OTHER ROAD.
OH, I THOUGHT IT WAS MAYBE LIKE AN *X-FILES* KINDA THING.
NOTHING SO EXCITING, I'M AFRAID.
LAUNDRY

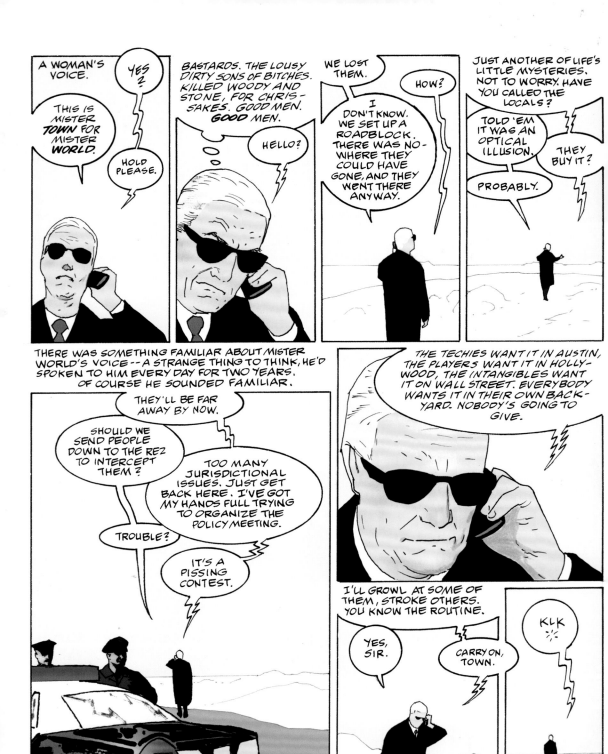

A WOMAN'S VOICE.

THIS IS MISTER *TOWN* FOR MISTER *WORLD*.

YES?

HOLD PLEASE.

BASTARDS. THE LOUSY DIRTY SONS OF BITCHES. KILLED WOODY AND STONE, FOR CHRIS-SAKES. GOOD MEN. *GOOD* MEN.

HELLO?

WE LOST THEM.

HOW?

I DON'T KNOW. WE SET UP A ROADBLOCK. THERE WAS NO-WHERE THEY COULD HAVE GONE, AND THEY WENT THERE ANYWAY.

JUST ANOTHER OF LIFE'S LITTLE MYSTERIES. NOT TO WORRY. HAVE YOU CALLED THE LOCALS?

TOLD 'EM IT WAS AN OPTICAL ILLUSION.

THEY BUY IT?

PROBABLY.

THERE WAS SOMETHING FAMILIAR ABOUT MISTER WORLD'S VOICE -- A STRANGE THING TO THINK, HE'D SPOKEN TO HIM EVERY DAY FOR TWO YEARS. OF COURSE HE SOUNDED FAMILIAR.

THEY'LL BE FAR AWAY BY NOW.

SHOULD WE SEND PEOPLE DOWN TO THE REZ TO INTERCEPT THEM?

TOO MANY JURISDICTIONAL ISSUES. JUST GET BACK HERE. I'VE GOT MY HANDS FULL TRYING TO ORGANIZE THE POLICY MEETING.

TROUBLE?

IT'S A PISSING CONTEST.

THE TECHIES WANT IT IN AUSTIN, THE PLAYERS WANT IT IN HOLLY-WOOD, THE INTANGIBLES WANT IT ON WALL STREET. EVERYBODY WANTS IT IN THEIR OWN BACK-YARD. NOBODY'S GOING TO GIVE.

I'LL GROWL AT SOME OF THEM, STROKE OTHERS. YOU KNOW THE ROUTINE.

YES, SIR.

CARRY ON, TOWN.

KLK

WE SHOULD HAVE HAD A SWAT TEAM PICK OFF THAT FUCKING WINNEBAGO, OR LAND MINES IN THE ROAD. THAT WOULD'VE SHOWN THOSE BASTARDS WE MEAN BUSINESS.

WE'RE WRITING THE FUTURE IN LETTERS OF FIRE.

LIKE MISTER WORLD SAID...

AND IT WAS THEN

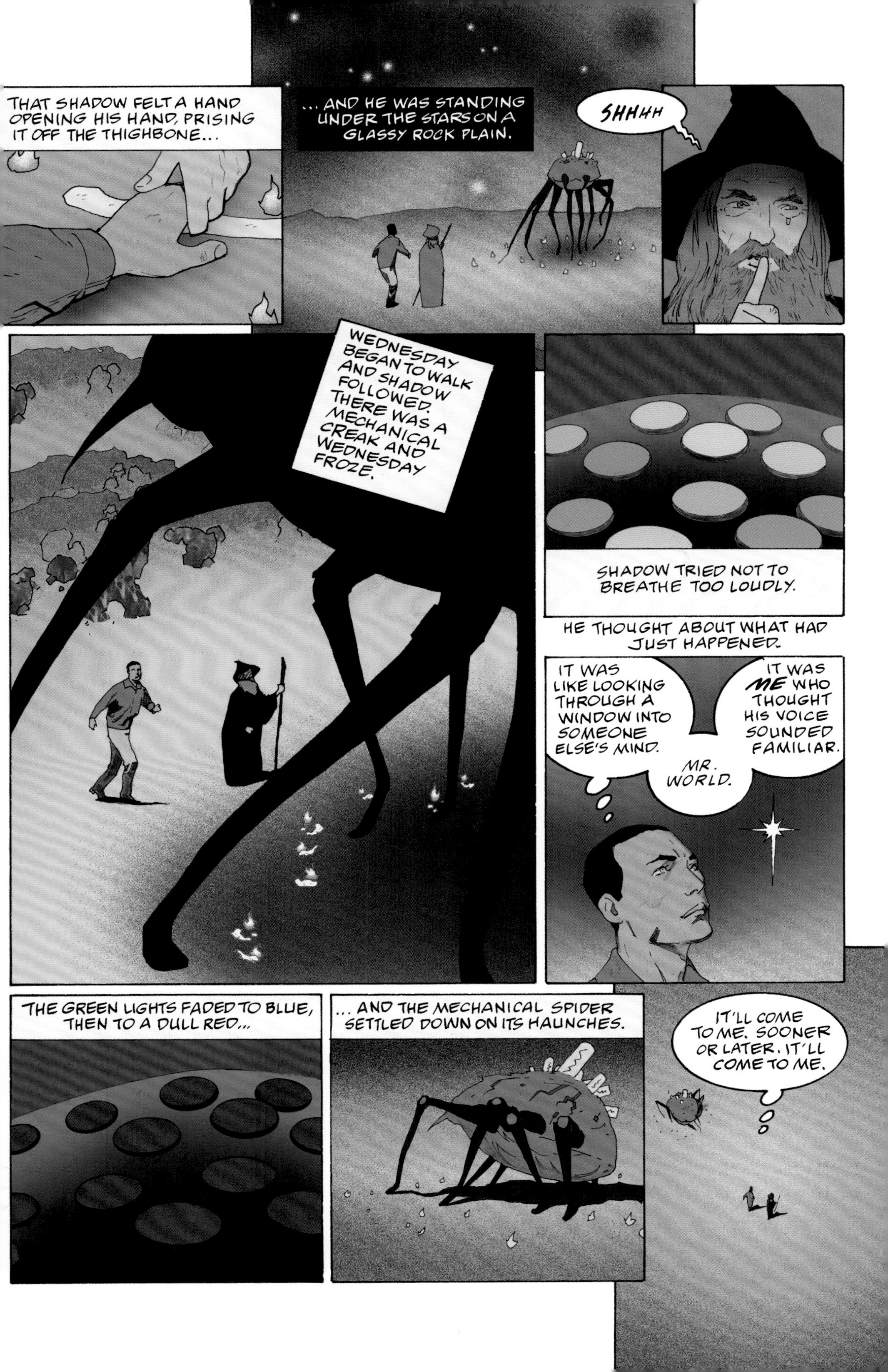
THAT SHADOW FELT A HAND OPENING HIS HAND, PRISING IT OFF THE THIGHBONE...
...AND HE WAS STANDING UNDER THE STARS ON A GLASSY ROCK PLAIN.
SHHHH
WEDNESDAY BEGAN TO WALK AND SHADOW FOLLOWED. THERE WAS A MECHANICAL CREAK AND WEDNESDAY FROZE.
SHADOW TRIED NOT TO BREATHE TOO LOUDLY.
HE THOUGHT ABOUT WHAT HAD JUST HAPPENED.
IT WAS LIKE LOOKING THROUGH A WINDOW INTO SOMEONE ELSE'S MIND.
IT WAS ME WHO THOUGHT HIS VOICE SOUNDED FAMILIAR.
MR. WORLD.
THE GREEN LIGHTS FADED TO BLUE, THEN TO A DULL RED...
...AND THE MECHANICAL SPIDER SETTLED DOWN ON ITS HAUNCHES.
IT'LL COME TO ME. SOONER OR LATER. IT'LL COME TO ME.

IT SHOULD BE SAFE TO SPEAK NOW.

WHERE ARE WE?

BEHIND THE SCENES.

THINK OF IT AS BEING IN A THEATRE. I JUST PULLED US OUT OF THE AUDIENCE AND NOW WE'RE WALKING ABOUT BACKSTAGE. IT'S A SHORT-CUT.

WHEN I TOUCHED THAT BONE I WAS IN THE MIND OF A GUY NAMED TOWN. HE'S WITH THAT SPOOKSHOW. HE HATES US.

YES.

HE'S GOT A BOSS NAMED MISTER WORLD. HE REMINDS ME OF SOMEONE, BUT I DON'T KNOW WHO.

DO THEY KNOW WHERE WE'RE HEADED?

I THINK THEY'RE CALLING OFF THE HUNT. THEY DIDN'T WANT TO FOLLOW US TO THE RESERVATION. IS THAT WHERE WE'RE GOING?

MAYBE.

WHAT WAS THAT SPIDER-THING?

" A PATTERN MANIFESTATION. A SEARCH ENGINE."

ARE THEY DANGEROUS?

YOU ONLY GET TO MY AGE BY ASSUMING THE WORST.

AND HOW OLD WOULD THAT BE?

OLD AS MY TONGUE AND A FEW YEARS OLDER THAN MY TEETH.

YOU PLAY YOUR CARDS SO CLOSE TO THE VEST THAT I'M NOT EVEN SURE THAT THEY'RE REALLY CARDS AT ALL.

MPH.

SHADOW BEGAN TO FEEL HEADACHY. THERE WAS A POUNDING QUALITY TO THE STARLIGHT THAT RESONATED WITH THE PULSE IN HIS TEMPLES.

I ...

BLARGH

TAKE A SIP OF THIS, ONLY A SIP.

IT'S NOT GOOD FOR THE AUDIENCE TO FIND THEMSELVES WALKING ABOUT BACKSTAGE. THAT'S WHY YOU'RE FEELING SICK. WE NEED TO HURRY TO GET YOU OUT OF HERE.

THERE, BETWEEN THOSE TWO MOUNDS.

WALK BESIDE ME.

THEY WALKED, AND THE COLD AIR AND BRIGHT DAYLIGHT SMASHED INTO SHADOW'S FACE AT THE SAME TIME.

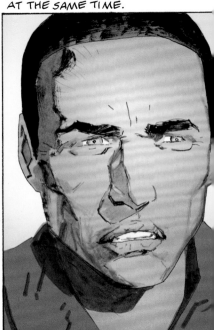

OVER HERE.

EYAH, I HEARD THAT THERE WERE TWO WHITE MEN IN A WINNEBAGO ON THEIR WAY TO SEE ME. AND I HEARD THEY GOT LOST, LIKE WHITE MEN ALWAYS GET LOST IF THEY DON'T PUT UP THEIR SIGNS EVERYWHERE.

YOU KNOW YOU'RE ON LAKOTA LAND?

SINCE WHEN WERE YOU LAKOTA, WHISKEY JACK, YOU OLD FRAUD? I'M STARVING, AND MY FRIEND JUST THREW UP HIS BREAKFAST. ARE YOU GOING TO INVITE US IN?

COME IN, WHITE MEN WHO LOST THEIR WINNEBAGO.

WELL, WHISKEY JACK AND APPLE JOHNNY. TWO BIRDS WITH ONE STONE.

WRONG. I STILL GOT BOTH OF MY STONES.

I'M JOHN CHAPMAN. DON'T MIND ANYTHING YOUR BOSS SAYS ABOUT ME.

HE'S AN ASSHOLE.

ALWAYS GOING TO BE. SOME PEOPLE IS JES' ASSHOLES AND THAT'S AN END OF IT.

MIKE AINSEL.

AINSEL, THAT'S NOT A NAME, BUT IT'LL DO AT A PINCH. WHAT DO THEY CALL YOU?

SHADOW.

I'LL CALL YOU SHADOW, THEN.

HEY, WHISKEY JACK, HOW'S THE FOOD LOOKING?

IT'S READY FOR EATING.

LOOKS LIKE PISS.

IT'S A SOFT APPLE CIDER. I NEVER BELIEVED IN HARD LIQUOR. MAKES MEN MAD.

DAME RUMOR SAYS YOU'VE BEEN OUT TALKING TO ALL MANNER OF FOLK. SAYS YOU'RE TAKING THE OLD FOLKS ON THE WAR PATH.

I THINK THAT'S A FAIR AND JUDICIOUS SUMMARY OF EVENTS.

THEY WILL WIN. THEY WON ALREADY. YOU LOST ALREADY. LIKE THE WHITE MAN AND MY PEOPLE. THEY WON. I'M NOT FIGHTING FOR ANOTHER LOST CAUSE.

AND IT'S NO USE YOU LOOKING AT ME. I'M NO USE TO YOU.

MANGY, RAT-TAILED BASTARDS JES' PICKED ME OFF AND CLEAN FORGOT ME.

PAUL BUNYON.

PAULLLLL BUNYON.

PAUL BUNYON?

HE TOOK UP HEAD SPACE.

IT'S LIKE THE IDIOTS WHO WANT TO SPARE HUMMINGBIRDS THE EVILS OF SUGAR. THEY FILL THE FEEDERS WITH FUCKIN' *NUTRASWEET*. NO CALORIES IN THEIR FOOD AND THE BIRDS DIE.

THAT'S PAUL BUNYON FOR YOU.

HE CAME STAGGERING OUT OF A NEW YORK AD AGENCY IN 1910, AND FILLED THE NATION'S MYTH STOMACH WITH EMPTY CALORIES.

I LIKE PAUL BUNYON. I WENT ON HIS RIDE AT THE MALL OF AMERICA. I DON'T MIND THAT HE NEVER EXISTED. MEANS THAT HE NEVER CUT DOWN ANY TREES.

YOU SAID A MOUTH-FUL.

DAMN IT. THAT'S NOT THE POINT AND YOU KNOW IT.

I'M NOT GOING TO HELP YOU, BUT WHEN YOU GET YOUR ASS KICKED, YOU CAN COME BACK HERE AND I'LL FEED YOU AGAIN.

ALL THE ALTERNATIVES ARE WORSE.

YOU HAVE NO IDEA WHAT THE ALTERNATIVES ARE.

AND *YOU*. YOU ARE HUNTING.

I'M WORKING.

YOU ARE ALSO HUNTING SOMETHING. THERE IS A DEBT THAT YOU WISH TO PAY.

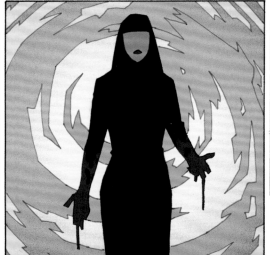

YES.

LISTEN...

"FOX WAS HERE FIRST, AND HIS BROTHER WAS THE WOLF. FOX SAID PEOPLE WILL LIVE FOREVER. WOLF SAID, NO, ALL THINGS THAT LIVE MUST DIE, OR THEY WILL SPREAD AND COVER THE WORLD, AND EAT ALL THE SALMON. NOW, ONE DAY WOLF DIED, AND HE SAID TO THE FOX, 'BRING ME BACK TO LIFE.' AND FOX SAID, 'NO, THE DEAD MUST STAY THAT WAY, YOU CONVINCED ME.' AND HE WEPT AS HE SAID THIS. NOW WOLF RULES THE WORLD OF THE DEAD, AND FOX LIVES UNDER THE SUN AND THE MOON, AND HE STILL MOURNS HIS BROTHER."

IF YOU WON'T PLAY, YOU WON'T PLAY. WE'LL BE MOVING ON.

I'M TALKING TO THIS YOUNG MAN.

HE IS NOT.

YOU ARE BEYOND HELP.

YOU KNOW, YOU CANNOT COME HERE UNLESS I WISH IT.

YES.

TELL ME YOUR DREAM.

"I WAS CLIMBING A TOWER OF SKULLS. THERE WERE HUGE BIRDS FLYING AROUND IT. THEY HAD LIGHTNING IN THEIR WINGS. THEY WERE ATTACKING ME. THE TOWER FELL."

EVERYBODY DREAMS. CAN WE HIT THE ROAD?

NOT EVERYBODY DREAMS OF THE WAKINYAU, THE THUNDER-BIRDS. WE FELT THE ECHOES OF IT HERE.

I TOLD YOU.

JESUS!

THERE'S A CLUTCH OF THUNDERBIRDS IN WEST VIRGINIA AND A BREEDING PAIR IN THE LAND THEY USED TO CALL THE STATE OF FRANKLIN.

WHISKEY JACK TOUCHED SHADOW'S FACE, GENTLY.

EYAH, IT'S TRUE. IF YOU HUNT THE THUNDERBIRD YOU COULD BRING YOUR WOMAN BACK.

"BUT SHE BELONGS TO THE WOLF, IN THE DEAD PLACES, NOT WALKING THE LAND."

HOW DO YOU *KNOW*?

WHISKEY JACK'S LIPS DID NOT MOVE.

THE MOMENT PASSED.

"WHAT DID THE BUFFALO TELL YOU?"
"TO BELIEVE."
"GOOD ADVICE. ARE YOU GOING TO TAKE IT?"
"KIND OF. I GUESS."
"WHEN YOU FIND YOUR TRIBE, COME BACK AND SEE ME."
"I WILL."

SHADOW WONDERED IF, FOR THE OTHER TWO MEN IN THE ROOM, THEY WERE STANDING, UNMOVING, FOR A HEART-BEAT, OR FOR A FRACTION OF A HEARTBEAT.

ARE YOU GOING TO FETCH YOUR HO CHUNK?

MY WHAT?

HO CHUNK. IT'S WHAT THE WINNEBAGO CALL THEM-SELVES.

IT'S TOO RISKY. THEY'LL BE LOOKING FOR IT.

IS IT STOLEN?

NOT A BIT.

AND THE KEYS?

I'VE GOT THEM.

MY NEPHEW, HARRY BLUEJAY, HAS AN '81 BUICK, HE'LL TRADE IT FOR YOUR CAMPER.

!

WHAT KIND OF A *TRADE* IS THAT?

I'M DOING YOU A FAVOR. TAKE IT OR LEAVE IT.

I DON'T CARE.

HHH HH H.

SHADOW, GIVE THE MAN THE KEYS TO THE WINNEBAGO.

JOHNNY, WILL YOU TAKE THESE MEN DOWN TO FIND HARRY BLUEJAY? TELL HIM I SAID TO GIVE THEM HIS CAR.

BE MY PLEASURE.

HEY!

DON'T COME BACK HERE! YOU ARE NOT WELCOME!

ROTATE ON THIS.

THEY WALKED DOWNHILL THROUGH THE SNOW. CHAPMAN WALKED IN FRONT, HIS BARE FEET RED AGAINST THE CRUST-TOPPED SNOW.

AREN'T YOU COLD?

MY WIFE WAS CHOCTAW.

AND SHE TAUGHT YOU MYSTICAL WAYS TO KEEP OUT THE COLD?

NOPE. SHE THOUGHT I WAS CRAZY.

SHE'S DEAD NOW, A' COURSE. WHEN SHE DIED I GUESS MAYBE I WENT A MITE CRAZY. IT COULD HAPPEN TO ANYONE.

IT COULD HAPPEN TO YOU.

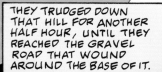

THEY TRUDGED DOWN THAT HILL FOR ANOTHER HALF HOUR, UNTIL THEY REACHED THE GRAVEL ROAD THAT WOUND AROUND THE BASE OF IT.

YOU BOZOS NEED A RIDE?

YOU ARE VERY GRACIOUS, MADAM. WE'RE LOOKING FOR A MISTER HARRY BLUEJAY.

HE'LL BE DOWN AT THE RECITAL HALL. GET IN.

SO WHERE DID YOU THREE COME FROM?

JUST VISITING WITH A FRIEND.

LIVES ON THE HILL BACK THERE.

WHAT HILL?

THERE WAS NO HIGH HILL BACK THERE.

WHISKEY JACK.

WE CALL HIM INKTOMI, HERE.

YOU KNOW THE WHITE POPULATION ALL AROUND HERE IS FALLING? YOU GO OUT THERE, YOU FIND GHOST TOWNS.

AND IT'S NOT WORTH ANYONE'S WHILE TO FARM THE BADLANDS, ANYHOW. THEY TOOK OUR LANDS, THEY SETTLED HERE, NOW THEY'RE LEAVING.

THEY GO SOUTH, THEY GO WEST.

MAYBE IF WE WAIT FOR ENOUGH OF THEM TO MOVE TO NEW YORK AND MIAMI AND L.A., WE CAN TAKE THE WHOLE OF THE MIDDLE BACK WITHOUT A FIGHT.

GOOD LUCK.

HO HOKA, HARRY BLUEJAY.

FUCK OFF, YOU CRAZY, BAREFOOT WHITE GHOST. YOU GIVE ME THE CREEPS.

I GOT A MESSAGE FROM YOUR UNCLE. HE SAYS YOU'RE TO GIVE THESE TWO YOUR CAR.

YOU WANT TO TELL YOUR UNCLE THAT? HE SAYS YOU'RE THE ONLY REASON HE STAYS AMONG THE LAKOTA.

HE'S NOT MY UNCLE.

WHISKEY JACK SAYS A LOT OF THINGS.

WHISKEY JACK SOUNDS LIKE WISAKEDJAK WHEN HE SAYS IT.

AND ONE OF THE THINGS HE SAID WAS THAT WE'RE TRADING OUR WINNEBAGO FOR YOUR BUICK.

I DON'T SEE A WINNEBAGO.

HE'LL BRING YOU THE WINNEBAGO. YOU KNOW HE WILL.

I'M NOT THE OLD FOX'S NEPHEW. I WISH HE'D STOP SAYING THAT.

BETTER A LIVE FOX THAN A DEAD WOLF. NOW, WILL YOU SELL US YOUR CAR?

SURE, SURE. I WAS ONLY KIDDING. I KID A LOT, ME.

IT'S JUST DOWN THE ROAD.

GOOD DAY TO YOU, FATHER!

I TOLD YOU NOT TO GIVE HIM THOSE PAMPHLETS.

IT IS *HE* THAT IS IN ERROR, NOT *ME*. IF HE'D JES' READ THE *SWEDENBORG* I GAVE HIM HE'D KNOW THAT. IT'D BRING LIGHT INTO HIS LIFE.

HARRY BLUEJAY'S CAR WAS MISSING ITS SIDE MIRRORS AND ITS TIRES WERE PERFECTLY SMOOTH BLACK RUBBER.

IT DRINKS OIL, BUT AS LONG AS YOU KEEP POURING OIL IN, IT WILL KEEP RUNNING FOREVER.

UNLESS IT STOPS.

SORRY I WAS JERKING YOUR CHAIN BEFORE...

...YOU KNOW WHEN I'LL GET THE WINNE-BAGO?

ASK YOUR UNCLE. HE'S THE FUCKING USED-CAR DEALER.

HE'S *NOT MY UNCLE.*

THEY DROPPED JOHNNY CHAPMAN IN SIOUX FALLS.

WEDNESDAY SAID NOTHING ON THE DRIVE. HE WAS BROODING.

JUST OUTSIDE ST. PAUL.

OLLIE'S
A FAMILY RESTAURANT

?

LOOK AT THIS.

"FATHER AND SON CATCH RECORD NORTHERN PIKE."

DELIGHTFUL.

NOT THAT. *LOOK*, IT SAYS IT'S THE FOURTEENTH OF FEBRUARY.

HAPPY VALENTINE'S DAY.

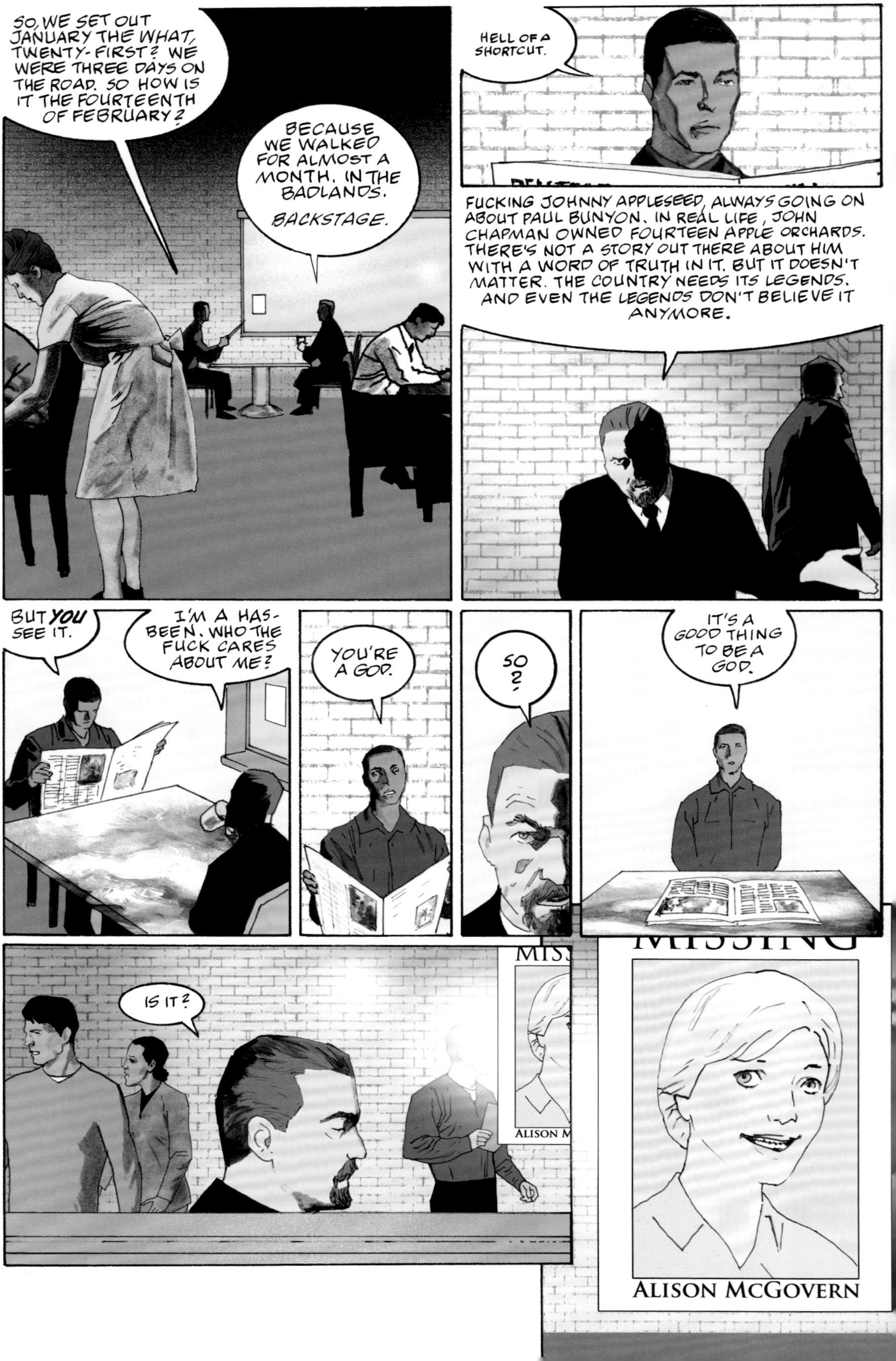
SO, WE SET OUT JANUARY THE WHAT, TWENTY-FIRST? WE WERE THREE DAYS ON THE ROAD. SO HOW IS IT THE FOURTEENTH OF FEBRUARY?
BECAUSE WE WALKED FOR ALMOST A MONTH. IN THE BADLANDS.
BACKSTAGE.
HELL OF A SHORTCUT.
FUCKING JOHNNY APPLESEED, ALWAYS GOING ON ABOUT PAUL BUNYON. IN REAL LIFE, JOHN CHAPMAN OWNED FOURTEEN APPLE ORCHARDS. THERE'S NOT A STORY OUT THERE ABOUT HIM WITH A WORD OF TRUTH IN IT. BUT IT DOESN'T MATTER. THE COUNTRY NEEDS ITS LEGENDS. AND EVEN THE LEGENDS DON'T BELIEVE IT ANYMORE.
BUT YOU SEE IT.
I'M A HAS-BEEN. WHO THE FUCK CARES ABOUT ME?
YOU'RE A GOD.
SO?
IT'S A GOOD THING TO BE A GOD.
IS IT?
MISSING
ALISON McGOVERN

CHAPTER SEVEN

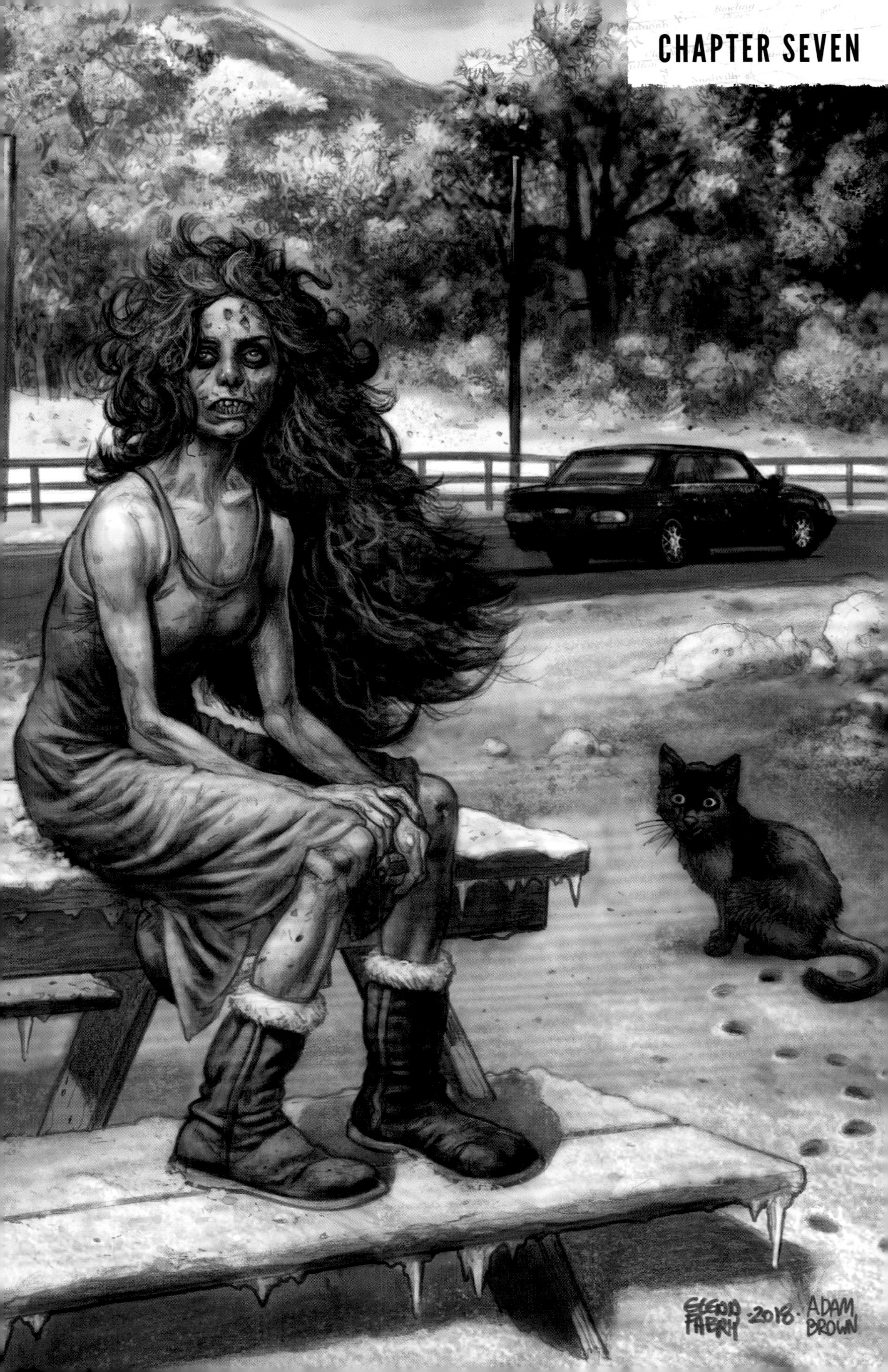

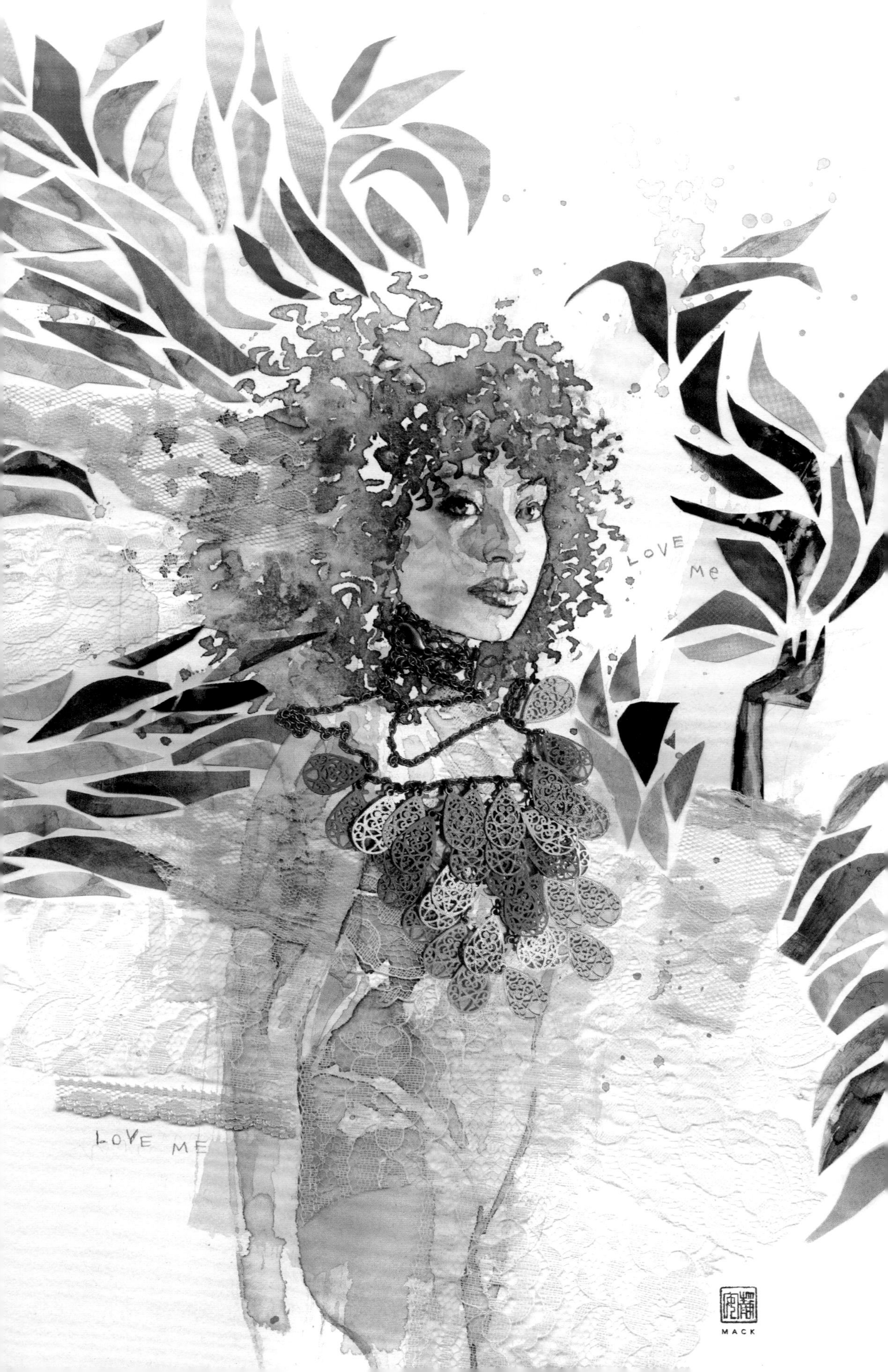
LOVE
ME
LOVE ME
MACK

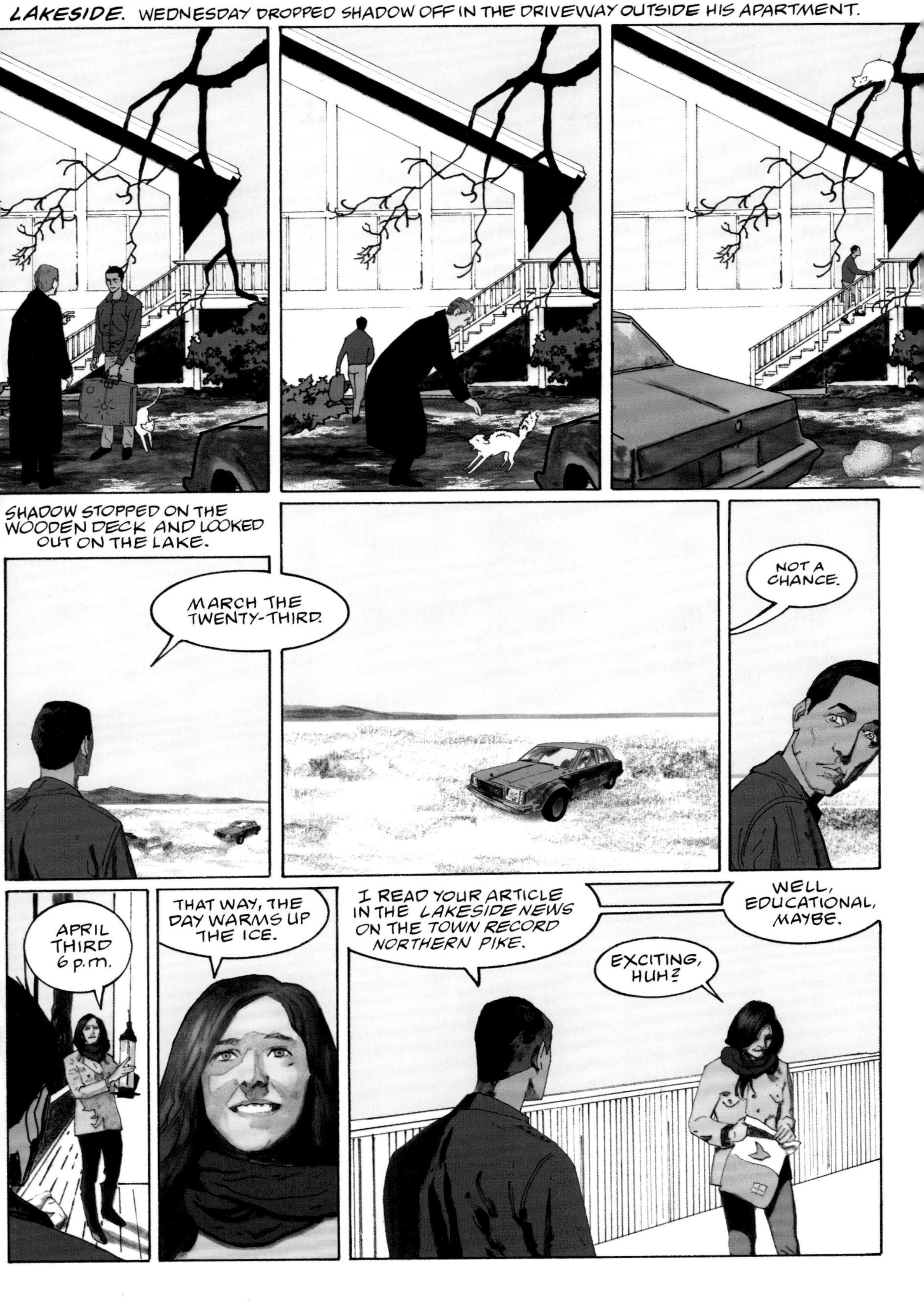
LAKESIDE. WEDNESDAY DROPPED SHADOW OFF IN THE DRIVEWAY OUTSIDE HIS APARTMENT.
SHADOW STOPPED ON THE WOODEN DECK AND LOOKED OUT ON THE LAKE.
MARCH THE TWENTY-THIRD.
NOT A CHANCE.
APRIL THIRD 6 p.m.
THAT WAY, THE DAY WARMS UP THE ICE.
I READ YOUR ARTICLE IN THE LAKESIDE NEWS ON THE TOWN RECORD NORTHERN PIKE.
EXCITING, HUH?
WELL, EDUCATIONAL, MAYBE.

I THOUGHT YOU WEREN'T COMING BACK TO US. YOU WERE GONE FOR A WHILE.

I DIDN'T SEE ANYTHING IN THE PAPER ABOUT ALISON McGOVERN.

THERE WASN'T ANYTHING IN THE PAPER TO REPORT. SHE'S STILL MISSING. THERE WAS A RUMOR THAT SOMEONE HAD SEEN HER IN DETROIT, BUT IT TURNED OUT TO BE A FALSE ALARM.

POOR KID.

I HOPE SHE'S DEAD.

WHY?

BECAUSE THE ALTERNATIVES ARE WORSE.

YOU AREN'T THINKING OF ALISON, YOU'RE THINKING OF YOUR SON. YOU'RE THINKING OF SANDY.

HE REMEMBERED SOMEONE SAYING...

I MISS SANDY.

WHO WAS THAT?

GOOD TALKING TO YOU.

YEAH, YOU TOO.

FEBRUARY PASSED IN A SUCCESSION OF SHORT, GRAY DAYS. SOME DAYS THE SNOW FELL. SHADOW STAYED IN THE APARTMENT UNTIL IT BEGAN TO FEEL LIKE A PRISON CELL. ON THE GOOD DAYS, WHEN IT GOT ABOVE FREEZING, HE BEGAN TO WALK.

IF HE WALKED, HE DID NOT HAVE TO THINK. HIS MIND DID NOT GO TO PLACES THAT MADE HIM UNCOMFORTABLE. WHEN HE WAS EXHAUSTED, HIS THOUGHTS DID NOT GO TO LAURA.

CHIEF MULLIGAN.

MIKE.

GEORGE'S BARBER SHOP

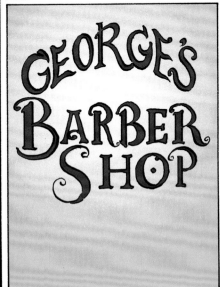

I DUNNO...

IT LOOKS GOOD.

WOULD IT LOOK GOOD TO YOU IF YOU WERE A WOMAN?

I GUESS.

HEY, MIKE-- HAVE YOU EVER THOUGHT ABOUT A CAREER IN LAW ENFORCEMENT?

I CAN'T SAY I HAVE.

est. 1937

George's Barber

YOU KNOW THE MAIN PART OF POLICE WORK? IT'S JUST KEEPING YOUR HEAD. SOMEBODY'S SCREAMING BLUE MURDER AT YOU, SIMPLY SAY YOU'LL SORT IT ALL OUT IF THEY JUST STEP OUTSIDE QUIETLY. AND YOU HAVE TO BE ABLE TO MEAN IT.

AND *THEN* YOU SORT IT OUT?

MOSTLY, THAT'S WHEN YOU PUT THE HANDCUFFS ON THEM. LET ME KNOW IF YOU WANT A JOB. WE'RE HIRING.

TWO HOT CHOCO-LATES.

SAY, MIKE --

WHAT WOULD YOU DO IF YOU HAD A COUSIN-- LIKE A *WIDOW*--AND SHE STARTED CALLING YOU--?

CALLING YOU HOW?

ON THE PHONE. LONG DISTANCE. SHE LIVES OUT OF STATE.

I SAW HER LAST YEAR AT A FAMILY WEDDING. SHE WAS MARRIED BACK THEN. HER HUSBAND WAS STILL ALIVE, AND SHE'S FAMILY, NOT A FIRST COUSIN. PRETTY DISTANT.

YOU GOT A THING FOR HER?

HEH. I DON'T KNOW ABOUT THAT.

WELL, THEN PUT IT ANOTHER WAY. DOES SHE HAVE A THING FOR *YOU*?

WELL, SHE'S SAID A FEW THINGS WHEN SHE CALLED. I COULD ASK HER OUT HERE, COULDN'T I? SHE'S KIND OF SAID SHE'D LIKE TO COME UP HERE.

YOU'RE BOTH ADULTS. I'D SAY GO FOR IT.

HEH.

THE TELEPHONE IN SHADOW'S APARTMENT WAS SILENT AND DEAD.

HE THOUGHT OF GETTING IT CONNECTED, BUT COULD THINK OF NO ONE HE WANTED TO CALL.

LATE ONE NIGHT, HE PICKED IT UP AND LISTENED, AND WAS CONVINCED HE COULD HEAR A WIND BLOWING AND A DISTANT CONVERSATION BETWEEN A GROUP OF PEOPLE WHOSE VOICES WERE TOO FAINT TO DISTINGUISH.

HELLO?

WHO'S THERE?

BUT THERE WAS NO REPLY, ONLY A SUDDEN SILENCE, AND THEN THE FARAWAY SOUND OF LAUGHTER, SO FAINT THAT HE WAS NOT SURE THAT HE WAS NOT IMAGINING IT.

SHADOW MADE MORE JOURNEYS WITH WEDNESDAY.

RHODE ISLAND.

SHADOW LISTENED AS WEDNESDAY ARGUED WITH A WOMAN WHO WOULD NOT GET OUT OF BED, NOR LET WEDNESDAY OR SHADOW LOOK AT HER FACE.

IN THE REFRIGERATOR WAS A PLASTIC BAG FILLED WITH CRICKETS AND ANOTHER WITH THE CORPSES OF BABY MICE.

SEATTLE.

SHADOW WATCHED WEDNESDAY SHOUT HIS GREETING TO A YOUNG WOMAN WITH SHORT RED HAIR AND BLUE SPIRAL TATTOOS.

WEDNESDAY CAME AWAY FROM THE TALK GRINNING.

DALLAS.

DRIVE!

FUCKING ALBANIANS. LIKE ANYBODY CARES.

BOULDER.

THEY HAD A PLEASANT LUNCH WITH FIVE YOUNG JAPANESE WOMEN.

Rigdon's

IT WAS A MEAL OF PLEASANTRIES AND POLITENESS, AND SHADOW LEFT UNSURE IF ANYTHING HAD BEEN AGREED TO.

WEDNESDAY, THOUGH, SEEMED HAPPY ENOUGH.

SHADOW HAD BEGUN TO LOOK FORWARD TO RETURNING TO LAKESIDE. THERE WAS A PEACE THERE, AND A WELCOME, THAT HE APPRECIATED.

LAKESIDE. MORNING.

HEY, MIKE, WHERE YOU GOING TODAY?

I DON'T KNOW. MAYBE THE WILDERNESS TRAIL AGAIN.

YOU EVER GONE EAST ON COUNTY **Q**? IT'S KIND OF PRETTY OUT THATAWAY. STARTS ACROSS FROM THE CARPET STORE ON 20TH AVENUE.

NO, NEVER HAVE.

WELL, IT'S KIND OF PRETTY.

IT WAS EXTREMELY PRETTY.

HEY, CAT.

HHHHSSSSSS

THE CAT HISSED--NOT AT HIM, BUT AT SOMETHING ACROSS THE ROAD, SOMETHING HE COULD NOT SEE.

AROUND THE NEXT BEND IN THE ROAD...

HE REMOVED A PASTY FROM HIS POCKET AND BROKE OFF THE TOP.

IT BREATHED A FAINT WISP OF STEAM INTO THE WINTRY AIR. IT SMELLED REALLY GOOD AND HE BIT INTO IT.

THEN HE SMELLED PERFUME, AND UNDER THE PERFUME THE SCENT OF SOMETHING ROTTEN.

PLEASE DON'T LOOK AT ME.

SHADOW LOOKED AT HER IN THE DAYLIGHT. HER EYES HAD NOT CHANGED, NOR THE CROOKED HOPEFULLNESS OF HER SMILE. AND SHE WAS, VERY OBVIOUSLY, VERY DEAD.

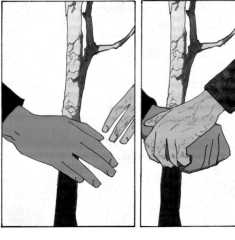

HE COULD FEEL HIS HEART BEATING IN HIS CHEST. WHAT SCARED HIM WAS THE NORMALITY OF THE MOMENT. WITH HER AT HIS SIDE, HE WOULD HAVE BEEN WILLING TO STAND THERE FOREVER.

I MISS YOU.

I'M HERE.

THAT'S WHEN I MISS YOU THE MOST-- WHEN YOU'RE HERE. WHEN YOU AREN'T, YOU'RE JUST A GHOST FROM THE PAST--A DREAM FROM ANOTHER LIFE. IT'S EASIER THEN.

SO ...

HOW'S DEATH?

HARD. IT JUST KEEPS GOING.

YOU WANT TO GO FOR A WALK?

SURE.

WHERE HAVE YOU BEEN?

HERE, MOSTLY.

SINCE CHRISTMAS, I KIND OF LOST YOU. SOMETIMES I WOULD KNOW WHERE YOU WERE FOR A FEW DAYS. YOU'D BE ALL OVER, THEN YOU'D FADE AWAY AGAIN.

I WAS HERE IN LAKESIDE. IT'S A GOOD LITTLE TOWN.

OH.

NICE BOOTS, BY THE WAY.

AREN'T THEY GREAT? I FOUND THEM IN THIS LITTLE STORE IN CHICAGO.

SO, WHAT MADE YOU COME UP FROM CHICAGO?

WHEN THE *CALL* CAME I HAD TO HURRY BACK. I WAS HEADING SOUTH. THE COLD WAS BOTHERING ME. SOMETHING TO DO WITH BEING DEAD, I GUESS. YOU DON'T FEEL IT AS COLD. YOU FEEL IT AS A SORT OF *NOTHING.*

CALL?

IT *FELT* LIKE A CALL. I STARTED TO THINK ABOUT HOW MUCH I NEEDED TO SEE YOU. IT WAS LIKE A *HUNGER.*

YOU KNEW I WAS *HERE* THEN.

YES. SUDDENLY, I DID. I THOUGHT YOU WERE CALLING ME, BUT IT WASN'T YOU, WAS IT?

NO.

YOU DIDN'T WANT TO SEE ME?

NO. I DIDN'T WANT TO SEE YOU. IT HURTS TOO MUCH.

IT MUST BE HARD, NOT BEING ALIVE.

YOU MEAN IT'S HARD FOR *YOU* TO BE DEAD.

LOOK, I'M STILL GOING TO FIGURE OUT HOW TO BRING YOU BACK...

NO. I WAS TALKING ABOUT YOU.

I'M ALIVE. I'M NOT DEAD. REMEMBER?

YOU'RE NOT DEAD. BUT I'M NOT SURE THAT YOU'RE ALIVE, EITHER. NOT REALLY.

I LOVE YOU. YOU'RE MY PUPPY. BUT WHEN YOU'RE DEAD, YOU SEE THINGS CLEARER.

YOU'RE LIKE THIS BIG SOLID MAN-SHAPED HOLE IN THE WORLD.

"EVEN WHEN WE WERE TOGETHER, SOMETIMES I'D GO INTO A ROOM AND I WOULDN'T THINK ANY-ONE WAS IN THERE. AND I'D TURN THE LIGHT ON OR OFF, AND I'D REALIZE YOU WERE IN THERE, SITTING ON YOUR OWN, NOT READING, NOT WATCHING T.V., NOT DOING ANYTHING."

THE BEST THING ABOUT ROBBIE WAS THAT HE WAS SOMEBODY. HE WAS A JERK SOMETIMES AND HE LOVED TO HAVE MIRRORS AROUND WHEN WE MADE LOVE SO HE COULD WATCH HIM-SELF FUCKING ME...

BUT HE WAS ALIVE, PUPPY. HE WANTED THINGS.

HE FILLED THE SPACE.

I'M SORRY. DID I HURT YOUR FEELINGS?

NO.

SHADOW FELT THAT HE NEEDED TO SAY SOMETHING: *I LOVE YOU*, OR *PLEASE DON'T GO*. INSTEAD, HE SAID:

I'M NOT DEAD.

MAYBE NOT. BUT ARE YOU SURE YOU'RE ALIVE?

LOOK AT ME.

THAT'S NOT AN ANSWER.

YOU'LL KNOW IT WHEN YOU ARE.

WHAT NOW?

WELL, I'VE SEEN YOU NOW. I'M GOING SOUTH AGAIN.

I HAVE TO WAIT HERE UNTIL MY BOSS NEEDS ME.

THAT'S NOT LIVING.

WILL I SEE YOU AGAIN?

I GUESS SO. IN THE END, NOTHING'S FINISHED YET, IS IT?

NO. IT'S NOT.

THE WAR HAD BEGUN AND NOBODY SAW IT. WARS ARE BEING FOUGHT ALL THE TIME: THE WARS ON CRIME, POVERTY, DRUGS. THIS WAR WAS SMALLER, AND HUGER, THAN THOSE...

...BUT IT WAS AS REAL AS ANY.

A FALLING GIRDER IN MANHATTAN CLOSED A STREET FOR TWO DAYS. IT KILLED TWO PEDESTRIANS, AN ARABIC CAB DRIVER, AND THE TAXI-DRIVER'S PASSENGER.

A TRUCKER IN DENVER WAS FOUND DEAD IN HIS HOME. THE BACK OF HIS HEAD WAS COMPLETELY DESTROYED, AND SEVERAL WORDS IN A FOREIGN ALPHABET WERE WRITTEN ON THE BATHROOM MIRROR IN BROWN LIPSTICK.

IN A POSTAL SORTING STATION IN PHOENIX, ARIZONA, A MAN WENT CRAZY-- **WENT POSTAL**--AND SHOT *'TERRY THE TROLL EVENSEN!* SEVERAL OTHER PEOPLE WERE FIRED ON, BUT ONLY EVENSEN WAS KILLED. THE MAN WHO FIRED THE SHOTS--FIRST THOUGHT TO BE A DISGRUNTLED POSTAL WORKER-- WAS NOT CAUGHT AND WAS NEVER IDENTIFIED.

A COMMUNITY OF NINE ANCHORITES IN MONTANA WAS FOUND DEAD.
REPORTERS SPECULATED THAT IT WAS MASS SUICIDE...

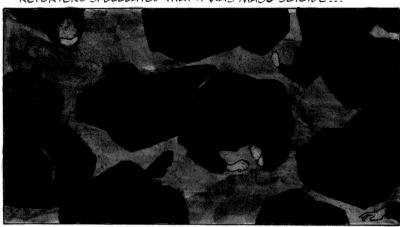

BUT SOON, THE CAUSE OF DEATH WAS REPORTED AS CARBON MONOXIDE POISONING FROM AN ELDERLY FURNACE.

A LOBSTER TANK WAS SMASHED IN THE LOBBY OF AN ATLANTA SEAFOOD RESTAURANT.

A CRYPT WAS DEFILED IN THE KEY WEST GRAVEYARD.

AN *AMTRAK* PASSENGER TRAIN HIT A *U.P.S.* TRUCK IN IDAHO, KILLING THE DRIVER OF THE TRUCK, NO PASSENGERS WERE SERIOUSLY INJURED.

IT WAS STILL A COLD WAR AT THIS STAGE. A PHONY WAR, NOTHING THAT COULD BE TRULY WON OR LOST. THE WIND STIRRED THE BRANCHES OF THE TREE.

THE STORM WAS COMING.

THE QUEEN OF SHEBA, HALF-DEMON, THEY SAID, ON HER FATHER'S SIDE, WHO RULED SHEBA WHEN SHEBA WAS THE RICHEST LAND THERE EVER WAS, WHO WAS WORSHIPPED AS A LIVING GODDESS BY THE WISEST OF KINGS, STANDS ON THE SIDEWALK OF SUNSET BOULEVARD AT 2:00 A.M. LIKE A SLUTTY PLASTIC BRIDE ON A NEW WEDDING CAKE. SHE STANDS AS IF SHE OWNS THE SIDEWALK AND THE SURROUNDING NIGHT.

IT'S BEEN A LONG NIGHT AND A LONG FOUR THOUSAND YEARS.

WHEN SOMEONE LOOKS STRAIGHT AT HER, HER LIPS MOVE AS IF SHE IS TALKING TO HERSELF.

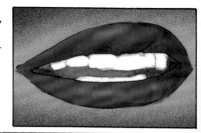

WHEN MEN IN CARS DRIVE PAST, SHE MAKES EYE-CONTACT AND SMILES. SHE IGNORES THE MEN WHO WALK PAST HER ON THE SIDE-WALK, PRETENDS THAT THEY ARE NOT THERE.

SHE IS PROUD SHE OWES NOTHING TO ANYONE. THE OTHER GIRLS ON THE STREET, THEY HAVE PIMPS, HABITS, CHILDREN, PEOPLE WHO TAKE WHAT THEY MAKE.

NOT HER.

THERE IS NOTHING HOLY LEFT IN HER PROFESSION. NOT ANYMORE.

A WEEK AGO THE RAINS BEGAN IN LOS ANGELES, CRUMBLING THE MUD FROM THE HILLSIDES AND TOPPLING HOUSES INTO CANYONS.

BILQUIS HAS SPENT THE LAST WEEK INSIDE CURLED UP IN HER BED, LISTENING TO THE RAIN AND PLACING PERSONALS ON THE INTERNET FROM AN ANONYMOUS E-MAIL ADDRESS.

SHE HAS AVOIDED ANYTHING THAT MIGHT LEAVE A PAPER TRAIL, PREFERRING TO PICK OUT HER OWN CUSTOMERS...

...TO FIND THE ONES WHO WILL WORSHIP HER AS SHE NEEDS TO BE WORSHIPPED...

...THE ONES WHO WILL LET HER TAKE THEM ALL THE WAY.

AND IT OCCURS TO HER NOW, STANDING AND SHIVERING ON THE STREET CORNER, THAT SHE HAS A HABIT AS BAD AS THE CRACK WHORES AND HER LIPS BEGIN TO MOVE.

I WILL RISE AND GO NOW ABOUT THE CITY IN THE STREETS, AND IN THE BROAD WAYS I WILL SEEK THE ONE I LOVE. I AM MY BELOVED'S AND MY BELOVED IS MINE.

ONCE A MONTH SHE PAYS OFF AN OFFICER IN THE L.A.P.D. SHE USED TO PAY OFF A DIFFERENT OFFICER IN THE L.A.P.D., BUT HE HAD VANISHED.

THAT MAN'S NAME WAS JERRY LE BEC, AND HIS DISAPPEARANCE HAD BEEN A MYSTERY TO THE L.A.P.D.

HE HAD BECOME OBSESSED WITH BILQUIS AND HAD TAKEN TO FOLLOWING HER ON FOOT.

ONE AFTERNOON SHE WOKE, STARTLED BY A NOISE.

THE NOISE WAS THE NOISE OF HIS HEAD, THUMPING AGAINST HER DOOR AS HE ROCKED BACK AND FORTH ON HIS KNEES.

COME INSIDE.

LATER SHE PUT HIS CLOTHES IN A GARBAGE BAG AND TOSSED THEM IN A DUMPSTER.

SHE KEPT NO SOUVENIRS.

THE ORANGE NIGHT-SKY GLIMMERS TO THE WEST WITH DISTANT LIGHTNING, SOMEWHERE OUT TO SEA, AND BILQUIS KNOWS THAT THE RAIN WILL BE STARTING SOON.

"BY NIGHT ON MY BED I SOUGHT HIM WHOM MY SOUL LOVETH."

"LET HIM KISS ME WITH THE KISSES OF HIS MOUTH."

"MY BELOVED IS MINE AND I AM HIS"

SHE TURNS TO AN APPROACHING CAR AND SMILES. HER SMILE FREEZES WHEN SHE SEES IT'S A STRETCH LIMO. MEN IN STRETCH LIMOS WANT TO FUCK IN STRETCH LIMOS, NOT IN BILQUIS'S SHRINE. STILL, IT MIGHT BE AN INVESTMENT IN THE FUTURE.

HEY, HONEY. YOU LOOKING FOR SOMETHING?

SWEET LOVING

HOW MUCH?

DEPENDS ON WHAT YOU WANT AND HOW LONG YOU WANT IT FOR.

SHE CAN SMELL SOMETHING LIKE BURNING WIRES AND OVERHEATING CIRCUIT BOARDS DRIFTING OUT THE WINDOW.

I CAN PAY FOR ANYTHING I WANT. I'M RICHER THAN RICH.

MMM. MAKES ME HOT, HONEY.

YOU MUST BE ONE OF THEM DOT-COMS I READ ABOUT.

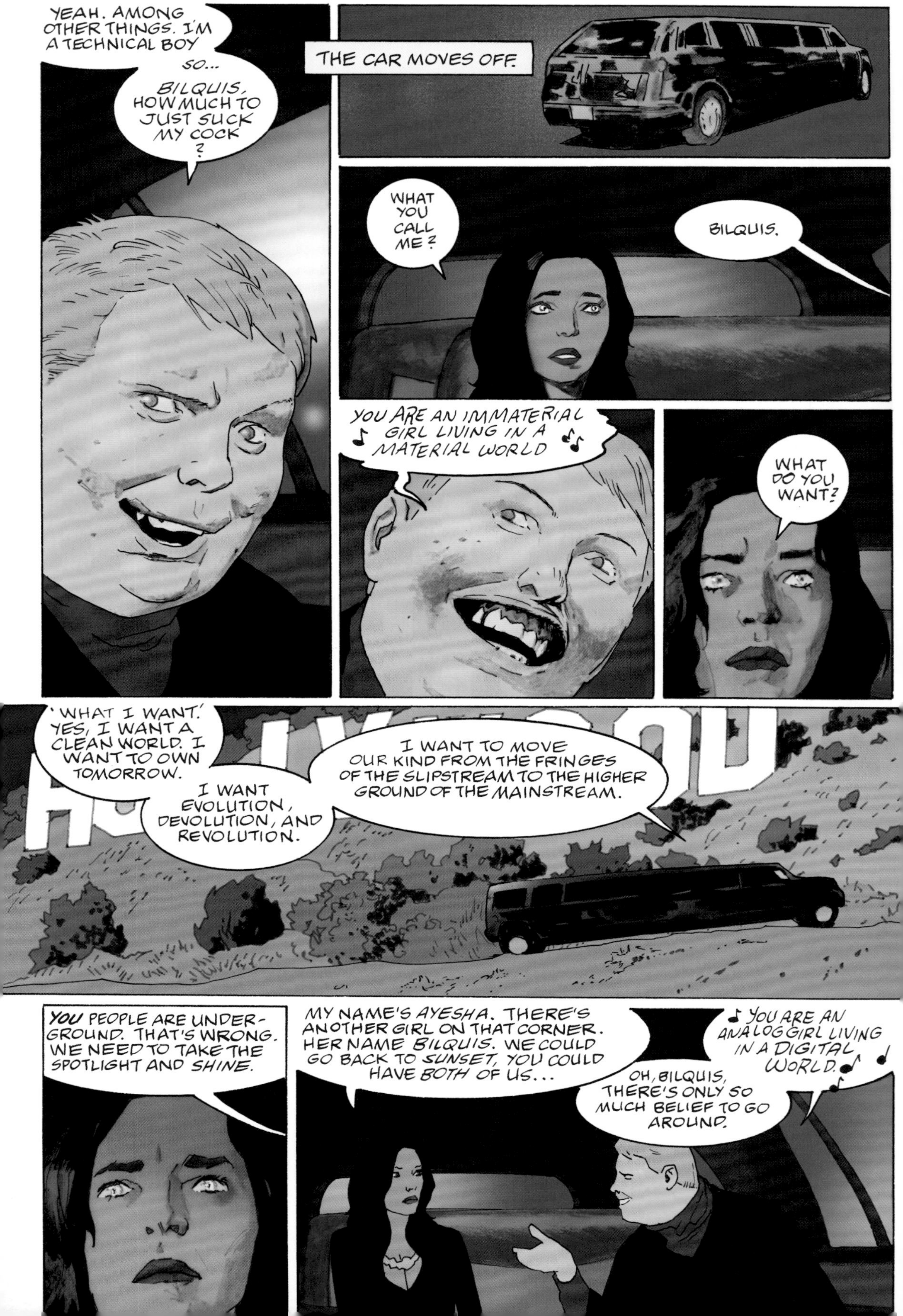

YEAH. AMONG OTHER THINGS. I'M A TECHNICAL BOY
SO... BILQUIS, HOW MUCH TO JUST SUCK MY COCK?
THE CAR MOVES OFF.
WHAT YOU CALL ME?
BILQUIS.
YOU ARE AN IMMATERIAL GIRL LIVING IN A MATERIAL WORLD
WHAT DO YOU WANT?
'WHAT I WANT.' YES, I WANT A CLEAN WORLD. I WANT TO OWN TOMORROW.
I WANT EVOLUTION, DEVOLUTION, AND REVOLUTION.
I WANT TO MOVE OUR KIND FROM THE FRINGES OF THE SLIPSTREAM TO THE HIGHER GROUND OF THE MAINSTREAM.
YOU PEOPLE ARE UNDERGROUND. THAT'S WRONG. WE NEED TO TAKE THE SPOTLIGHT AND SHINE.
MY NAME'S AYESHA. THERE'S ANOTHER GIRL ON THAT CORNER. HER NAME BILQUIS. WE COULD GO BACK TO SUNSET, YOU COULD HAVE BOTH OF US...
YOU ARE AN ANALOG GIRL LIVING IN A DIGITAL WORLD.
OH, BILQUIS, THERE'S ONLY SO MUCH BELIEF TO GO AROUND.

THE LIMO TAKES A CORNER TOO FAST, AND AN IRRATIONAL CONVICTION STRIKES HER, THAT NOBODY IS DRIVING THE CAR...

... AND SHE PUSHES OPEN THE DOOR, AND HALF-JUMPS, HALF-FALLS OUT ONTO THE BLACKTOP.

I AM THE ROSE OF SHARON AND THE LILY OF THE VALLEY...

STAY ME WITH FLAGONS, COMFORT ME WITH APPLES...

..."FOR I AM SICK OF LOVE."

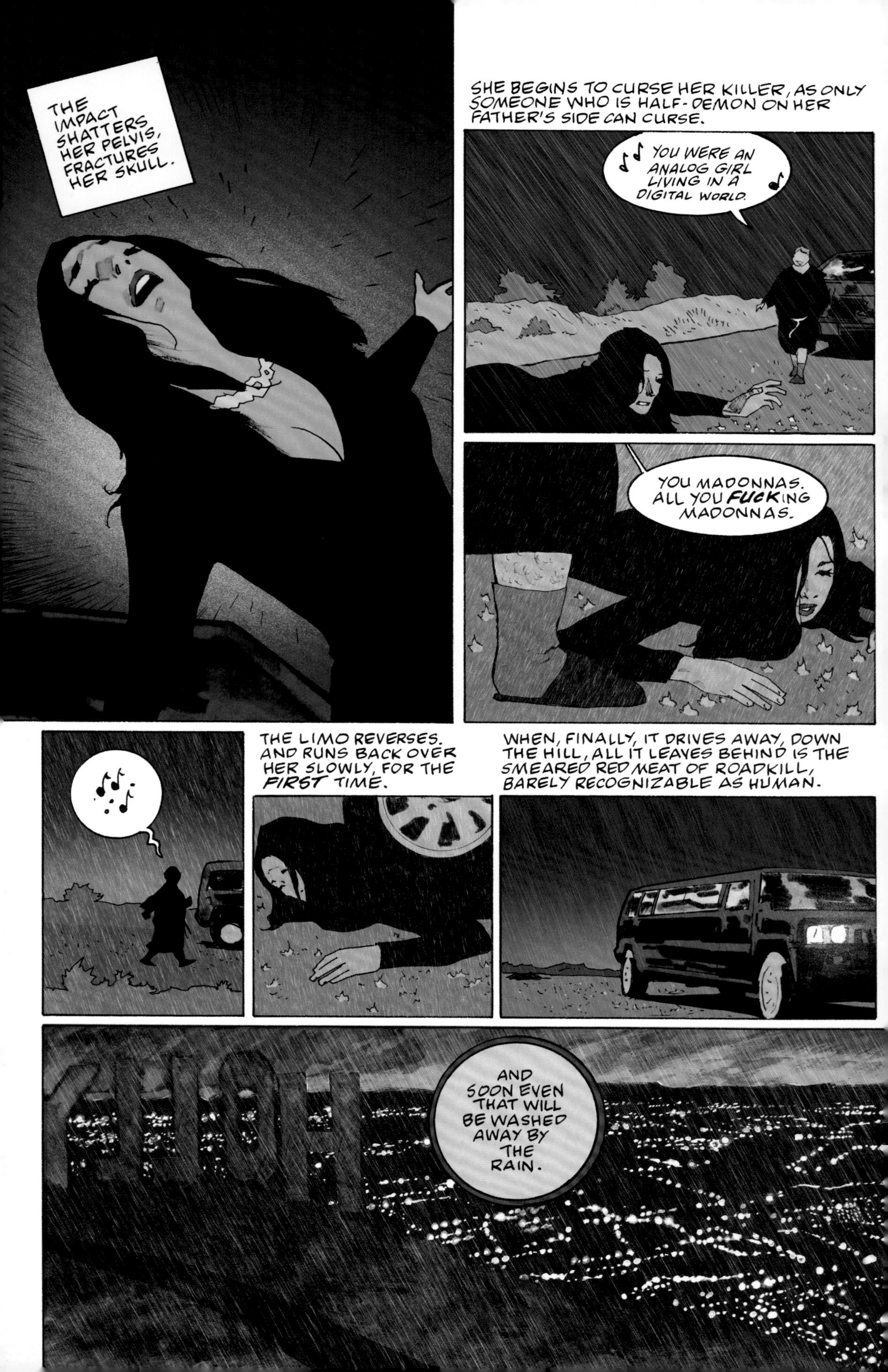

THE IMPACT SHATTERS HER PELVIS, FRACTURES HER SKULL.
SHE BEGINS TO CURSE HER KILLER, AS ONLY SOMEONE WHO IS HALF-DEMON ON HER FATHER'S SIDE CAN CURSE.
♪♪ YOU WERE AN ANALOG GIRL LIVING IN A DIGITAL WORLD. ♪
YOU MADONNAS. ALL YOU FUCKING MADONNAS.
THE LIMO REVERSES. AND RUNS BACK OVER HER SLOWLY, FOR THE FIRST TIME.
WHEN, FINALLY, IT DRIVES AWAY, DOWN THE HILL, ALL IT LEAVES BEHIND IS THE SMEARED RED MEAT OF ROADKILL, BARELY RECOGNIZABLE AS HUMAN.
AND SOON EVEN THAT WILL BE WASHED AWAY BY THE RAIN.

CHAPTER EIGHT

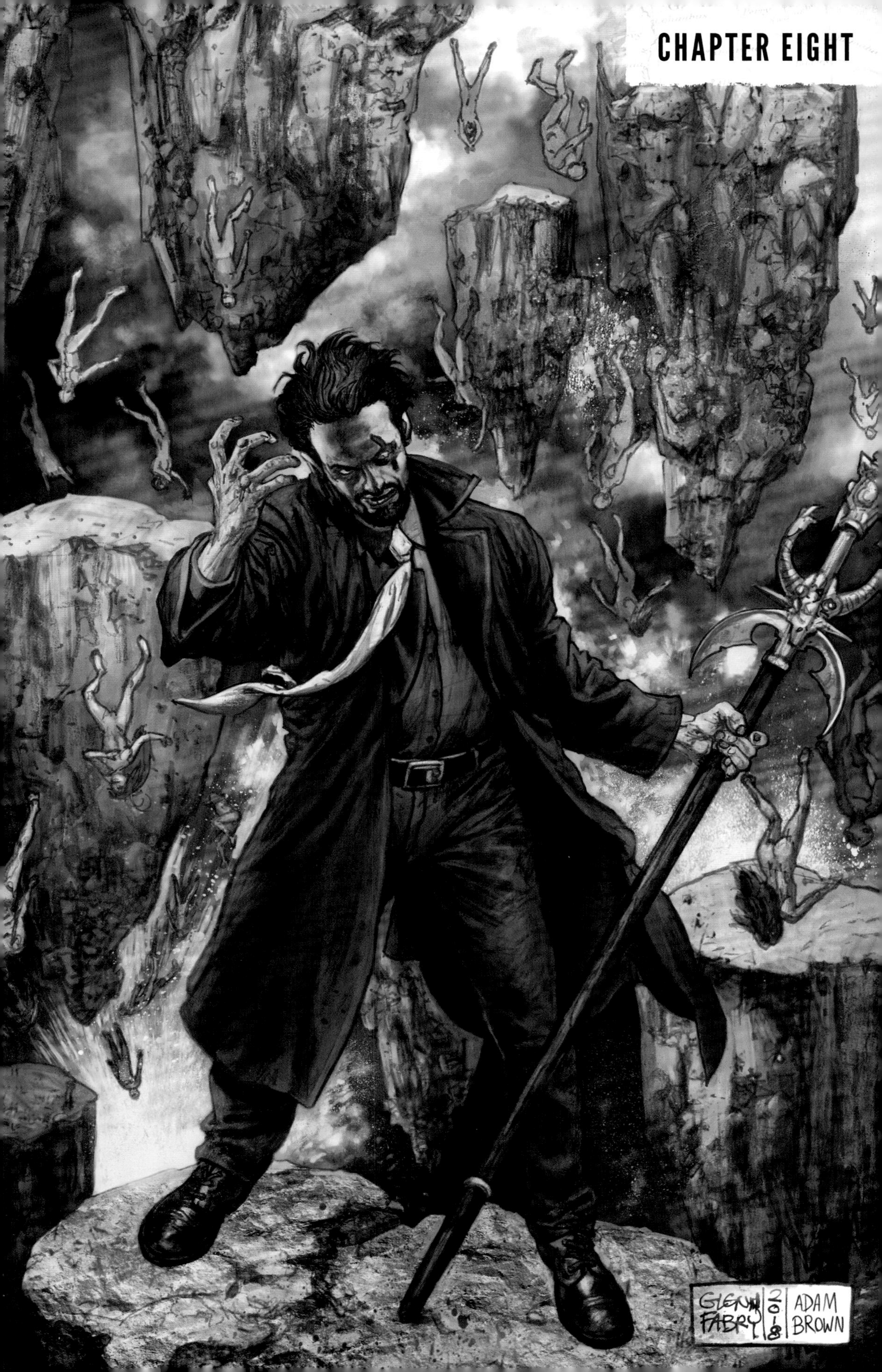
GLENN FABRY
2018
ADAM BROWN

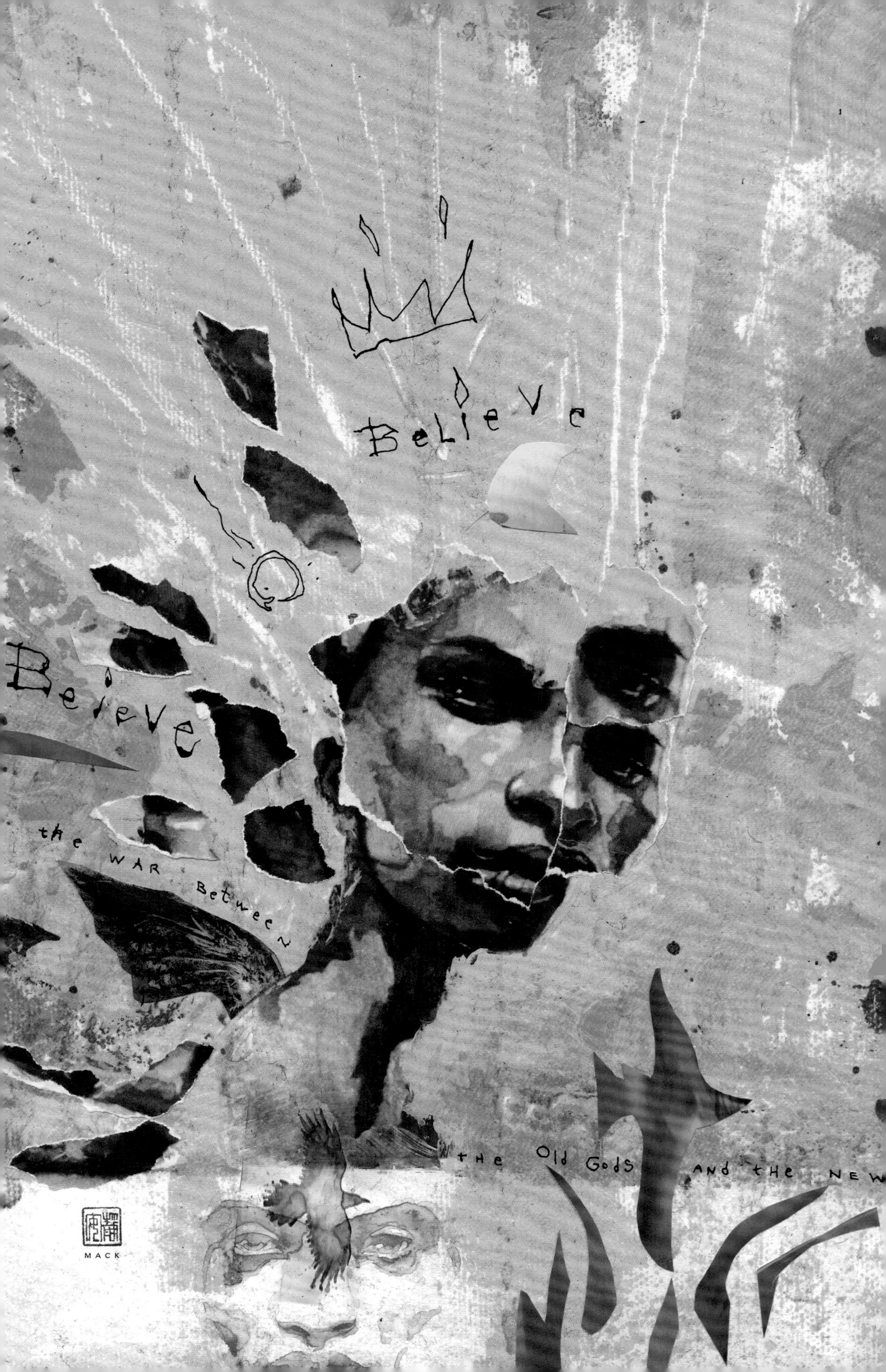
Believe
Believe
the WAR Between
the Old Gods and the new
MACK

HI, SAMANTHA.

MAGS? IS THAT YOU?

WHO ELSE? LEON SAID THAT *AUNT SAMMY* CALLED WHEN I WAS IN THE SHOWER.

WE HAD A GOOD TALK. HE'S SUCH A SWEET KID.

YEAH, I THINK I'LL KEEP HIM.

SO... HOW'S SCHOOL?

THEY'RE GIVING US A WEEK OFF. FURNACE PROBLEMS. SO HOW'S THINGS IN YOUR NECK OF THE NORTH-WOODS?

WELL, I'VE GOT A NEW NEXT-DOOR NEIGHBOR. HE DOES COIN TRICKS.

THE *LAKESIDE NEWS* CURRENTLY FEATURES A BLISTERING DEBATE ON THE RE-ZONING OF TOWN LAND BY THE OLD CEME-TERY ON THE SOUTH-EAST SHORE OF THE LAKE.

AND YOURS TRULY HAS TO WRITE A STRIDENT EDITORIAL SUMMARIZING THE PAPER'S POSITION WITHOUT OFFENDING ANYBODY, OR IN FACT, GIVING ANYONE ANY IDEA WHAT OUR POSITION IS ON THIS.

SOUNDS LIKE FUN.

IT'S NOT. ALISON McGOVERN VANISHED LAST WEEK. NICE KID. SHE BABYSAT FOR LEON A FEW TIMES.

THAT'S *AWFUL*.

YES.

SO... WHAT'S HIS NAME?

WHO?

THE *NEIGHBOR*.

HIS NAME'S MIKE AINSEL. HE'S OKAY. BIG GUY, LOOKS... WHAT'S THE WORD? BEGINS WITH AN *M*... MEAN? MOODY?

MARRIED? HA! YES, I GUESS HE DOES LOOK MARRIED. BUT THE WORD I WAS THINKING OF WAS MELANCHOLY. HE LOOKS MELANCHOLY.

"WHEN HE MOVED IN, HE SEEMED KIND OF HELPLESS-- HE DIDN'T EVEN KNOW HOW TO HEAT-SEAL THE WINDOWS. I'VE SEEN HIM OUT WALKING FROM TIME TO TIME. HE'S NO TROUBLE."

LISTEN, MAGS, HOW ARE *YOU*? ARE *YOU* OKAY?

REALLY?

YEAH.

NO.

...

I'M COMING UP TO SEE YOU.

SAMMY, NO.

IT'LL BE FUN. YOU CAN INVITE THE MYSTERIOUS NEIGHBOR OVER FOR DINNER ONE NIGHT.

SAM, YOU'RE MATCH-MAKING.

WHO'S MATCHMAKING? AFTER *CLAUDINE*-- THE *BITCH FROM HELL*, MAYBE I'M READY TO GO BACK TO BOYS. I MET A NICE STRANGE BOY WHEN I HITCHHIKED DOWN TO *EL PASO* FOR CHRISTMAS.

OH, LOOK, SAM, YOU'VE GOT TO STOP HITCHHIKING. ALISON McGOVERN WAS HITCHHIKING. EVEN IN A TOWN LIKE THIS, IT'S NOT SAFE. I'LL WIRE YOU THE MONEY. YOU CAN TAKE THE BUS.

OKAY, MAGS-- WIRE ME THE MONEY IF IT'LL LET YOU SLEEP EASIER.

YOU KNOW IT WILL.

OKAY, BOSSY BIG SISTER, GIVE LEON A HUG AND TELL HIM HIS AUNTIE SAMMY'S COMING UP.

SO WHEN SHOULD I EXPECT YOU?

TOMORROW NIGHT. YOU DON'T HAVE TO MEET ME AT THE BUS STATION. I'LL ASK HINZELMANN TO RUN ME OVER IN TESSIE.

TOO LATE. TESSIE'S IN MOTHBALLS FOR THE WINTER. BUT HINZELMANN WILL GIVE YOU A RIDE ANYWAY. HE LIKES YOU TO LISTEN TO HIS STORIES.

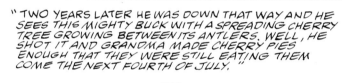

MAYBE YOU SHOULD GET HINZELMANN TO WRITE YOUR EDITORIAL FOR YOU.

LET'S SEE...

"ON THE REZONING OF THE LAND BY THE OLD CEMETERY, IT SO HAPPENS THAT MY GRAMPA SHOT A STAG DOWN BY THE OLD CEMETERY. HE WAS OUT OF BULLETS, SO HE USED A CHERRY STONE. CREASED THE SKULL OF THAT STAG AND IT SHOT OFF LIKE A BAT OUT OF HECK.

" TWO YEARS LATER HE WAS DOWN THAT WAY AND HE SEES THIS MIGHTY BUCK WITH A SPREADING CHERRY TREE GROWING BETWEEN ITS ANTLERS. WELL, HE SHOT IT AND GRANDMA MADE CHERRY PIES ENOUGH THAT THEY WERE STILL EATING THEM COME THE NEXT FOURTH OF JULY. "

AND THEY BOTH LAUGHED, THEN.

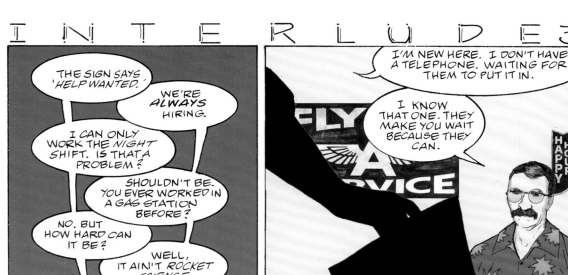

THE SIGN SAYS 'HELP WANTED.'

WE'RE *ALWAYS* HIRING.

I CAN ONLY WORK THE *NIGHT* SHIFT. IS THAT A PROBLEM?

SHOULDN'T BE. YOU EVER WORKED IN A GAS STATION BEFORE?

NO. BUT HOW HARD CAN IT BE?

WELL, IT AIN'T *ROCKET SCIENCE.*

I'M NEW HERE. I DON'T HAVE A TELEPHONE. WAITING FOR THEM TO PUT IT IN.

I KNOW THAT ONE. THEY MAKE YOU WAIT BECAUSE THEY CAN.

YOU KNOW, MA'AM, YOU DON'T MIND MY SAYING THIS, BUT YOU DO *NOT* LOOK WELL.

I KNOW. IT'S A MEDICAL CONDITION...LOOKS WORSE THAN IT IS. NOTHING LIFE-THREATENING.

HOT FOAM SHAVE

OKAY. WE ARE REALLY SHORT-HANDED ON THE LATE SHIFT. WE CALL IT THE *ZOMBIE* SHIFT... UH... *LARNA*...

LAURA.

LAURA. OKAY...I HOPE YOU DON'T MIND DEALING WITH WEIRDOS, BECAUSE THEY COME OUT AT NIGHT.

I'M SURE THEY DO. I CAN COPE.

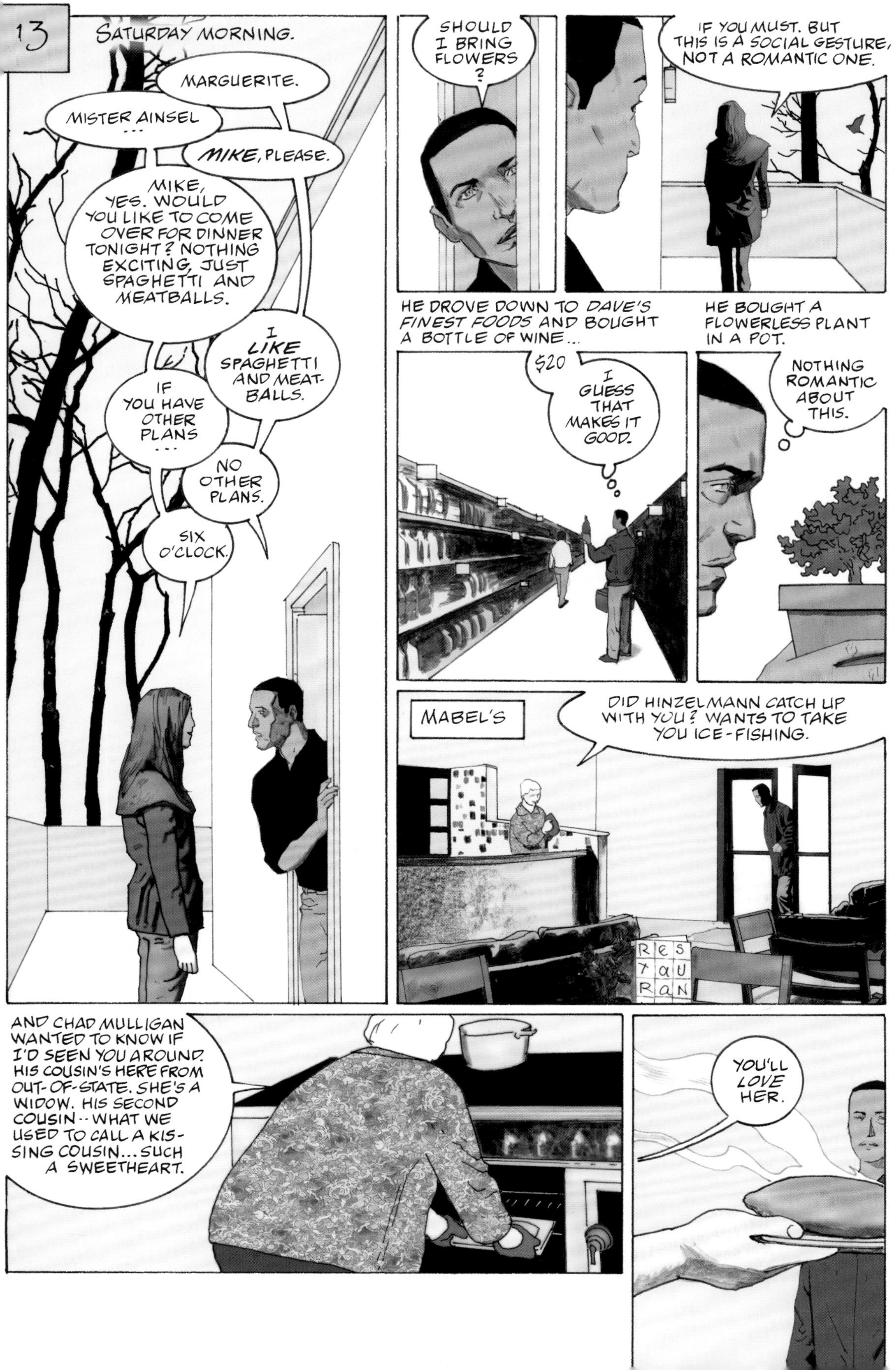
13
SATURDAY MORNING.
MISTER AINSEL ...
MARGUERITE.
MIKE, PLEASE.
MIKE, YES. WOULD YOU LIKE TO COME OVER FOR DINNER TONIGHT? NOTHING EXCITING, JUST SPAGHETTI AND MEATBALLS.
I LIKE SPAGHETTI AND MEAT-BALLS.
IF YOU HAVE OTHER PLANS ...
NO OTHER PLANS.
SIX O'CLOCK.
SHOULD I BRING FLOWERS ?
IF YOU MUST. BUT THIS IS A SOCIAL GESTURE, NOT A ROMANTIC ONE.
HE DROVE DOWN TO DAVE'S FINEST FOODS AND BOUGHT A BOTTLE OF WINE...
$20
I GUESS THAT MAKES IT GOOD.
HE BOUGHT A FLOWERLESS PLANT IN A POT.
NOTHING ROMANTIC ABOUT THIS.
MABEL'S
DID HINZELMANN CATCH UP WITH YOU? WANTS TO TAKE YOU ICE-FISHING.
RES TAU RAN
AND CHAD MULLIGAN WANTED TO KNOW IF I'D SEEN YOU AROUND. HIS COUSIN'S HERE FROM OUT-OF-STATE. SHE'S A WIDOW. HIS SECOND COUSIN -- WHAT WE USED TO CALL A KIS-SING COUSIN... SUCH A SWEETHEART.
YOU'LL LOVE HER.

SHADOW DROVE THE LONG WAY HOME. THERE WAS A LOT OF TIME TO KILL BEFORE SIX.

HE WISHED HE COULD COMFORTABLY WATCH TELEVISION ONCE MORE.

DO YOU WANT TO SEE LUCY'S TITS?

NOT REALLY.

SHE TOLD ME TO BE THERE AT SIX.

DID SHE MEAN SIX *EXACTLY?*

SHOULD I BE THERE A LITTLE EARLY?

A LITTLE LATE?

I'LL WALK OVER AT FIVE PAST SIX.

YEAH?

THAT'S NO WAY TO ANSWER THE PHONE.

WHEN I GET MY TELEPHONE CONNECTED, I'LL ANSWER IT POLITELY. CAN I HELP YOU?

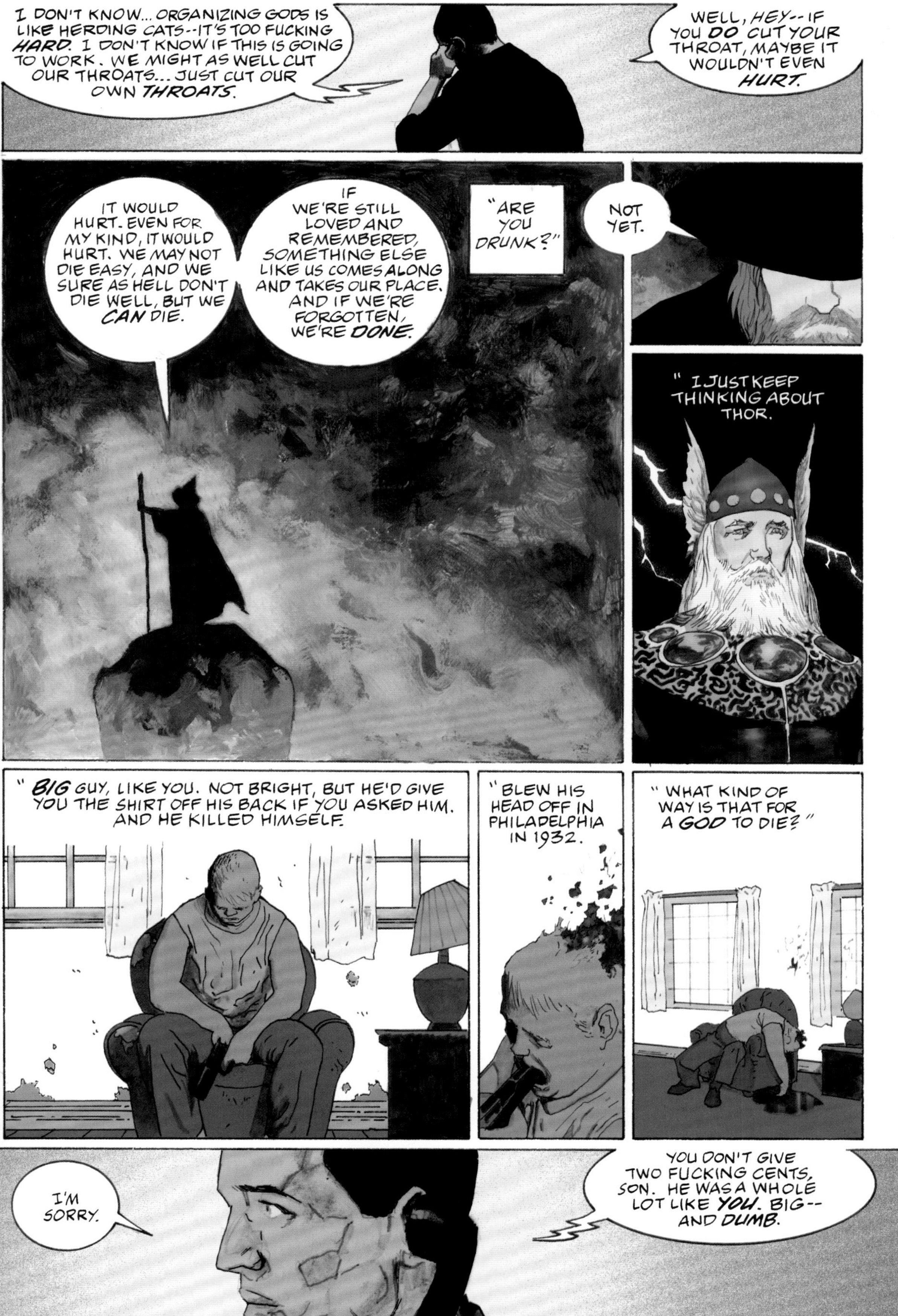
I DON'T KNOW... ORGANIZING GODS IS LIKE HERDING CATS--IT'S TOO FUCKING *HARD*. I DON'T KNOW IF THIS IS GOING TO WORK. WE MIGHT AS WELL CUT OUR THROATS... JUST CUT OUR OWN *THROATS*.
WELL, *HEY*--IF YOU ***DO*** CUT YOUR THROAT, MAYBE IT WOULDN'T EVEN *HURT*.
IT WOULD HURT. EVEN FOR MY KIND, IT WOULD HURT. WE MAY NOT DIE EASY, AND WE SURE AS HELL DON'T DIE WELL, BUT WE ***CAN*** DIE.
IF WE'RE STILL LOVED AND REMEMBERED, SOMETHING ELSE LIKE US COMES ALONG AND TAKES OUR PLACE. AND IF WE'RE FORGOTTEN, WE'RE ***DONE***.
"ARE YOU DRUNK?"
NOT YET.
" I JUST KEEP THINKING ABOUT THOR.
" ***BIG*** GUY, LIKE YOU. NOT BRIGHT, BUT HE'D GIVE YOU THE SHIRT OFF HIS BACK IF YOU ASKED HIM. AND HE KILLED HIMSELF.
" BLEW HIS HEAD OFF IN PHILADELPHIA IN 1932.
" WHAT KIND OF WAY IS THAT FOR A ***GOD*** TO DIE? "
I'M SORRY.
YOU DON'T GIVE TWO FUCKING CENTS, SON. HE WAS A WHOLE LOT LIKE ***YOU***. BIG--AND ***DUMB***.

THE OPPOSITION GOT IN TOUCH. THEY WANT TO DISCUSS A TRUCE. PEACE TALKS. LIVE AND LET FUCKING LIVE.

"SO WHAT HAPPENS NOW?"

NOW I GO AND DRINK BAD COFFEE WITH THE MODERN ASSHOLES IN A KANSAS CITY MASONIC HALL.

YOU STAY HERE AND YOU KEEP YOUR HEAD DOWN. DON'T GET INTO ANY *TROUBLE*, YOU HEAR ME?

BUT...

CLICK

THE LINE WENT DEAD AND *STAYED* DEAD. THERE WAS NO DIAL TONE, BUT THEN, THERE *NEVER* WAS.

NOTHING BUT TIME TO KILL.

Minutes of The Lakeside City Council 1872-18

JULY, 1874

"IT IS TO BE EXPECTED THAT THE NUISANCES ATTENDANT TO THE DAMMING OF *MILL CREEK* WILL ABATE ONCE THE MILL POND HAS BECOME A LAKE."

THE LAKE WAS MAN-MADE? WHY CALL THE TOWN LAKESIDE WHEN THE LAKE BEGAN AS A DAMNED MILL POND?

"MR. HINZELMANN IS IN CHARGE OF THE LAKE-BUILDING PROJECT. THE CITY COUNCIL HAS GRANTED HIM THE SUM OF $370 TOWARD THE PROJECT."

THEY HAD DEDICATED THE LAKE IN THE SPRING OF 1876. A VOTE OF THANKS TO MR. HINZELMANN WAS TAKEN BY THE COUNCIL.

I WONDER IF HINZELMANN KNOWS HIS FAMILY WAS INSTRUMENTAL IN BUILDING THE LAKE?

OH! THANK YOU.

MIKE AINSEL.

WATCH.

I MADE IT DISAPPEAR, MIKE AINSEL.

YOU DID. AFTER WE'VE EATEN, IF IT'S OKAY WITH YOUR MOTHER, I'LL SHOW YOU HOW TO DO IT EVEN SMOOTHER THAN THAT.

DO IT NOW IF YOU WANT. WE'RE STILL WAITING FOR SAMANTHA. I SENT HER OUT FOR SOUR CREAM.

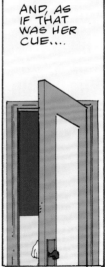

AND, AS IF THAT WAS HER CUE....

I DIDN'T KNOW IF YOU WANTED THE KIND WITH CALORIES, OR THE KIND THAT TASTES LIKE WALLPAPER PASTE, SO I WENT WITH THE KIND WITH CALORIES.

THAT'S FINE, SAM. THIS IS MY NEIGHBOR, MIKE AINSEL.

MIKE, THIS IS SAMANTHA BLACK CROW, MY SISTER.

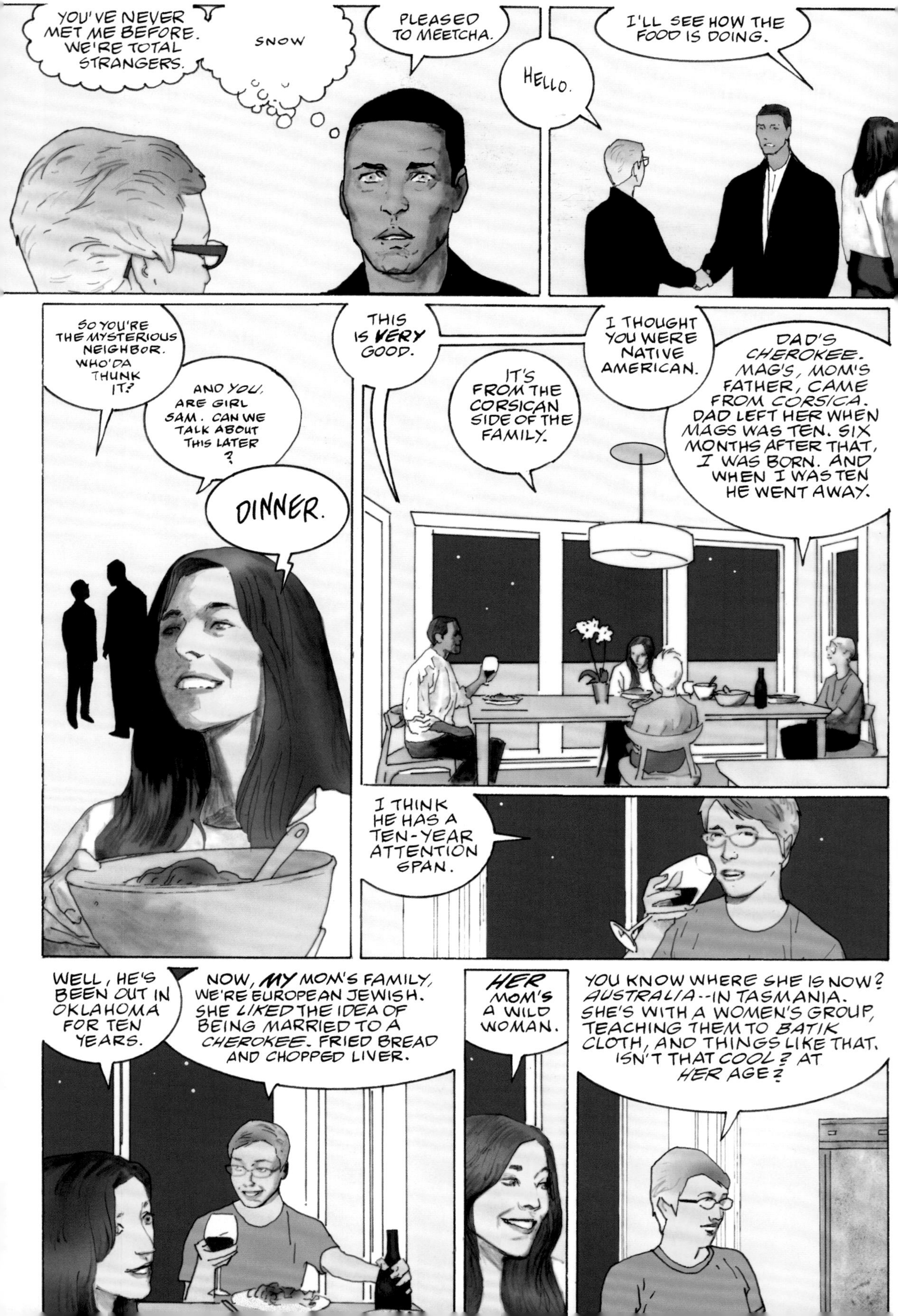
YOU'VE NEVER MET ME BEFORE. WE'RE TOTAL STRANGERS.
SNOW
PLEASED TO MEETCHA.
HELLO.
I'LL SEE HOW THE FOOD IS DOING.
SO YOU'RE THE MYSTERIOUS NEIGHBOR. WHO'DA THUNK IT?
AND YOU, ARE GIRL SAM. CAN WE TALK ABOUT THIS LATER ?
DINNER.
THIS IS VERY GOOD.
IT'S FROM THE CORSICAN SIDE OF THE FAMILY.
I THOUGHT YOU WERE NATIVE AMERICAN.
DAD'S CHEROKEE. MAG'S, MOM'S FATHER, CAME FROM CORSICA. DAD LEFT HER WHEN MAGS WAS TEN. SIX MONTHS AFTER THAT, I WAS BORN. AND WHEN I WAS TEN HE WENT AWAY.
I THINK HE HAS A TEN-YEAR ATTENTION SPAN.
WELL, HE'S BEEN OUT IN OKLAHOMA FOR TEN YEARS.
NOW, MY MOM'S FAMILY, WE'RE EUROPEAN JEWISH. SHE LIKED THE IDEA OF BEING MARRIED TO A CHEROKEE. FRIED BREAD AND CHOPPED LIVER.
HER MOM'S A WILD WOMAN.
YOU KNOW WHERE SHE IS NOW? AUSTRALIA--IN TASMANIA. SHE'S WITH A WOMEN'S GROUP, TEACHING THEM TO BATIK CLOTH, AND THINGS LIKE THAT. ISN'T THAT COOL? AT HER AGE?

SO, **MIKE**, TELL US ABOUT YOUR FAMILY. WHAT ARE THE AINSELS LIKE?

DULL. SO YOU'RE AT SCHOOL IN MADISON. WHAT'S THAT LIKE?

YOU KNOW. I'M STUDYING ART HISTORY, WOMEN'S STUDIES, CASTING MY OWN BRONZES.

WHEN I GROW UP, I'M GOING TO DO MAGIC. *POOF.*

WILL YOU TEACH ME, MIKE AINSEL?

SURE. IF YOUR MOM DOESN'T MIND.

YOU KNOW HOW TO MAKE THE COIN DISAPPEAR, ALREADY. THAT'S HALF OF IT. THE OTHER HALF IS THIS: PUT YOUR ATTENTION ON THE PLACE WHERE THE COIN *OUGHT* TO BE. FOLLOW IT WITH YOUR EYES AND NO ONE WILL EVEN LOOK AT YOUR LEFT HAND.

BUT YOU **MUST** REMEMBER THAT A MASTER MAGICIAN **NEVER** TELLS ANYONE HOW IT'S DONE.

I PROMISE.

MAGS, I THINK I'M GOING TO GET MIKE TO TAKE ME TO *THE BUCK STOPS HERE* FOR AN HOUR OR SO.

I THINK HE'S INTERESTING.

AND WE HAVE LOTS TO TALK ABOUT.

WELL...

YOU'RE GROWN-UPS.

C'MON. YOU'RE TAKING *ME* TO *THE BUCK STOPS HERE*.

THANKS FOR DINNER.

HOLD ON. I NEED TO GET SOMETHING.

HINZELMANN MIGHT BE DOWN AT THE BUCK. I HAVE SOMETHING HE MIGHT BE INTERESTED IN.

OMIGOD. PAUL GUNTHER'S CAR. YOU BOUGHT PAUL GUNTHER'S CAR? OMIGOD.

YOU KNOW THE CAR?

IT WAS ME THAT PERSUADED HIM TO PAINT IT *PURPLE*.

OH. IT'S GOOD TO HAVE SOMEONE TO BLAME.

SUDDENLY THIS FEELS LIKE A STUPID THING TO DO. GETTING INTO A CAR WITH A PSYCHO-KILLER.

I GOT YOU HOME SAFE LAST TIME.

YOU KILLED TWO MEN. YOU'RE WANTED BY THE FEDS. AND NOW I FIND OUT YOU'RE LIVING UNDER AN ASSUMED NAME NEXT DOOR TO MY SISTER. UNLESS MIKE AINSEL IS YOUR *REAL* NAME?

NO. HHHHH, IT'S NOT.

THOSE MEN CAME TO MY HOUSE, SAID WE'D BEEN SEEN TOGETHER, SHOWED ME THE PHOTOGRAPS OF YOU. IT WAS LIKE *THE FUGITIVE*. BUT I SAID I HADN'T SEEN YOU.

THANK *YOU*. AND I'VE NEVER KILLED ANYBODY

REALLY.

NOW I'M GOING TO TAKE YOU TO THE *BUCK*. I'LL BUY YOU A DRINK IF YOU'RE ACTUALLY OLD ENOUGH TO DRINK. THEN I'LL TAKE YOU BACK TO MARGUERITE, SAFE AND SOUND, AND HOPE YOU AREN'T GOING TO CALL THE COPS.

YOU WOULDN'T BELIEVE ME IF I TOLD YOU.

WHO *DID* KILL THOSE MEN?

I *WOULD*. YOU HAVE NO *IDEA* WHAT I CAN BELIEVE.

REALLY?

I CAN BELIEVE THINGS THAT ARE TRUE, AND I CAN BELIEVE THINGS THAT AREN'T TRUE, AND THINGS WHERE NOBODY KNOWS IF THEY'RE TRUE OR NOT, SANTA CLAUS AND THE EASTER BUNNY, AND MARILYN MONROE, AND THE BEATLES AND ELVIS AND *MISTER ED.*

"I BELIEVE THAT PEOPLE ARE PERFEC-TABLE, THAT KNOWLEDGE IS *INFINITE*...

"THAT THE WORLD IS RUN BY SECRET BANKING CARTELS...

".'AND IS VISITED BY ALIENS, CUTE ONES THAT LOOK LIKE *LEMURS*...

"... AND BAD ONES WHO MUTILATE CATTLE AND WANT OUR WOMEN.

"I BELIEVE THAT THE FUTURE SUCKS...

"AND I BELIEVE THAT THE FUTURE ROCKS...

"AND I BELIEVE THAT ONE DAY *WHITE BUFFALO WOMAN* IS GOING TO COME BACK AND KICK EVERYONE'S ASS.

"I BELIEVE THAT ALL POLITICIANS ARE CROOKS, AND I STILL BELIEVE THEY ARE BETTER THAN THE ALTERNATIVE.

"I BELIEVE CALIFORNIA IS GOING TO SINK INTO THE SEA, WHILE FLORIDA DISSOLVES INTO MAD-NESS, ALLIGATORS, AND TOXIC WASTE.

"I BELIEVE THAT ANTI-BACTERIAL SOAP IS DESTROYING OUR RESISTANCE TO DIRT AND DISEASE SO THAT ONE DAY WE'LL ALL BE WIPED OUT BY THE COMMON COLD LIKE THE MARTIANS IN *THE WAR OF THE WORLDS*.

" I BELIEVE IN A PERSONAL GOD WHO CARES ABOUT ME AND WORRIES AND OVERSEES EVERYTHING I DO.

"AND I BELIEVE IN AN EMPTY AND GODLESS UNIVERSE OF CASUAL CHAOS.

"I BELIEVE THAT ANYONE WHO SAYS SEX IS OVERRATED, HASN'T *DONE* IT PROPERLY.

" I BELIEVE IN ABSOLUTE HONESTY AND SENSIBLE SOCIAL LIES.

"I BELIEVE IN A WOMAN'S RIGHT TO CHOOSE, A BABY'S RIGHT TO LIVE, THAT WHILE ALL HUMAN LIFE IS SACRED, THERE'S NOTHING WRONG WITH THE *DEATH PENALTY* IF YOU CAN TRUST THE LEGAL SYSTEM IMPLICITLY.

" AND THAT NO ONE BUT A MORON WOULD EVER TRUST THE LEGAL SYSTEM."

I BELIEVE THAT LIFE IS A GAME.

LIFE IS A CRUEL JOKE.

AND THAT LIFE IS WHAT HAPPENS WHEN YOU ARE *ALIVE*--AND THAT YOU MIGHT AS WELL LIE BACK AND *ENJOY* IT.

=WHEW=

HA! BRAVO! SO, IF I TELL YOU WHAT I LEARNED, YOU WON'T THINK THAT I'M A NUT?

MAYBE. TRY ME.

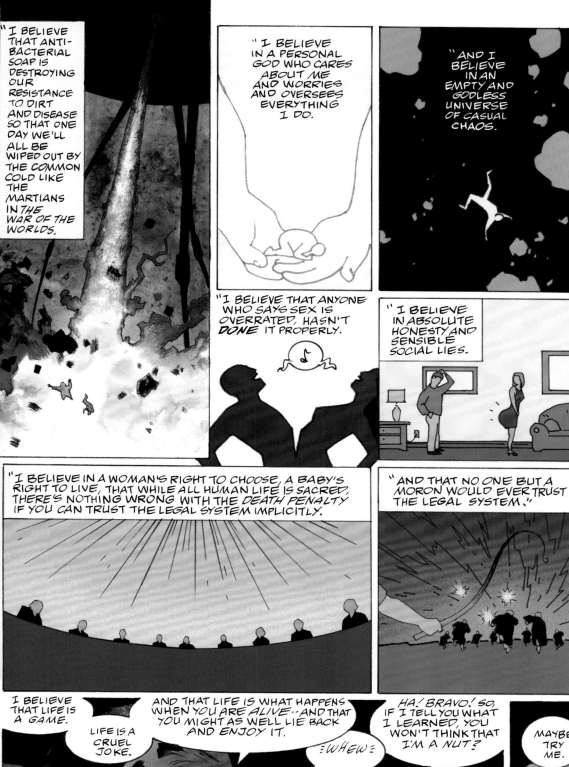

" WOULD YOU BELIEVE THAT ALL THE GODS THAT PEOPLE HAVE EVER IMAGINED ARE STILL WITH US TODAY?"

" MAYBE."

" AND THAT THERE ARE NEW GODS OUT THERE, GODS OF COMPUTERS AND TELEPHONES AND WHATEVER AND THAT THEY ALL SEEM TO THINK THERE ISN'T ROOM FOR THEM BOTH IN THIS WORLD? AND THAT SOME KIND OF WAR IS LIKELY?"

"AND THESE GODS KILLED THOSE TWO MEN?"

" NO. MY WIFE KILLED THOSE TWO MEN."

" I THOUGHT YOU SAID YOUR WIFE WAS DEAD?"

"SHE *IS*."

"SHE KILLED THEM BEFORE SHE DIED?"

"*AFTER*. DON'T ASK ."

" WHY WOULD THEY HAVE A WAR? WHAT IS THERE TO WIN?"

"I DON'T KNOW."

"IT'S EASIER TO BELIEVE IN ALIENS THAN IN GODS. MAYBE MISTER TOWN AND MISTER WHATEVER WERE *MEN IN BLACK*, ONLY THE *ALIEN* KIND."

"MAYBE THEY WERE, AT THAT. "

JUST TELL ME YOU'RE ONE OF THE *GOOD* GUYS.

I CAN'T. I WISH I COULD. BUT I'M DOING MY BEST.

The BUCK Stops Here

HMM.

GOOD ENOUGH. I WON'T TURN YOU IN. YOU CAN BUY ME A BEER.

THERE'S CHAD MULLIGAN. LOOKS LIKE HE HAS HIS KISSING COUSIN WITH HIM. I WONDER WHAT SHE LOOKS LIKE?

AND *HINZELMANN* DOESN'T SEEM TO BE HERE.

SPITTING ON SIDEWALKS PROHIBITED TY $5 TO $100

CLIMAX PLUG TOBACCO

LOOKS LIKE A FREE TABLE AT THE BACK.

HE STARTED WALKING TOWARD IT.

THEN SOMEBODY BEGAN TO SCREAM.

IT WAS A **BAD** SCREAM, A FULL-THROATED, SEEN-A-GHOST HYSTERICAL SCREAM, WHICH SILENCED ALL CONVERSATION.

GET HIM! OH, FOR GOD'S SAKE, SOMEBODY **STOP HIM!**

DON'T LET HIM **GETAWAY!** PLEASE!

HHHSSSSSSSSSS,

IT WAS A VOICE HE KNEW.

AUDREY? AUDREY BURTON?

MURDERER!

MIKE.

CHAD.

SHADOW. YOU BASTARD. YOU MURDEROUS EVIL BASTARD.

ARE YOU SURE THAT YOU KNOW THIS MAN, HON?

ARE YOU CRAZY?

HE WORKED FOR ROBBIE FOR YEARS!

HIS SLUTTY WIFE WAS MY BEST FRIEND!

HE'S WANTED FOR MURDER.

I HAD TO ANSWER QUESTIONS.

HE'S AN ESCAPED CONVICT.

IT'S PROBABLY A MISTAKE. I'M SURE WE CAN SORT THIS ALL OUT. IT'S ALL FINE. NOTHING TO WORRY ABOUT.

LET'S STEP OUTSIDE, MIKE.

SURE.

SHADOW FELT A HAND TOUCH HIS HAND.

I DON'T KNOW WHO YOU ARE...

BUT

YOU

ARE

SUCH

A CUNT.

!

THEN SHE KISSED HIM HARD ON THE LIPS, A FLAG-WAVING KISS, TO LET THEM KNOW SHE HAD PICKED SIDES. EVEN THEN, HE WAS CERTAIN SHE DIDN'T LIKE HIM. WELL, NOT LIKE *THAT*.

STILL, THERE WAS A TALE HE HAD READ ONCE, LONG AGO: THE STORY OF A TRAVELER WHO HAD SLIPPED DOWN A CLIFF WITH MAN-EATING TIGERS ABOVE HIM AND A LETHAL FALL BELOW HIM. THERE WAS A CLUMP OF STRAWBERRIES BESIDE HIM.

"WHAT SHOULD HE DO?" WENT THE QUESTION.

AND THE REPLY WAS...

...EAT THE STRAWBERRIES.

C'MON, MIKE. *PLEASE.* LET'S TAKE IT OUTSIDE.

NOT BAD. YOU KISS GOOD FOR A BOY.

OKAY. GO PLAY OUTSIDE.

BUT *YOU* ARE STILL A *CUNT*.

YOU WANT TO TALK ABOUT THIS?

AM I UNDER *ARREST*?

HE *KILLED* TWO MEN, CHAD. THE *F.B.I.* CAME TO MY DOOR. HE'S A *PSYCHO*. I'LL COME DOWN TO THE STATION WITH YOU IF YOU WANT.

YOU'VE CAUSED ENOUGH TROUBLE, MA'AM. PLEASE GO AWAY.

CHAD? DID YOU *HEAR* THAT? HE THREATENED ME!

GET BACK INSIDE, AUDREY.

WOULD YOU LIKE TO COMMENT ON ANYTHING SHE SAID?

I'VE NEVER KILLED ANYONE.

I BELIEVE YOU. I'M SURE WE CAN DEAL WITH THESE ALLEGATIONS EASILY ENOUGH. IT'S PROBABLY NOTHING. YOU WON'T GIVE ME ANY TROUBLE, WILL YOU, MIKE?

NO TROUBLE. THIS IS ALL A MISTAKE.

EXACTLY. SO I FIGURE WE OUGHT TO HEAD DOWN TO MY OFFICE AND SORT IT ALL OUT THERE.

AM I UNDER ARREST?

NOT UNLESS YOU WANT TO BE. YOU COME WITH ME OUT OF A SENSE OF CIVIC DUTY, AND WE'LL DO ALL WE CAN TO STRAIGHTEN THIS OUT.

CHAD PATTED SHADOW DOWN, FOUND NO WEAPONS. THEY GOT INTO MULLIGAN'S CAR. AGAIN, SHADOW SAT IN THE BACK, LOOKING OUT THROUGH THE METAL CAGE.

S.O.S.   MAY-DAY.   HELP.

CHAPTER NINE

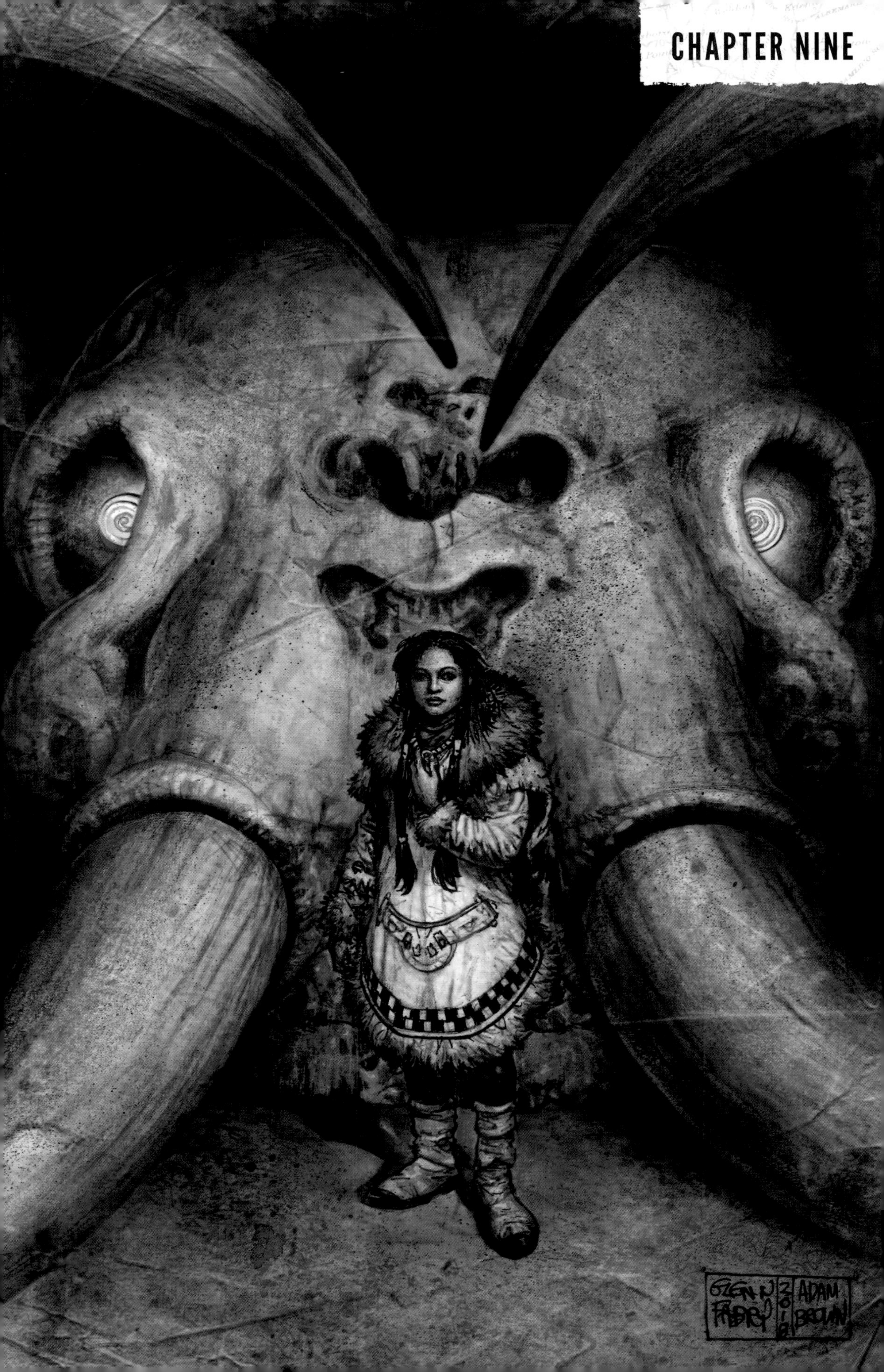
GLENN FABRY
2018
ADAM BROWN

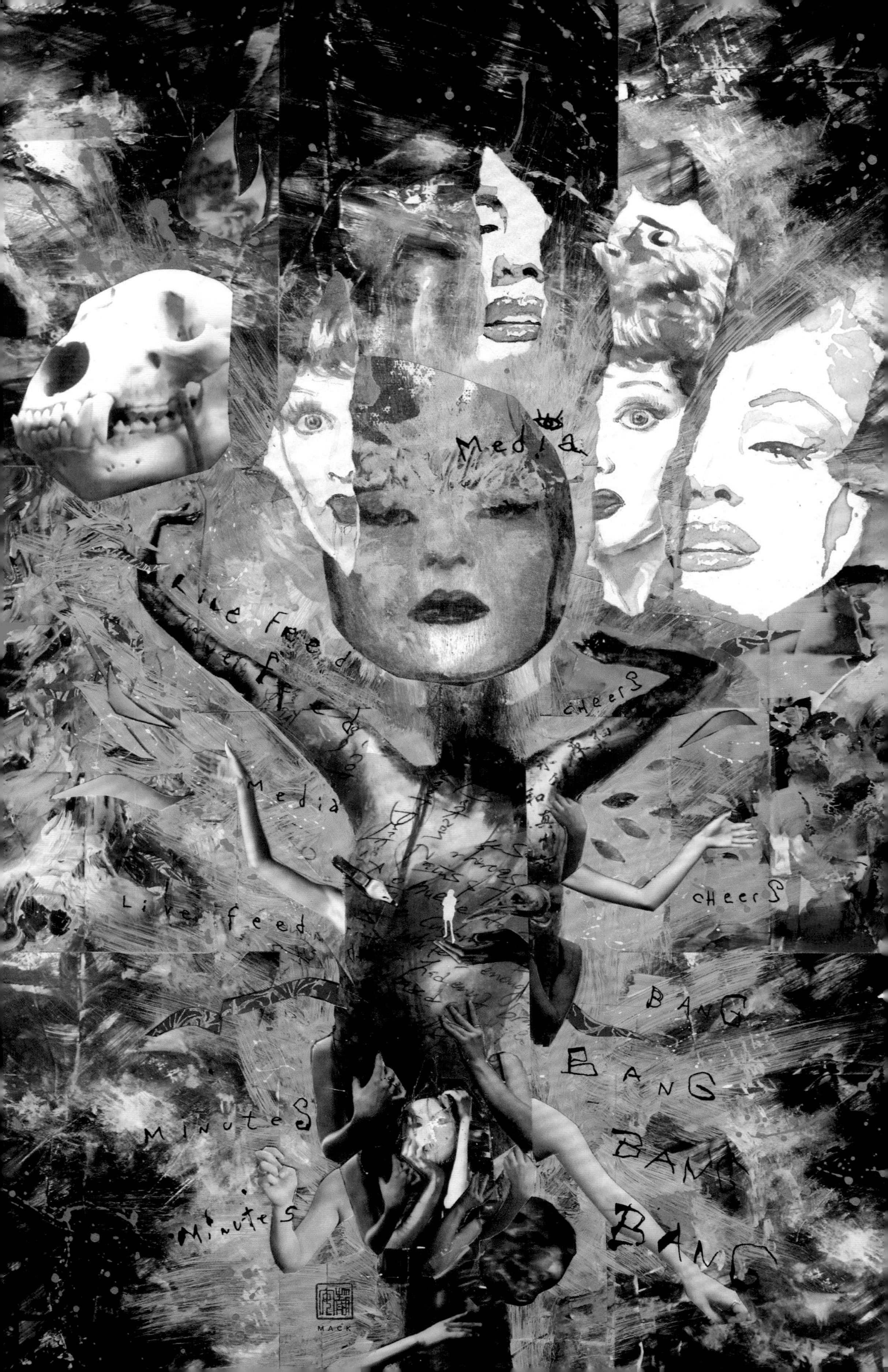
Media
Media
cheerS
Live feed
cheerS
BANG
BANG
BANG
BANG
MinuteS
MinuteS
MACK

I FIGURE IT WAS A GOOD IDEA TO GET YOU OUT OF THERE. ALL YOU NEEDED WAS SOME LOUD-MOUTH DECIDING THAT YOU WERE ALISON McGOVERN'S KILLER AND WE'D HAVE A LYNCH MOB ON OUR HANDS.

POINT TAKEN.

SO, YOU'RE SURE THERE'S NOTHING YOU WANT TO TELL ME?

NOPE. NOTHING TO SAY. SHOULD I CALL A LAWYER?

YOU AREN'T ACCUSED OF ANYTHING. UP TO YOU.

TAKE A SEAT OVER THERE.

MISSING

MINUTES PASSED, AND HOURS IN THAT ROOM. SHADOW READ
TWO OUTDATED ISSUES OF *SPORTS ILLUSTRATED* AND ONE
OF *NEWSWEEK*. FROM TIME TO TIME, CHAD WOULD COME
THROUGH TO SEE IF HE NEEDED TO USE THE RESTROOM,
ONCE TO OFFER HIM A HAM ROLL AND CHIPS.

WE'LL KNOW PRETTY SOON. IT DOESN'T LOOK LIKE YOU CAME BY THE NAME MIKE AINSEL LEGALLY.

THANKS. AM I UNDER ARREST?

ON THE OTHER HAND, YOU CAN CALL YOURSELF WHATEVER YOU WANT IN THIS STATE. IF IT'S NOT FOR FRAUDULENT PURPOSES.

CAN I MAKE A PHONE CALL?

LOCAL?

LONG DISTANCE.

IT'LL SAVE MONEY IF I PUT IT ON MY CALLING CARD.

YEAH, AND YOU'LL KNOW THE NUMBER I DIALED AND YOU'LL LISTEN IN ON THE EXTENSION.

GREAT.

YOU CAN USE THIS EMPTY OFFICE.

THANKS.

JACQUEL AND IBIS. CAN I HELP YOU?

HI. MISTER IBIS, THIS IS MIKE AINSEL. I HELPED OUT THERE FOR A FEW DAYS OVER CHRISTMAS.

OF COURSE. MIKE. HOW ARE YOU?

NOT GREAT, MISTER IBIS. IN A PATCH OF TROUBLE. ABOUT TO BE ARRESTED. HOPING YOU'D SEEN MY UNCLE ABOUT, OR MAYBE YOU COULD GET A MESSAGE TO HIM.

I CAN CERTAINLY ASK AROUND.

HOLD ON, UH, MIKE--THERE'S SOMEONE WHO WANTS TO TALK TO YOU.

HI, HONEY. I MISS YOU. WHO WAS THAT GIRL YOU WERE KISSING? YOU TRYING TO MAKE ME JEALOUS, HON'?

HE'D NEVER HEARD THAT VOICE BEFORE, BUT HE WAS CERTAIN THAT HE KNEW HER.

LET IT HAPPEN.

WE'RE JUST FRIENDS. I THINK SHE WAS TRYING TO PROVE A POINT. HOW DID YOU KNOW SHE KISSED ME?

I GOT EYES WHEREVER MY FOLK WALK. YOU TAKE CARE NOW, HON.

MIKE?

YES?

THERE'S A PROBLEM GETTING AHOLD OF YOUR UNCLE. HE SEEMS TO BE KIND OF TIED UP. BUT I'LL TRY TO GET A MESSAGE TO YOUR AUNT NANCY. GOOD LUCK.

THE LINE WENT DEAD.

SHADOW SAT IN THE EMPTY OFFICE, WAITING FOR CHAD TO RETURN.

HE PICKED UP THE MINUTES ONCE MORE.

DECEMBER, 1876

"FIRE AT OLSEN'S LIVERY STABLE WAS EXTINGUISHED. NO INJURY OR LOSS OF LIFE, HUMAN OR EQUINE.

"ORDINANCE PROHIBITING EXPECTORATION ON SIDE-WALKS INTRODUCED AND PASSED, EIGHT TO FOUR.

"LEMMI HAUTALA, TWELVE YEARS OLD, WANDERED AWAY IN A FIT OF DELIRIUM, SEARCH EFFECTED, BUT IMPEDED BY SNOWS. COUNCIL VOTED TO SEND HAUTALA FAMILY THEIR CONDOLENCES."

NO FURTHER MENTION OF LEMMI HAUTALA.

AND THEN, ON SOMETHING SLIGHTLY MORE THAN A WHIM, HE FLIPPED FORWARD TO THE WINTER OF...

1877.

"JESSIE LOVAT, A NEGRO CHILD, VANISHED ON THE NIGHT OF THE TWENTY-EIGHTH OF DECEMBER, BELIEVED SHE MIGHT HAVE BEEN ABDUCTED BY TRAVELLING PEDLARS RUN OUT OF TOWN THE PREVIOUS WEEK, SAID TO BE MAKING FOR ST. PAUL. TELEGRAMS SENT TO ST. PAUL. NO RESULTS REPORTED.

CONDOLENCES WERE NOT SENT TO THE LOVAT FAMILY.

OKAY. FORWARD TO WINTER OF 1878.

MISTER AINSEL.

MIKE, I'M TRULY SORRY. I APPRECIATE HOW EASY YOU'VE BEEN ABOUT ALL THIS. PERSONALLY, I LIKE YOU. BUT THAT DOESN'T CHANGE ANYTHING, YOU KNOW?

I KNOW.

I GOT NO CHOICE IN THE MATTER BUT TO PLACE YOU UNDER ARREST FOR VIOLATING YOUR PAROLE.

THEN POLICE CHIEF CHAD MULLIGAN READ SHADOW HIS RIGHTS. HE FILLED OUT SOME PAPERWORK. HE TOOK SHADOW'S PRINTS. HE WALKED HIM DOWN THE HALL TO THE COUNTY JAIL, ON THE OTHER SIDE OF THE BUILDING.

A SLEEPY-LOOKING WOMAN WATCHING JAY LENO ON A PORTABLE TELEVISION TOOK THE PAPERS FROM CHAD, AND SIGNED FOR SHADOW. CHAD HUNG AROUND, FILLED IN MORE PAPERS.

THE WOMAN PATTED SHADOW DOWN ...

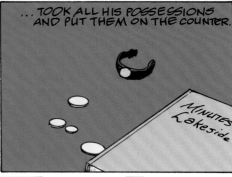

... TOOK ALL HIS POSSESSIONS AND PUT THEM ON THE COUNTER.

MINUTES Lakeside

YOU TAKE CARE OF THIS. MY WHOLE LIFE IS IN HERE.

IT'LL BE SAFE WITH US. AM I RIGHT, CHAD?

NEVER LOST A PRISONER'S POSSESSIONS YET.

YOU CAN CHANGE IN THERE. YOU CAN KEEP YOUR OWN UNDER-WEAR AND SOCKS.

SHADOW SLIPPED THE FOUR HUNDRED-DOLLAR BILLS HE HAD PALMED FROM HIS WALLET, ALONG WITH THE SILVER LIBERTY DOLLAR INTO HIS SOCK.

THE WOMAN PUT HIS CLOTHES INTO THE PLASTIC BAG WITH THE REST OF HIS POSSESSIONS. SHE HAD HIM SIGN FOR THEM.

Mike Ainsel

SHADOW WAS ALREADY THINKING OF MIKE AINSEL AS SOMEONE HE HAD LIKED WELL ENOUGH IN THE PAST, BUT WOULD NO LONGER BE SEEING IN THE FUTURE.

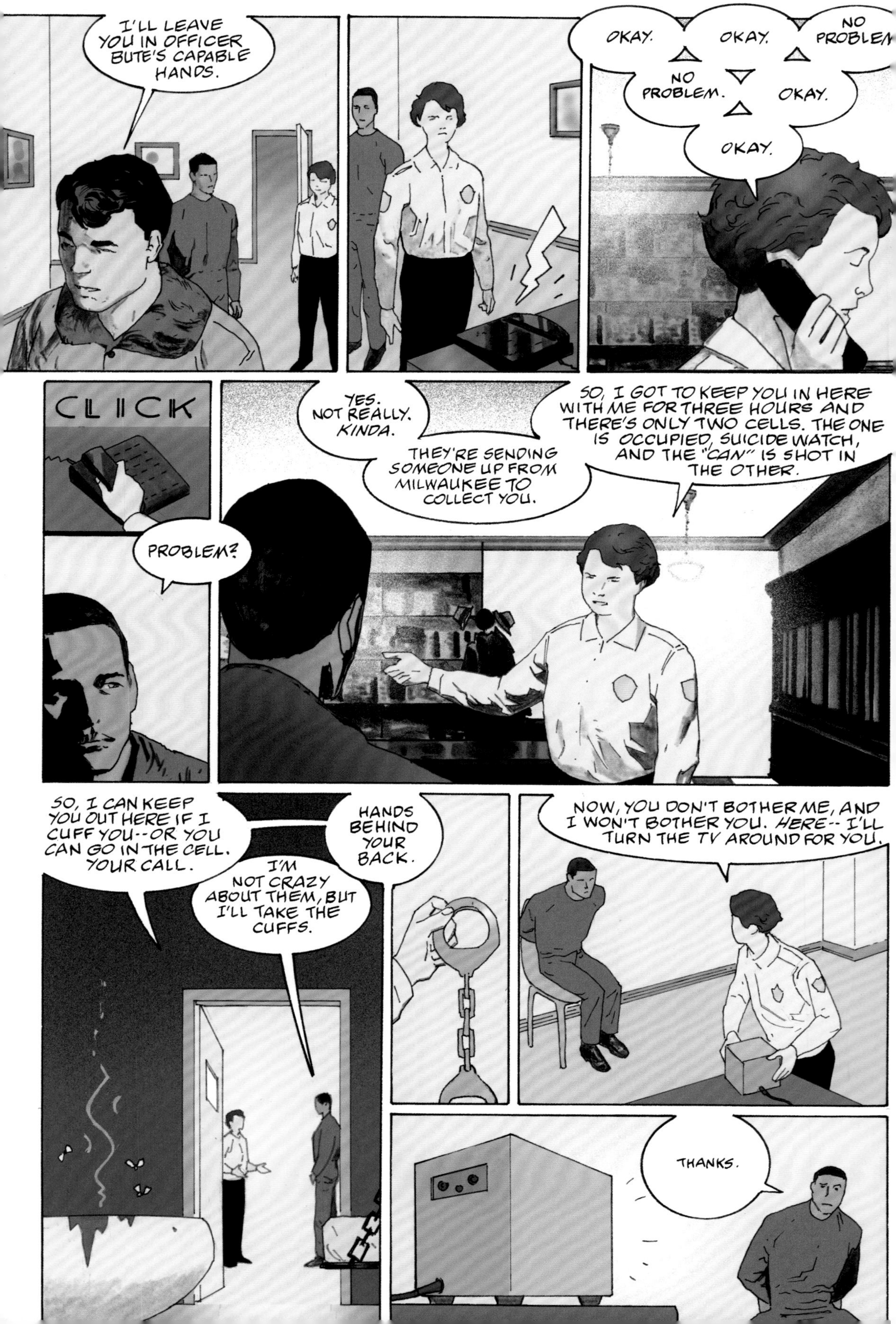
I'LL LEAVE YOU IN OFFICER BUTE'S CAPABLE HANDS.
OKAY.
OKAY.
NO PROBLEM
NO PROBLEM.
OKAY.
OKAY.
CLICK
PROBLEM?
YES. NOT REALLY. KINDA.
THEY'RE SENDING SOMEONE UP FROM MILWAUKEE TO COLLECT YOU.
SO, I GOT TO KEEP YOU IN HERE WITH ME FOR THREE HOURS AND THERE'S ONLY TWO CELLS. THE ONE IS OCCUPIED, SUICIDE WATCH, AND THE "CAN" IS SHOT IN THE OTHER.
SO, I CAN KEEP YOU OUT HERE IF I CUFF YOU--OR YOU CAN GO IN THE CELL. YOUR CALL.
I'M NOT CRAZY ABOUT THEM, BUT I'LL TAKE THE CUFFS.
HANDS BEHIND YOUR BACK.
NOW, YOU DON'T BOTHER ME, AND I WON'T BOTHER YOU. HERE-- I'LL TURN THE TV AROUND FOR YOU.
THANKS.

AN EPISODE OF CHEERS WAS JUST BEGINNING. OFFICER LIZ BUTE SAT BACK IN HER CHAIR, NOT DOZING BUT BY NO MEANS AWAKE. SO, SHE DID NOT NOTICE WHEN THE GANG AT CHEERS STOPPED GETTING OFF ONE-LINERS, AND JUST STARTED STARING OUT OF THE SCREEN AT SHADOW.

SHADOW. WE WERE SO WORRIED ABOUT YOU. YOU'D FALLEN OFF THE WORLD.

IT'S SO *GOOD* TO SEE YOU AGAIN--ALBEIT IN BONDAGE AND *COUNTY COUTURE.*

WELL, YOU'VE LED US A *MERRY CHASE.*

AH..., CAT GOT YOUR TONGUE, I SEE.

HEY-- *JERK-WAD!*

WE INTERRUPT THIS *BROADCAST* TO SHOW YOU SOMETHING THAT'S GOING TO MAKE YOU *PISS* IN YOUR *FRIGGIN' PANTS.* YOU *READY?*

THE SCREEN FLICKERED AND WENT BLACK, A SOFT FEMALE VOICE SAID IN VOICE-OVER...

THE PICTURE LURCHED FORWARD IN THE MANNER OF A HAND-HELD CAMERA.

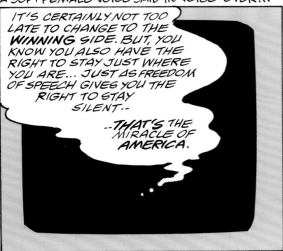

IT'S CERTAINLY NOT TOO LATE TO CHANGE TO THE *WINNING* SIDE. BUT, YOU KNOW YOU ALSO HAVE THE RIGHT TO STAY JUST WHERE YOU ARE... JUST AS FREEDOM OF SPEECH GIVES YOU THE RIGHT TO STAY SILENT--

--*THAT'S* THE *MIRACLE* OF *AMERICA.*

TERRORISM IS TOO EASY A WORD TO BANDY ABOUT. THEY ARE *MURDERING SCUM,* PURE AND SIMPLE, HIDING BEHIND WEASEL-WORDS LIKE *FREEDOM FIGHTER.* WE'RE RISKING OUR LIVES, BUT AT LEAST WE KNOW WE'RE MAKING A *DIFFERENCE.*

I *KNOW* THAT VOICE. I'VE BEEN INSIDE THAT MAN'S HEAD. MR. TOWN. HE SOUNDS DIFFERENT FROM INSIDE. BUT THAT'S *HIM.*

LET'S SEE IF THE CAMERAS INSIDE THE HALL ARE WORKING.

THE CAMERA ZOOMED IN, IN A SERIES OF JAGGED MOVEMENTS.

FOR A MOMENT, THE INTERIOR WAS OUT OF FOCUS.

AND THEN IT BECAME SHARP ONCE MORE.

THAT'S WEDNESDAY.

THE SOUND CAME ON WITH A *POP*.

WE ARE OFFERING IS THE CHANCE TO END THIS HERE AND NOW, WITH NO MORE BLOODSHED, PAIN, OR LOSS OF LIFE. ISN'T THAT WORTH GIVING UP A LITTLE?

YOU ARE ASKING ME TO SPEAK FOR ALL OF US, WHICH IS NONSENSICAL. AND WHY SHOULD I BELIEVE THAT YOU PEOPLE ARE GOING TO KEEP YOUR WORD?

OBVIOUSLY, YOU PEOPLE HAVE NO LEADERS, BUT YOU'RE THE ONE THEY LISTEN TO. SOME OF YOUR PEOPLE ARE WATCHING AS WE SPEAK. THE CAMERA DOESN'T LIE.

EVERY-BODY LIES.

I KNOW THAT VOICE. IT'S MR. WORLD, THE ONE I SPOKE TO ON THE CELL PHONE WHILE I WAS IN MR. TOWN'S HEAD.

YOU DON'T BELIEVE THAT WE WILL KEEP OUR WORD?

I THINK YOUR PROMISES WERE MADE TO BE BROKEN AND YOUR OATHS TO BE FORSWORN. BUT *I* WILL KEEP *MY* WORD.

SAFE CONDUCT IS SAFE CONDUCT, AND A FLAG OF TRUCE IS WHAT WE AGREED. I SHOULD TELL YOU, BY THE WAY, THAT YOUR YOUNG *PROTEGÉ* IS ONCE MORE IN OUR CUSTODY.

PFF. NO, HE'S NOT.

WE WERE DISCUSSING THE WAYS TO DEAL WITH THE COMING PARADIGM SHIFT. WE DON'T *HAVE* TO BE ENEMIES. *DO* WE?

SOMETHING STRANGE ABOUT THE IMAGE OF WEDNESDAY ---

WHAT *IS* THAT?

A RED GLINT BURNED ON HIS LEFT EYE, THE GLASS ONE, A RED LASER-POINTED DOT. IT LEFT A PHOSPHOR-DOT AFTERIMAGE AS HE MOVED.

I WILL DO WHAT-EVER IS IN MY POWER...

HE DOESN'T KNOW. HE DOESN'T SEE IT.

HE MOVED HIS HEAD...

IT'S A *BIG* COUN-TRY...

AND THE SCARLET GLITTER-BLUR SLIPPED TO HIS CHEEK.

THEN IT EDGED UP TO HIS GLASS EYE ONCE MORE.

"THERE IS ROOM FOR..."

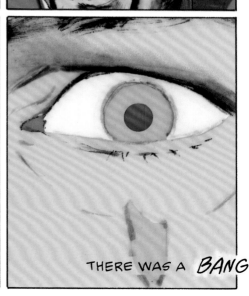

THERE WAS A *BANG*

"LET'S SEE THAT AGAIN, IN SLOW MOTION THIS TIME--

"YES, IT'S STILL GOD'S OWN COUNTRY.

THE ONLY QUESTION IS...

...WHICH GODS?

" WE NOW RETURN YOU TO YOUR REGULARLY SCHEDULED PROG

AH!

OKAY.
OKAY.

YES.

OKAY, I'LL BE OVER THERE.

SORRY, I'M GOING TO HAVE TO PUT YOU IN THE CELL. LET ME GET THOSE CUFFS OFF.

THE LAFAYETTE SHERRIF'S DEPARTMENT SHOULD BE HERE TO COLLECT YOU SOON.

THE SMELL WAS WORSE, NOW THAT THE DOOR WAS CLOSED.

I WONDER IF I'LL BE ONE OF THOSE GUYS WHO GETS LIFE FOR SOMETHING THEY DIDN'T DO. IF I EVEN **MAKE** IT THAT FAR.

IT DOESN'T SEEM AT ALL UNLIKELY.

FROM WHAT I'VE SEEN OF MR. WORLD AND MR. TOWN, MAYBE I'LL HAVE AN *UNFORTUNATE* ACCIDENT ON THE WAY TO THE HOLDING FACILITY.

THERE WAS A STIR OF ACTIVITY ON THE OTHER SIDE OF THE GLASS.

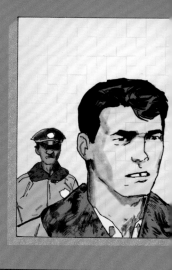

IT STINKS IN HERE.

TELL ME ABOUT IT.

OKAY. FOLK ARE HERE TO PICK YOU UP. SEEMS YOU'RE A MATTER OF NATIONAL SECURITY, YOU KNOW THAT?

IT'LL MAKE A GREAT FRONT-PAGE STORY FOR THE LAKESIDE NEWS.

THAT A DRIFTER GOT PICKED UP FOR PAROLE VIOLATIONS? NOT MUCH OF A STORY.

SO THAT'S THE WAY IT IS?

THAT'S THE WAY IT IS.

THEY'LL TAKE ME OUTSIDE--

--IN HOBBLES AND CUFFS AND LIGHT WEIGHT CLOTHES, OUT INTO THE SNOW.

MAYBE I CAN MAKE A BREAK FOR IT. SOME KIND OF A BREAK FOR IT...

AND EVEN AS HE THOUGHT IT, HE KNEW...

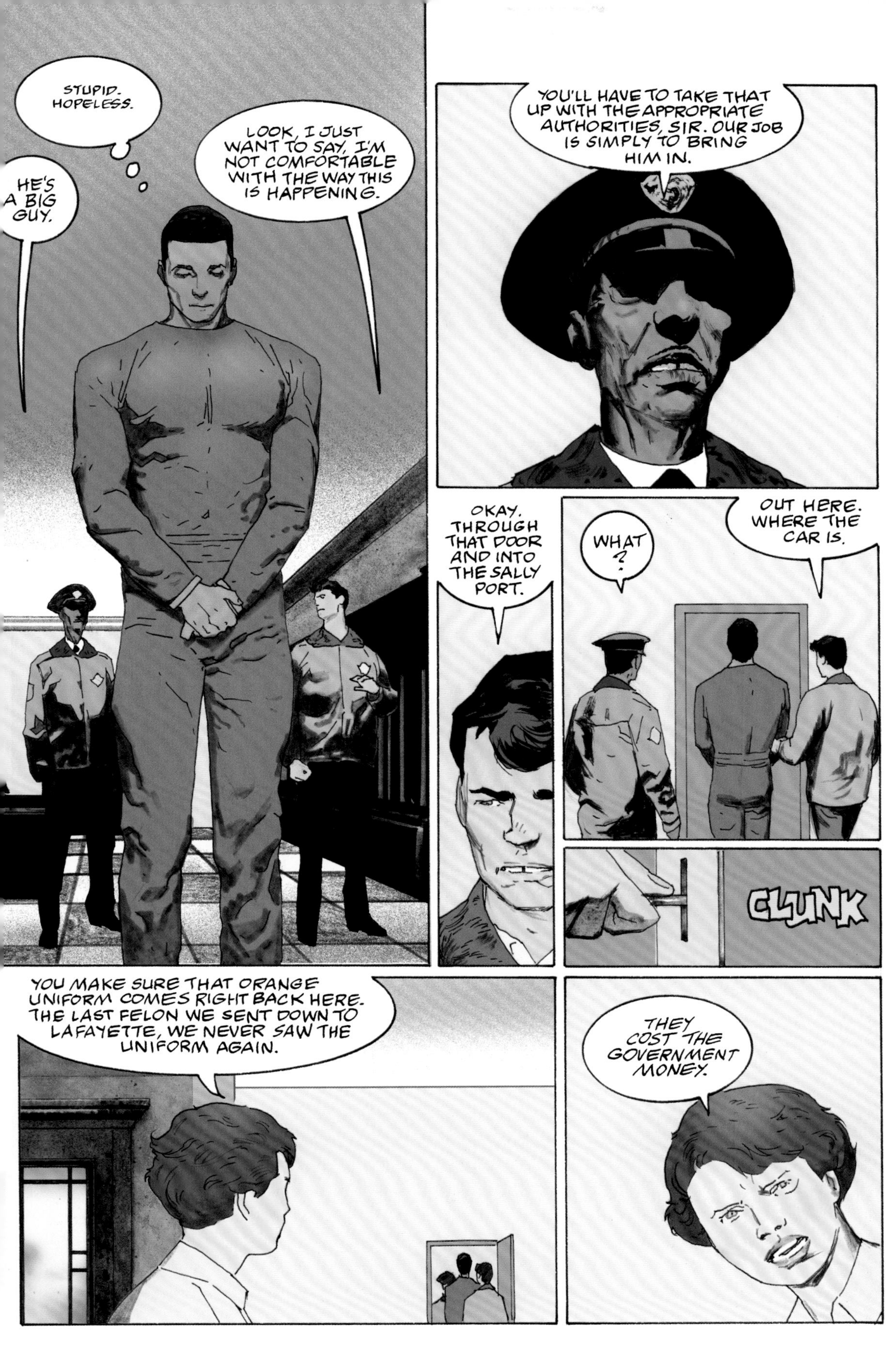
STUPID. HOPELESS.
HE'S A BIG GUY.
LOOK, I JUST WANT TO SAY, I'M NOT COMFORTABLE WITH THE WAY THIS IS HAPPENING.
YOU'LL HAVE TO TAKE THAT UP WITH THE APPROPRIATE AUTHORITIES, SIR. OUR JOB IS SIMPLY TO BRING HIM IN.
OKAY. THROUGH THAT DOOR AND INTO THE SALLY PORT.
WHAT?
OUT HERE. WHERE THE CAR IS.
CLUNK
YOU MAKE SURE THAT ORANGE UNIFORM COMES RIGHT BACK HERE. THE LAST FELON WE SENT DOWN TO LAFAYETTE, WE NEVER SAW THE UNIFORM AGAIN.
THEY COST THE GOVERNMENT MONEY.

THEY WALKED SHADOW OUT TO THE SALLY PORT, WHERE
ANOTHER DEPUTY STOOD WAITING BY A CAR. IT WAS NOT A
SHERIFF'S-DEPARTMENT CAR. IT WAS A BLACK TOWN-CAR.

OOF.

C'MON,
OPEN THE
DOOR.

TAP

TAP

TAP

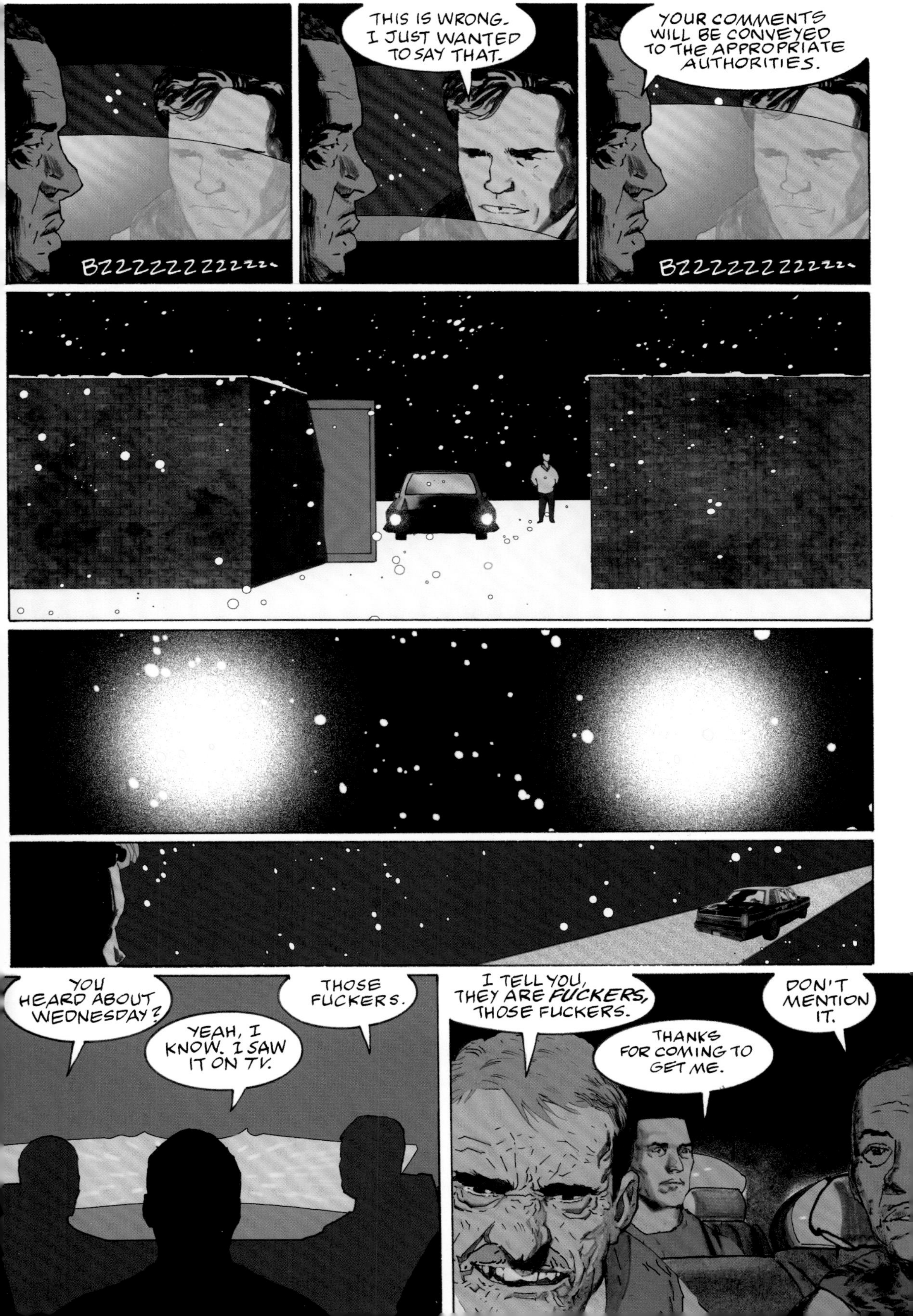
BZZZZZZZZZZzz-
THIS IS WRONG. I JUST WANTED TO SAY THAT.
YOUR COMMENTS WILL BE CONVEYED TO THE APPROPRIATE AUTHORITIES.
BZZZZZZZZZZzz-
YOU HEARD ABOUT WEDNESDAY?
YEAH, I KNOW. I SAW IT ON TV.
THOSE FUCKERS.
I TELL YOU, THEY ARE FUCKERS, THOSE FUCKERS.
THANKS FOR COMING TO GET ME.
DON'T MENTION IT.

IN THE LIGHT OF AN ONCOMING CAR, THE DRIVER'S FACE ALREADY LOOKED OLDER. THE LAST TIME SHADOW HAD SEEN HIM, HE HAD BEEN WEARING LEMON-YELLOW GLOVES AND A CHECK JACKET.

WE WERE IN MILWAUKEE. STILL HAD TO DRIVE LIKE DEMONS WHEN IBIS CALLED.

THE WHITE DEPUTY FUMBLED IN HIS POCKET.

YOU THINK WE LET THEM LOCK YOU UP WHEN I'M STILL WAITING TO BREAK YOUR HEAD WITH MY HAMMER?

THANK YOU.

I LIKE YOUR MOUSTACHE. IT SUITS YOU.

MR. NANCY WAS LOOKING MORE LIKE HIMSELF WITH EACH PASSING MOMENT.

THE *REAL* SHIT WILL HIT THE FAN WHEN THEY *REALLY* TURN UP TO COLLECT YOU. IN THE MEANTIME, WE'LL GET YOU OUT OF THOSE SHACKLES.

CZERNOBOG SMILED.

HAND-CUFF KEY.

WEDNESDAY. IS HE REALLY DEAD? THIS ISN'T SOME KIND OF TRICK, IS IT?

HE REALIZED THAT HE HAD BEEN HOLDING ON TO SOME KIND OF HOPE--FOOLISH THOUGH IT WAS. BUT THE EXPRESSION ON NANCY'S FACE TOLD HIM ALL HE NEEDED TO KNOW, AND THE HOPE WAS GONE.

COLD IT WAS, AND DARK, WHEN THE VISION CAME TO HER, FOR IN THE FAR NORTH, DAYLIGHT WAS A DIM TIME THAT CAME AND WENT.

THEY WERE NOT A LARGE TRIBE: NOMADS OF THE NORTHERN PLAINS. THEY HAD A GOD, WHO WAS THE SKULL OF A MAMMOTH AND THE HIDE OF A MAMMOTH FASHIONED INTO A CLOAK. *NUNYUNNINI*, THEY CALLED HIM.

SHE WAS THE HOLY WOMAN OF THE TRIBE AND HER NAME WAS *ATSULA*, THE FOX.

THERE WERE FOUR OF THEM INSIDE THE HOLY TENT: ATSULA; GUGWEI, THE ELDER; YANU, THE WAR LEADER; AND KALANU, THE SCOUT. KALANU WALKED AS A MAN AND HAD EVEN TAKEN THE MAIDEN, DALANI, AS HER WIFE.

ATSULA THREW SOME DRIED LEAVES INTO THE FIRE. THEY GAVE OFF AN ODOR THAT WAS SHARP AND STRANGE.

THEN SHE PASSED A WOODEN CUP TO GUGWEI. THE CUP WAS FILLED WITH A DARK YELLOW LIQUID.

ATSULA HAD FOUND THE *PUNGH* MUSHROOMS IN THE DARK OF THE MOON, AS ONLY A TRUE HOLY WOMAN COULD.

BEFORE SHE SLEPT, SHE ATE THREE OF THE DRIED MUSHROOM CAPS.

HER DREAMS HAD BEEN CONFUSED AND FEARFUL THINGS, OF ROCK MOUNTAINS AND LIGHTS SPEARING UP LIKE ICICLES.

SHE HAD WOKEN, SWEATING, AND NEEDING TO MAKE WATER. SHE SQUATTED OVER A WOODEN CUP.

THE CUP, SHE PLACED IN THE SNOW.

WHEN SHE WOKE, SHE PICKED OUT THE LUMPS OF ICE IN THE CUP, LEAVING A DARKER LIQUID BEHIND. IT WAS THIS LIQUID SHE PASSED AROUND THE TENT. EACH OF THEM TOOK A LARGE GULP OF THE LIQUID, ATSULA LAST OF ALL.

SHE POURED WHAT WAS LEFT ON THE GROUND, A LIBATION TO THEIR GOD.

THEY SAT IN THE SMOKY TENT, WAITING FOR THEIR GOD TO SPEAK.

KALANU BLINKED HER EYES TIGHTLY, THEN WALKED OVER TO THE MAMMOTH-SKULL.

SHE PULLED THE MAMMOTH-HIDE CLOAK OVER HERSELF, AND STOOD WITH HER HEAD INSIDE THE MAMMOTH-SKULL.

THERE IS EVIL IN THE LAND. EVIL, SUCH THAT IF YOU STAY YOU SHALL PERISH.

IS IT SLAVERS? IS IT THE GREAT WOLVES?

IT IS NOT THE SLAVERS. IT IS NOT THE WOLVES.

IS IT FAMINE?

NUNYUNNINI WAS SILENT.

KALANU CAME OUT OF THE SKULL AND WAITED.

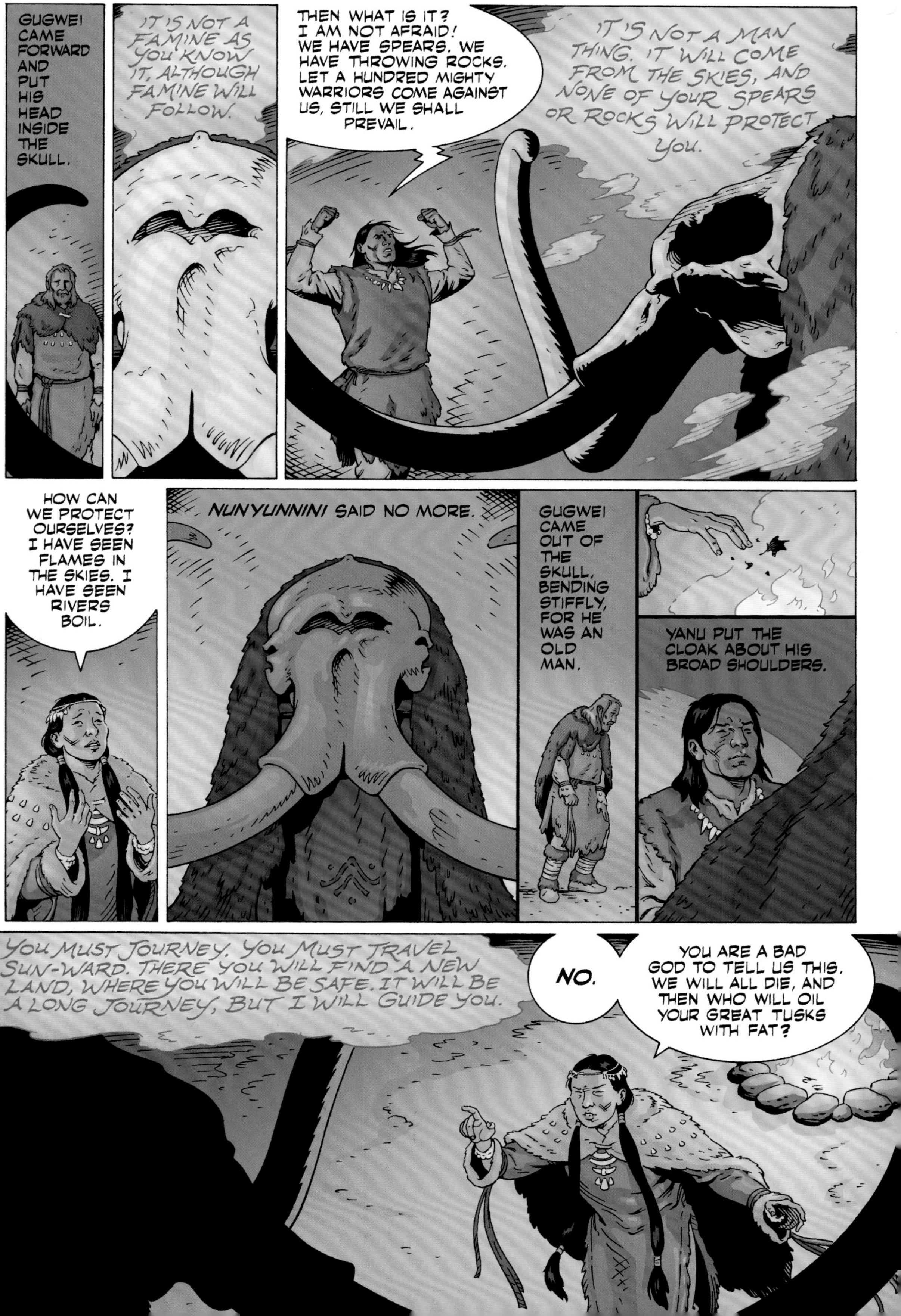
GUGWEI CAME FORWARD AND PUT HIS HEAD INSIDE THE SKULL.
IT'S NOT A FAMINE AS YOU KNOW IT, ALTHOUGH FAMINE WILL FOLLOW.
THEN WHAT IS IT? I AM NOT AFRAID! WE HAVE SPEARS. WE HAVE THROWING ROCKS. LET A HUNDRED MIGHTY WARRIORS COME AGAINST US, STILL WE SHALL PREVAIL.
IT'S NOT A MAN THING. IT WILL COME FROM THE SKIES, AND NONE OF YOUR SPEARS OR ROCKS WILL PROTECT YOU.
HOW CAN WE PROTECT OURSELVES? I HAVE SEEN FLAMES IN THE SKIES. I HAVE SEEN RIVERS BOIL.
NUNYUNNINI SAID NO MORE.
GUGWEI CAME OUT OF THE SKULL, BENDING STIFFLY, FOR HE WAS AN OLD MAN.
YANU PUT THE CLOAK ABOUT HIS BROAD SHOULDERS.
YOU MUST JOURNEY. YOU MUST TRAVEL SUN-WARD. THERE YOU WILL FIND A NEW LAND, WHERE YOU WILL BE SAFE. IT WILL BE A LONG JOURNEY, BUT I WILL GUIDE YOU.
NO.
YOU ARE A BAD GOD TO TELL US THIS. WE WILL ALL DIE, AND THEN WHO WILL OIL YOUR GREAT TUSKS WITH FAT?

ATSULA AND YANU EXCHANGED PLACES. NUNYUNNINI NOW SPOKE IN ATSULA'S VOICE.

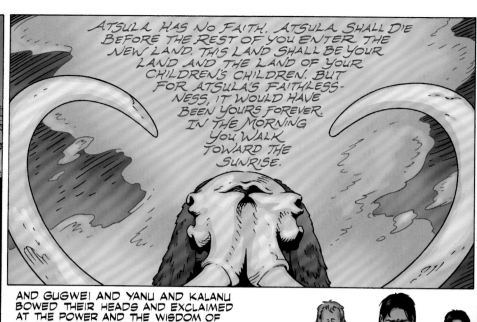

ATSULA HAS NO FAITH. ATSULA SHALL DIE BEFORE THE REST OF YOU ENTER THE NEW LAND. THIS LAND SHALL BE YOUR LAND AND THE LAND OF YOUR CHILDREN'S CHILDREN. BUT FOR ATSULA'S FAITHLESS-NESS, IT WOULD HAVE BEEN YOURS FOREVER. IN THE MORNING YOU WALK TOWARD THE SUNRISE.

AND GUGWEI AND YANU AND KALANU BOWED THEIR HEADS AND EXCLAIMED AT THE POWER AND THE WISDOM OF *NUNYUNNINI.*

THE MOON SWELLED AND WANED AND SWELLED AND WANED AGAIN. THE PEOPLE OF THE TRIBE HEADED EAST, THROUGH THE ICY WINDS.

THEY CROSSED THE LAND-BRIDGE.

KALANU HAD LEFT THEM AT FIRST LIGHT TO SCOUT THE WAY. BY THE TIME SHE RETURNED THE NIGHT SKY WAS ALIVE WITH LIGHTS, KNOTTING AND FLICKERING.

SOMETIMES, I FEEL I COULD SPREAD MY ARMS AND FALL INTO THE SKY.

THAT IS BECAUSE YOU ARE A SCOUT. WHEN YOU DIE, YOU SHALL FALL INTO THE SKY AND BECOME A STAR TO GUIDE US.

THERE ARE CLIFFS OF ICE TO THE EAST. TO CLIMB, IT WILL TAKE MANY DAYS.

YOU SHALL LEAD US SAFELY. I SHALL DIE AT THE FOOT OF THE CLIFF, AND THAT SHALL BE THE SACRIFICE THAT TAKES YOU INTO THE NEW LANDS.

TO THE WEST, BACK IN THE LANDS FROM WHICH THEY HAD COME, THERE WAS A FLASH OF LIGHT.

THE ROAR THAT ERUPTED FROM THE WEST WAS SO LOUD THAT EARS BLED.

THIS IS THE DOOM THAT *NUNYUNNINI* WARNED US OF. SURELY HE IS A WISE AND MIGHTY GOD.

HE IS THE BEST OF ALL GODS. IN OUR NEW LAND WE SHALL RAISE HIM UP ON HIGH AND TELL OUR CHILDREN'S CHILDREN THAT *NUNYUNNINI* IS THE GREATEST OF THE GODS AND SHALL NEVER BE FORGOTTEN.

GODS ARE GREAT. BUT THE HEART IS GREATER. FROM OUR HEARTS THEY COME, AND TO OUR HEARTS THEY RETURN...

ATSULA DIED AT THE FOOT OF THE CLIFFS. SHE DID NOT LIVE TO SEE THE NEW WORLD.

THE TRIBE WALKED INTO THOSE LANDS WITH NO HOLY WOMAN.

THEY WENT SOUTH AND WEST, UNTIL THEY FOUND A VALLEY WITH RIVERS THAT TEEMED WITH SILVER FISH.

DALANI GAVE BIRTH TO THREE BOYS. SOME SAID KALANU HAD THE MAGIC TO DO THE MAN-THING WITH HER BRIDE.

OTHERS SAID THAT OLD GUGWEI WAS NOT TOO OLD TO KEEP A YOUNG BRIDE COMPANY WHEN HER HUSBAND WAS AWAY.

AND CERTAINLY ONCE GUGWEI DIED, DALANI HAD NO MORE CHILDREN.

AND THE ICE TIMES CAME AND THE ICE TIMES WENT, AND THE PEOPLE SPREAD OUT ACROSS THE LAND, AND FORMED NEW TRIBES AND CHOSE NEW TOTEMS: RAVENS AND FOXES AND GROUND SLOTHS AND GREAT CATS AND BUFFALO, EACH A BEAST THAT MARKED A TRIBE'S IDENTITY, EACH BEAST A GOD.

THE MAMMOTHS OF THE NEW LAND WERE BIG AND SLOW, AND THE *PUNGH* WAS NOT TO BE FOUND, AND *NUNYUNNINI* NO LONGER SPOKE TO THE TRIBE.

AND IN THE DAYS OF THE GRANDCHILDREN OF DALANI AND KALANU'S GRANDCHILDREN, A BAND OF WARRIORS, MEMBERS OF A BIG AND PROSPEROUS TRIBE, FOUND THE VALLEY OF THE FIRST PEOPLE: THEY KILLED MOST OF THE MEN, AND THEY TOOK THE WOMEN AND THE CHILDREN CAPTIVE.

ONE OF THE CHILDREN, HOPING FOR CLEMENCY, TOOK THEM TO *NUNYUNNINI'S* SACRED CAVE.

SO THEY THREW THE OBJECTS INTO A DEEP RAVINE . . .

SOME OF THE WARRIORS WERE FOR TAKING THE SACRED OBJECTS. OTHERS SAID THAT WOULD BRING THE MALICE OF THEIR OWN GOD (FOR RAVENS ARE JEALOUS GODS).

. . . AND TOOK THEIR CAPTIVES WITH THEM ON THEIR LONG JOURNEY SOUTH.

AND THE RAVEN TRIBES, AND THE FOX TRIBES, GREW MORE POWERFUL IN THE LAND.

AND SOON *NUNYUNNINI* WAS ENTIRELY FORGOT.

AMERICAN GODS

SKETCHBOOK

NOTES BY **SCOTT HAMPTON**

The thing about Photoshop is it allows me to be really lazy about filling in black areas. If I need a large element to be black I put an X in it as a reminder for later. Jennifer Lange, the amazing colorist of "My Ainsel," alternates with me doing clean-up and preparing pages for compositing. Since she is much more thorough and meticulous than I am, she does a better job than I do, and really hates it when an area of black has a ghostly X in the middle. She always gets rid of them. They sometimes escape my notice, so if you see an X in the middle of someone's hair or costume, blame me.

Jennifer also modeled as Bilquis in this sequence and since the character had been designed by Craig Russell in chapter one, I had a preexisting look to try to match. The farther I need to deviate from the photo reference, the more likely it is that the character morphs from panel to panel. Is it just me, or does anyone else think Bilquis resembles Michael Jackson in the last shot?

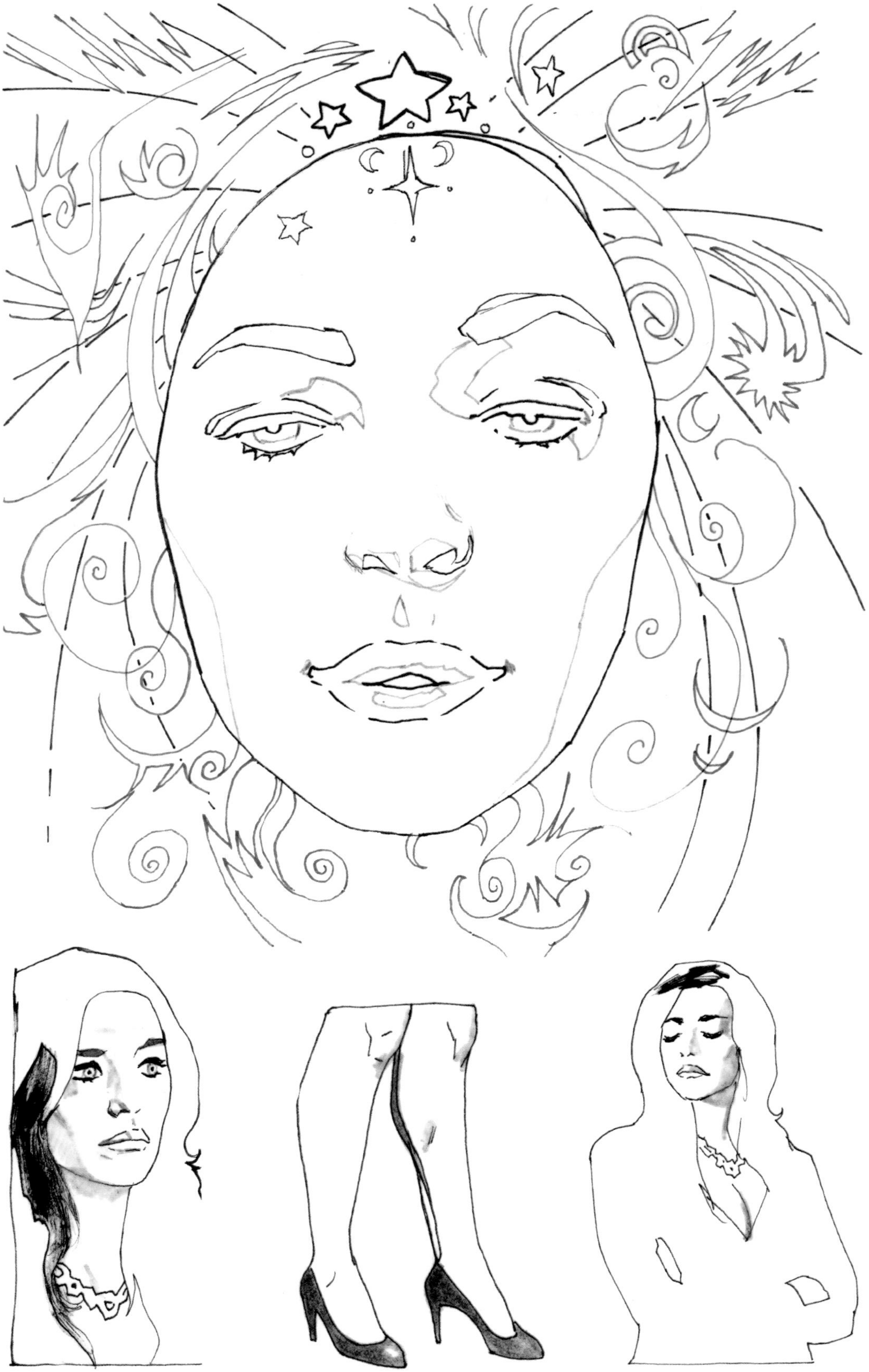

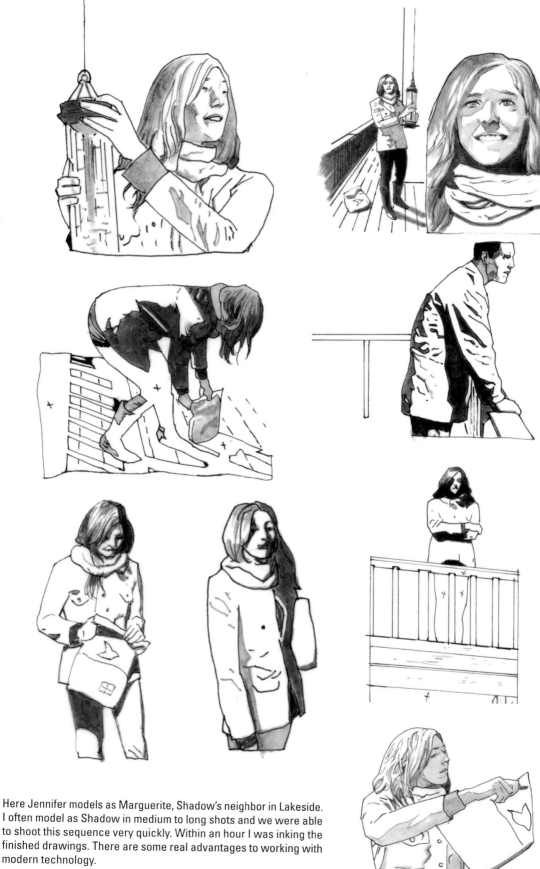

Here Jennifer models as Marguerite, Shadow's neighbor in Lakeside. I often model as Shadow in medium to long shots and we were able to shoot this sequence very quickly. Within an hour I was inking the finished drawings. There are some real advantages to working with modern technology.

The following pages feature layouts drawn by P. Craig Russell that were provided to Scott to draw from.

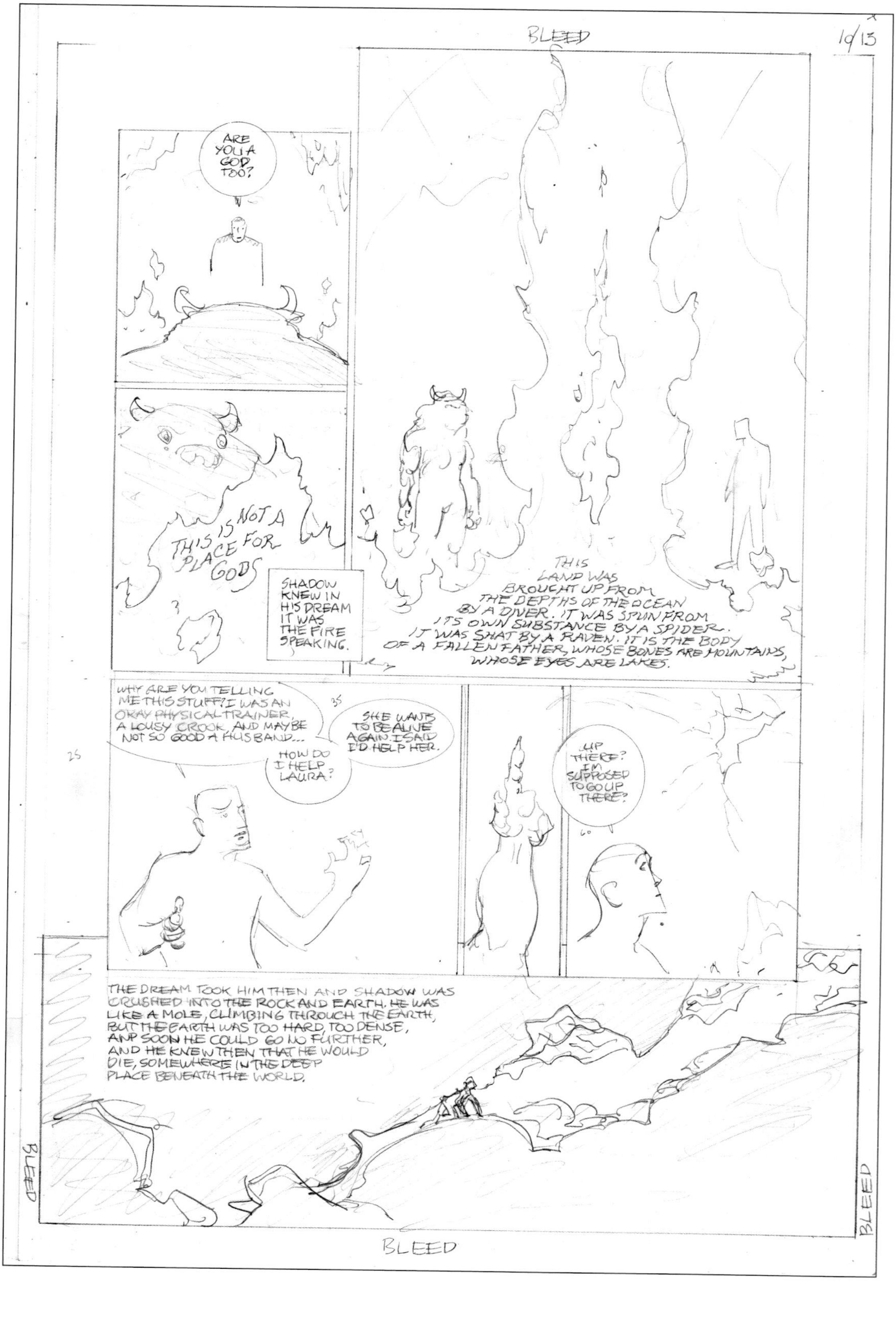
BLEED
10/13
ARE YOU A GOD TOO?
THIS IS NOT A PLACE FOR GODS
SHADOW KNEW IN HIS DREAM IT WAS THE FIRE SPEAKING.
THIS LAND WAS BROUGHT UP FROM THE DEPTHS OF THE OCEAN BY A DIVER. IT WAS SPUN FROM ITS OWN SUBSTANCE BY A SPIDER. IT WAS SHAT BY A RAVEN. IT IS THE BODY OF A FALLEN FATHER, WHOSE BONES ARE MOUNTAINS, WHOSE EYES ARE LAKES.
WHY ARE YOU TELLING ME THIS STUFF? I WAS AN OKAY PHYSICAL TRAINER, A LOUSY CROOK, AND MAYBE NOT SO GOOD A HUSBAND...
SHE WANTS TO BE ALIVE AGAIN. I SAID I'D HELP HER.
HOW DO I HELP LAURA?
UP THERE? I'M SUPPOSED TO GO UP THERE?
THE DREAM TOOK HIM THEN AND SHADOW WAS CRUSHED INTO THE ROCK AND EARTH. HE WAS LIKE A MOLE, CLIMBING THROUGH THE EARTH, BUT THE EARTH WAS TOO HARD, TOO DENSE, AND SOON HE COULD GO NO FURTHER, AND HE KNEW THEN THAT HE WOULD DIE, SOMEWHERE IN THE DEEP PLACE BENEATH THE WORLD.
BLEED
BLEED
BLEED

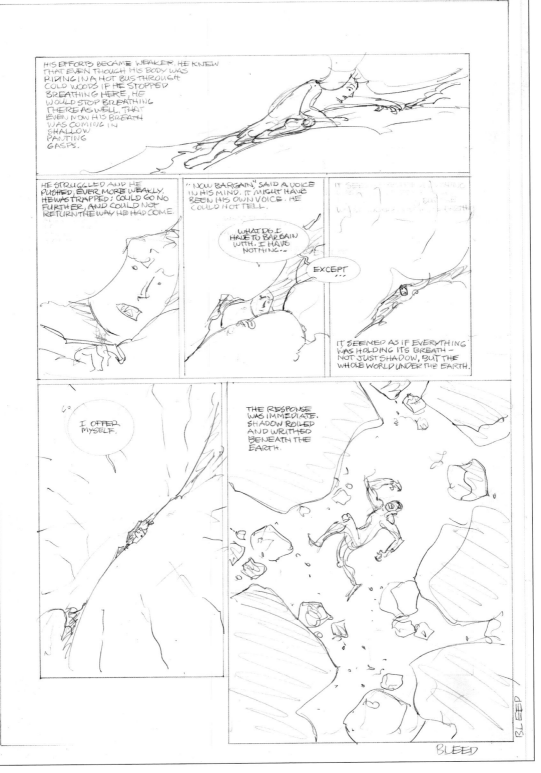

HIS EFFORTS BECAME WEAKER. HE KNEW THAT EVEN THOUGH HIS BODY WAS RIDING IN A HOT BUS THROUGH COLD WOODS IF HE STOPPED BREATHING HERE, HE WOULD STOP BREATHING THERE AS WELL, THAT EVEN NOW HIS BREATH WAS COMING IN SHALLOW PANTING GASPS.

HE STRUGGLED AND HE PUSHED, EVER MORE WEAKLY. HE WAS TRAPPED; COULD GO NO FURTHER, AND COULD NOT RETURN THE WAY HE HAD COME.

"NOW BARGAIN," SAID A VOICE IN HIS MIND. IT MIGHT HAVE BEEN HIS OWN VOICE. HE COULD NOT TELL.

WHAT DO I HAVE TO BARGAIN WITH. I HAVE NOTHING...

EXCEPT...

IT SEEMED AS IF EVERYTHING WAS HOLDING ITS BREATH — NOT JUST SHADOW, BUT THE WHOLE WORLD UNDER THE EARTH.

I OFFER MYSELF.

THE RESPONSE WAS IMMEDIATE. SHADOW ROILED AND WRITHED BENEATH THE EARTH.

BLEED

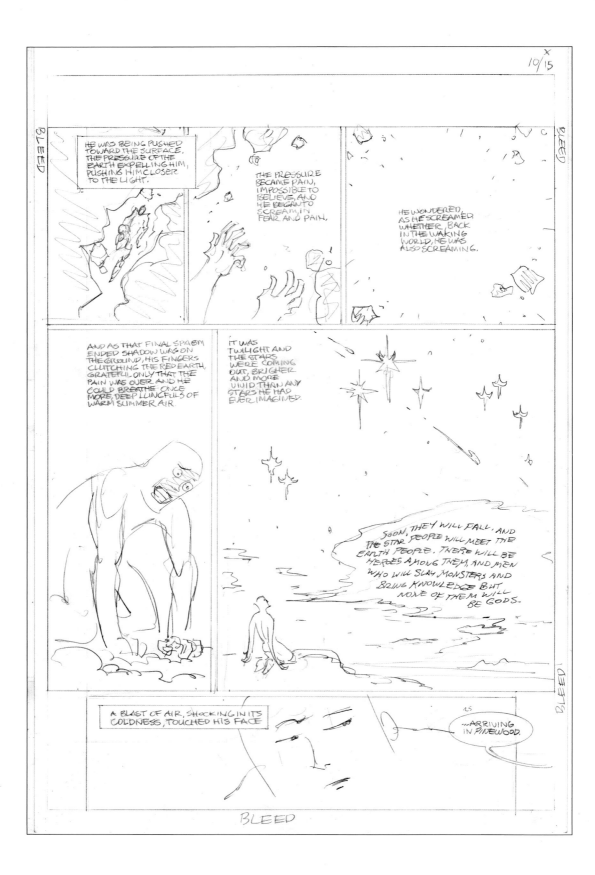

BLEED

BLEED

HE WAS BEING PUSHED TOWARD THE SURFACE, THE PRESSURE OF THE EARTH EXPELLING HIM, PUSHING HIM CLOSER TO THE LIGHT.

THE PRESSURE BECAME PAIN, IMPOSSIBLE TO BELIEVE, AND HE BEGAN TO SCREAM, IN FEAR AND PAIN.

HE WONDERED, AS HE SCREAMED WHETHER, BACK IN THE WAKING WORLD, HE WAS ALSO SCREAMING.

AND AS THAT FINAL SPASM ENDED SHADOW WAS ON THE GROUND, HIS FINGERS CLUTCHING THE RED EARTH, GRATEFUL ONLY THAT THE PAIN WAS OVER AND HE COULD BREATHE ONCE MORE, DEEP LUNGFULS OF WARM SUMMER AIR.

IT WAS TWILIGHT AND THE STARS WERE COMING OUT, BRIGHTER AND MORE VIVID THAN ANY STARS HE HAD EVER IMAGINED.

SOON, THEY WILL FALL, AND THE STAR PEOPLE WILL MEET THE EARTH PEOPLE. THERE WILL BE HEROES AMONG THEM, AND MEN WHO WILL SLAY MONSTERS AND BRING KNOWLEDGE BUT NONE OF THEM WILL BE GODS.

A BLAST OF AIR, SHOCKING IN ITS COLDNESS, TOUCHED HIS FACE

...ARRIVING IN PINEWOOD.

BLEED

BLEED

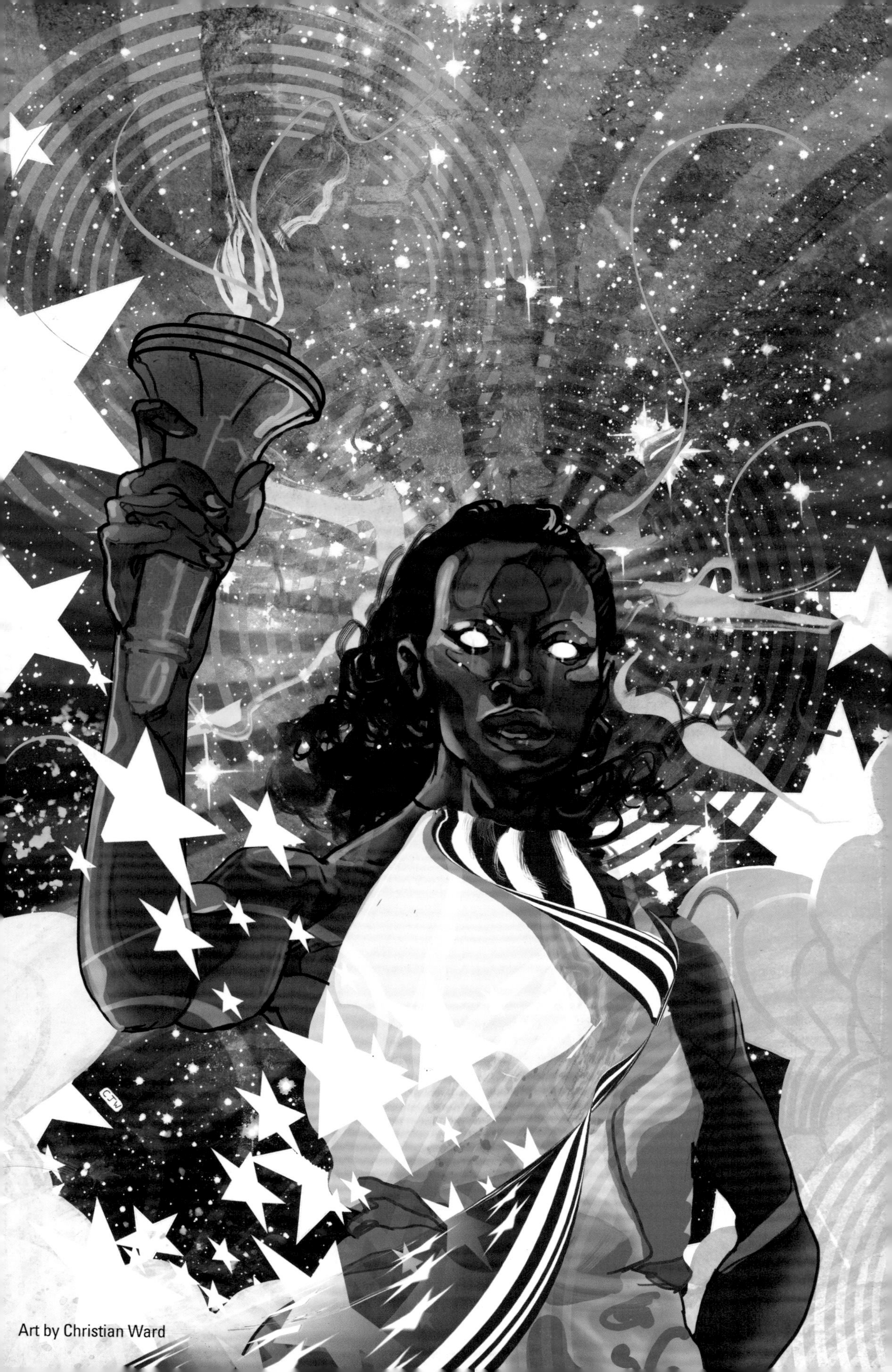

Art by Christian Ward

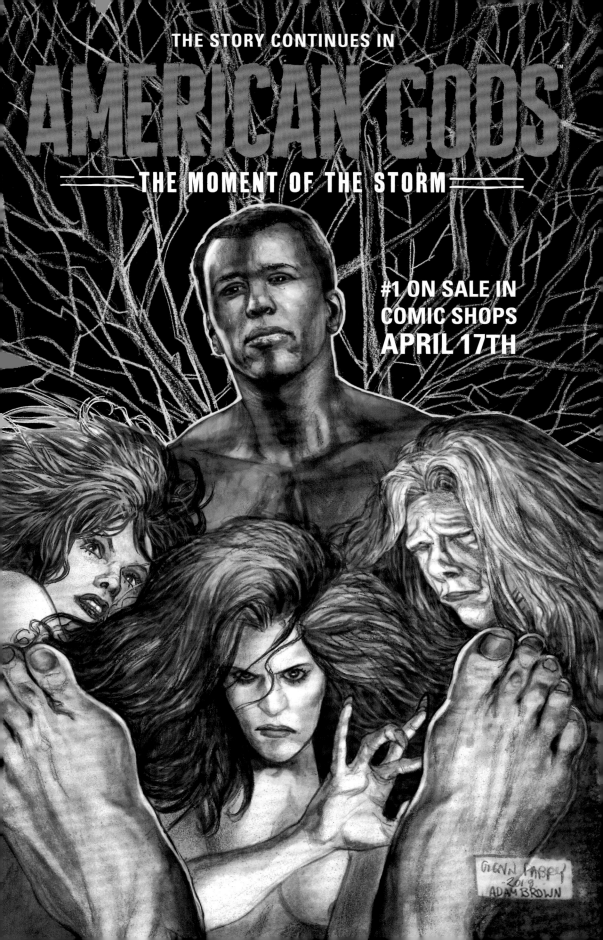

MORE TITLES FROM

THE NEIL GAIMAN LIBRARY

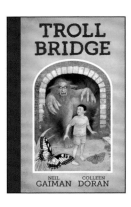

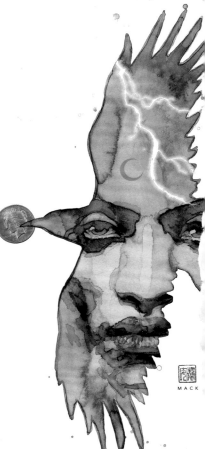

THE FACTS IN THE CASE OF THE DEPARTURE OF MISS FINCH
2nd Edition
Neil Gaiman and Michael Zulli
$13.99 | 978-1-61655-949-6

NEIL GAIMAN'S HOW TO TALK TO GIRLS AT PARTIES
Neil Gaiman, Fábio Moon, and Gabriel Bá
$17.99 | ISBN 978-1-61655-955-7

NEIL GAIMAN'S TROLL BRIDGE
Neil Gaiman and Colleen Doran
$14.99 | ISBN 978-1-50670-008-3

FORBIDDEN BRIDES OF THE FACELESS SLAVES IN THE SECRET HOUSE OF THE NIGHT OF DREAD DESIRE
Neil Gaiman and Shane Oakley
$17.99 | ISBN 978-1-50670-140-0

CREATURES OF THE NIGHT
2nd Edition
Neil Gaiman and Michael Zulli
$12.99 | ISBN 978-1-50670-025-0

SIGNAL TO NOISE
Neil Gaiman and Dave McKean
$24.99 | ISBN 978-1-59307-752-5

HARLEQUIN VALENTINE
2nd Edition
Neil Gaiman and John Bolton
$12.99 | ISBN 978-1-50670-087-8

AMERICAN GODS: SHADOWS
Neil Gaiman, P. Craig Russell, Scott Hampton, and others
$29.99 | ISBN 978-1-50670-386-2

NEIL GAIMAN'S A STUDY IN EMERALD
Neil Gaiman and Rafael Albuquerque
$17.99 | ISBN 978-1-50670-393-0

THE PROBLEM OF SUSAN AND OTHER STORIES
Neil Gaiman, P. Craig Russell, Paul Chadwick, and others
$17.99 | ISBN 978-1-50670-511-8